# ANALECTA BIBLICA

INVESTIGATIONES SCIENTIFICAE IN RES BIBLICAS

**103**

# Genesis

## An Authorship Study
## in
## Computer-Assisted Statistical Linguistics

ROMAE
E PONTIFICIO INSTITUTO BIBLICO
1985

YEHUDA T. RADDAY and HAIM SHORE
with
DIETER WICKMAN, MOSHE A. POLLATSCHEK
CHAIM RABIN and SHEMARYAHU TALMON

Preface by
DAVID NOEL FREEDMAN

# Genesis

## An Authorship Study
## in
## Computer-Assisted Statistical Linguistics

ROME
BIBLICAL INSTITUTE PRESS
1985

ISBN 88-7654-103-3

TIPOGRAFIA POLIGLOTTA DELLA PONTIFICIA UNIVERSITÀ GREGORIANA
PIAZZA DELLA PILOTTA, 4 - ROMA

## Acknowledgments

As its title indicates, this book is the result of a joint research project undertaken by a group of scholars in four different fields: Bible studies, linguistics, statistics and computer science. For geographical reasons, they regrettably never had opportunity to meet, all together, at the same time and place, one of the reasons why each is responsible only for the chapter or chapters where his participation is mentioned.

They all, though, are united in expressing their gratitude to the following for the help extended to them: The Technion — Israel Institute of Technology, Haifa; the Rheinisch-Westfälische Technische Hochschule as well as the now defunct Institut für Mathematisch-Empirische Systemforschung, both in Aachen; and the Katz Institute for Literary Research, Tel-Aviv University, especially its Director, Dr. Z. Malachi.

They also wish to acknowledge Ms. Edna Rothenstein-Widgerson's assistance in analyzing the Hebrew text of Genesis, and the skill of Mr. Uri Regev and Mr. Dov Barak, both formerly of the Technion Computer Center, who carried out most of the computer routines. The machines used were an IBM 370/168 in Haifa, a CDC 6600 in Tel-Aviv and a CYBER 175 in Aachen.

Less professional and more personal thanks are due to Ms. Amira Esser for more than two decades of support and encouragement.

Y. T. R.

H. S.

## Preface

The authors of this volume have produced a formidable work in the area of computer studies and the Bible. We are indebted to them for their pioneering efforts in this new and promising field of research. Radday's own earlier work, especially his classic study of literary characteristics and affinities in the Book of Isaiah, has initiated discussion and debate among scholars in these fields, and the immediate result has been a growing collection of articles and books responding to the first publications and extending the inquiry. As is inevitable in the early phases of a serious, scholarly enterprise, much controversy has arisen over principles and procedures, approaches and inferences. What is overwhelmingly important at this stage, however, is not the conclusions or claims, however interesting and exciting in themselves, but the great mass of useful data that has been collected, processed, classified, and organized in the course of this extended research. An enormous amount of such information is now or will shortly be available and accessible to scholars trained in both computer analysis and biblical studies.

There can be no question about the importance of the work undertaken by the present team of scholars, or about its bearing on basic questions of analysis and interpretation of the books of the Bible, quite apart from whether one agrees throughout with the approach, method, findings, and conclusions derived from the data. In this impressive volume especially Radday and Shore have mounted a major research project, an investigation into the so-called literary sources of the Pentateuch insofar as these are found in the Book of Genesis. While one may wish to quibble with the choices and decisions made as to specific assignment of passages and authorities used and cited, no one can doubt that this work makes an important contribution to the elucidation of this central issue in biblical studies.

Unlimited controversy will surely boil up over the conclusions reached by the authors, and that is all to the good. They have presented their effort to test the established views of generations of scholars and to put in their place, on the basis of material criteria and inductive considerations, a different hypothesis concerning the composition of the Book of Genesis and, by implication, other books of the Pentateuch or Hexateuch. Whether the contributors to this study have solved the problems, resolved the issues, and produced a better thesis about the literary character and characteristics of Genesis can only be settled through further testing and refining. But it will be impossible to ignore this work and others like it in the future, and those who deal with such literary questions will have to reckon with the methods, procedures, and, above all, data in this volume.

The results of this work are extremely provocative; they merit the attention, consideration, and reaction of scholars everywhere in our field. We are deeply indebted to Radday and his fellow-workers as they blaze a trail for the rest of us to follow.

David Noel Freedman

Professor of Biblical Studies
Dept. of Near Eastern Studies
University of Michigan, Ann Arbor

### Avant-propos by the Publishers

This book is a pioneer effort at studying an old problem, the authorship of Genesis (and eventually the Pentateuch), by means of a radically new, modern method, the employment of computers and statistical linguistics. The reliability of such a method is as yet imperfectly known since the whole science of computer linguistics is still developing with great speed. Hence *Analecta Biblica* cannot take full responsibility for all the methods and the conclusions they lead to here. Nevertheless we are proud to present this pioneering effort. We hope that reactions, even if they be critical, will stimulate discussion which can develop for the benefit of biblical and even linguistic science.

# Table of Contents

# List of Figures

# List of Tables

# List of Exhibits

PART ONE

# Introductory

YEHUDA T. RADDAY

## 1.1. The Problem

> This is one of the really few interesting cases of disputed authorship. What we are facing here is not a question of attributing a more or less obscure text to more or less forgotten author(s). We are dealing with a masterpiece in world literature translated into scores of languages and printed in hundreds of editions all over the world.

### 1.1.1. ANTECEDENTS AND FIRST DOUBTS

The above remarks are the opening sentences of a paper read a few years ago at a conference which I attended. I immediately made a note of it, certain that the speaker, whose name I forgot to write down, referred to the Torah, i.e., the Pentateuch. I was wrong: a few moments later it became clear that he had *The Quiet Don* in mind. If this book poses such a burning question, how much more so the Book of Genesis: Who wrote it? Is it of one cast? Or perhaps the work of several authors? If so, in what manner was it composed?

For the Jewish, and to an only somewhat lesser degree, Christian religions it is axiomatic that Moses, "our Master", wrote Genesis (and the four following parts of Torah), although this is nowhere therein stated explicitly. Nevertheless, the Divine origin and the authenticity of every single letter have since time immemorial been among the principal tenets of Judaism and were formally incorporated in the Thirteen Principles of Faith by Maimonides (d. 1204) in his commentary to the Mishnah (Sanh. 10). External evidence is most unlikely ever to turn up to prove or disprove Moses's authorship and the little internal evidence extant does not carry decisive weight.

The second and third of the above questions bring us closer to the issue at hand. How was Genesis written? All at once, as one of the Sages would have it ("Torah was handed down in one piece," TB Gittin 60a), or "scroll after scroll" (*ibid.*), as another Rabbi opined? Be it as it may, this problem was never of much centrality in traditional Jewish scholarship throughout the ages which rather chose to exert its intellectual efforts in others such as, What is the book's message, What exactly does it demand that the reader do, and, How can that reader, living in much changed circumstances, comply with the Divine precepts embodied in Scripture? It is in this latter sense that Torah in general and Genesis in particular has had an immense impact upon the daily lives, thoughts, emotions, arts and literatures of mankind for almost one hundred generations — infinitely more so than *The Quiet Don*.

However, and no matter whether the change is welcome or lamentable, the influence of the message of Scripture on the masses and particularly on the intelligentsia has diminished since the Age of Reason. With it, the absolute certainty about Moses' and, which amounts almost to the same, the single authorship and the homogeneity of Torah began to be doubted. Because of this doubt the otherwise quite irrelevant question of how else, if not by one man, this book was composed, has become so momentous. Growing rationalism and the concurrent decrease, temporary or permanent, of the part religious observance plays in life were responsible for the shift of interest from searching for the meaning of the Five Books toward inquiring into their composition, their history before and their transmission after their composition. Hence, matters of authorship and structure began to take precedence in Christian Biblical scholarship in the first place and, in its wake, in Jewish slightly later. Again, within this trend, interest was focused soon on Genesis: its stories were the best-known even among the less learned and the account it gives of Creation and the origin of Man, so strongly conflicting with nascent nineteenth century science, caused the gravest dilemmas of conscience to the erudite.

## 1.1.2. HIGHER PENTATEUCHAL CRITICISM

1.1.2.1. **Inconsistencies and Doublets.** Thus, this book and no other became the point of departure of what is commonly known as Higher Biblical and particularly Pentateuchal Criticism, an impressive edifice of eminent intellectual acumen. Because of a notable number of inconsistencies and repetitions, critics arrived at the conclusion that Genesis can not be a homogeneous book, but must be a patchwork of heterogeneous, though in most cases cleverly interlocked text blocks. If so, it was not Moses who wrote down what was revealed to him by God, but one or more editors who compiled Genesis. These could hardly have lived before King David's reign (fl. 1000 B.C.E.) and some may have lived as late as after the Babylonian exile (6th century B.C.E.). They incorporated in one book, it is said, *disiecta membra,* parts of older, perhaps oral popular traditions, and tried, with varying success, to harmonize them.

A few examples of contradictions and repetitions found in Genesis should suffice. Why was the city of Beer-Sheba named so by Isaac (26:33) when it had already received the same name a generation before by his father

Abraham (21:31)? Why was Jacob's name changed into Israel twice (32:29 and 35:10)? Could Sarah really have been taken away two times from her husband by force, once by Pharaoh (12:15) and another time by Abimelech (20:2), not to mention that the apparently same Abimelech committed the same outrage also against Isaac and Rebeccah (26:7-11)? Did Noah take seven (7:2) or two (7:9) of each kind of clean animals with him into the Ark? For how long did the Flood last: for forty days (7:4), one hundred and fifty days (7:24), or for a full year (7:11 and 8:13)? Were both sexes created at the same time, as told in ch. 1:27, or was woman created later from Adam's rib, as related in ch. 2:21-22?

This last instance is only one of the many contrasts between chs. 1 and 2. The contrasts are actually so numerous and the two chapters, taken *in toto,* so mutually contradictory that it seemed justified to speak of two different Accounts of Creation.[1]

1.1.2.2. **The Two Divine Names.** Yet the most blatant inconsistency is the alternate use of two Divine names, i.e., the Tetragrammaton *YHWH* and *Elohim.* This was what first drew the attention of scholars and led them to assume the pre-Biblical existence of two different oral traditions or written documents, each regularly employing only one of the two names. In accordance with this usage, the two hypothetical sources are today conventionally marked *J* (short for Jahwist) and *E* (short for Elohist). A third source, presumably interested less in the dramatic than in genealogies, cult and legal points, is the Priestly Writer, marked *P*. Finally, those passages that weave the various text stretches together are said to have been written by one or more editors (in German, *Redaktor* and hence they are denoted by the siglum *R*) who "inlibrated" the ancient material. Other sources conjectured by the proponents of *Quellenscheidung* — "source criticism" in English and from here on called the Documentary Hypothesis — may be neglected here since they are relatively rare and short in Genesis.

1.1.2.3.1. *The Documentary Hypothesis.* The Documentary School is generally named after J. Wellhausen (1844-1918), a Protestant professor of Oriental Studies in Germany, although he was responsible only for summing up, elaborating and spreading what had previously been suggested by his precursors. The earliest of these were K. D. Ilgen, M. de Wette, H. Hupfeld and K. H. Graf.[2]

---

[1] The subject of this collection which treats the linguistic aspects of a problem in Biblical philology by means of computer-aided statistics, is highly interdisciplinary. Readers will probably fall within four categories: Biblical scholars, linguists, statisticians and, perhaps, computer scientists. All four groups, it is easy to predict, will be dissatisfied with the manner in which their respective branches of knowledge were dealt with here, claiming that their own was neglected and the remaining three are overwritten. The editors and authors have no words of apology to offer for these deficiencies, but ask readers to make allowances: the field is too vast.

[2] The earliest to pay attention to the alternating use of the two Divine names and to surmise

In its later development, and much influenced by Hegelian thought, this school distinguished various layers within $J$ ($J_1$, $J_2$ etc.) and within $E$ ($E_1$, $E_2$ etc.), discerned various editorial hands ($R_{JE}$, $R_{JEP}$ etc.) and tentatively identified the Southern Kingdom of Judaea as the home of $J$ and the Northern of the Ten Tribes as that of $E$.   Critics were also capable of fixing the chronological order of the sources by investigating which presupposes which: $E$ seems to be acquainted with $J$ and must therefore follow him by perhaps no more than one century, whereas $P$ is still later — how much later has remained a bone of contention.

When Genesis was fragmented into sections purportedly belonging to $J$, $E$ or $P$ and when the respective sections were read consecutively, it was felt that each displayed certain stylistic properties not found in the other two.   On this aspect, we may let R. H. Pfeiffer, one of the advocates of the Documentary Hypothesis, speak for himself: [3]

> ... we note that $E$ lacks the epic scope, dramatic progress, and organic unity of $J$ ... $J$ is sculpture, $E$ is architecture; $J$ is like a river, $E$ like a canal ... $E$'s language is ... subtly different from that of $J$ ... The style of $E$ is less transparent, less spontaneous, less objective ... more deliberately musical, more delicately emotional ... There is classicism in $J$ and romanticism in $E$ ... $E$ is more detailed, but less lucid, more prolix, but less direct ... Occasionally, however, $E$ is laconic to the point of obscurity.

It is clear that for Pfeiffer the Jahwist and the Elohist stand at the two diametrically opposed ends of the literary spectrum.

As to $P$, the alleged authors of which were priests and lawyers, Pfeiffer calls its style "stereotyped, repetitious, intolerably explicit, pedantic, erudite, colorless, and schematic".   In some places, he says, "it reads like a municipal register ... or like a real estate deed", in others "like a textbook".[4]   It is "tedious ... and what is interesting is skipped over, what is indifferent is described exactly".[5]   One cannot fail to notice that Pfeiffer likes $J$ best, dislikes $P$, and is of two minds about the artistic quality of $E$.

---

from this fact the possible non-homogeneity of the Pentateuch was the 18th century French physician Jean Astruc whose family name may indicate that his ancestors were Jewish. His ideas were taken up by K. D. Ilgen, *Die Urkunden des Jerusalemer Tempelarchivs in ihrer Urgestalt* (1789). M. de Wette followed suit in his *Kritik der Israelitischen Geschichte*, I (1807). Independently of them, H. Hupfeld proposed a similar solution for the riddle of Genesis in *Die Quellen der Genesis und die Art ihrer Zusammensetzung*.   The source $P$ was first suggested by K. H. Graf, *Die geschichtlichen Bücher des Alten Testaments* (1866), while by others A. Kuenen is credited with discovering it, viz. W. v. d. Vlugt, *Levensbericht van Abraham Kuenen* (Leyden: Brill, 1893), 60-1. The last four may be seen as the fathers of the Documentary School.   Wellhausen's most influential work is his *Prolegomena zur Geschichte Israels*[4] (Berlin: Reimer, 1895).

[3] R. H. Pfeiffer, *Introduction to the Old Testament* (New York: Harper, 1941), 176.

[4] *Ibid.*, 208.

[5] Quoted by Pfeiffer (see note 3) from Wellhausen, *Prolegomena* (see note 2).

Each of the two main sources, *J* and *E,* also displays a predilection for a certain vocabulary. For instance, of the two Hebrew words for "handmaiden", one occurs exclusively in *J* and the other in *E*; the same mountain is called Sinai in *J,* but Horeb in *E*; the original inhabitants of the Promised Land are Canaanites for *J* and Amorites for *E*; and God "makes" or "establishes" His covenant with a person, depending on who the narrator is.

1.1.2.3.2. *An Example.* This short survey gives no more than the gist of a world-famous theory, does little justice to its ingenuity, and will rightly be considered much too concise by professional Biblicists. For the benefit of readers less than familiar with the intricacies of the questions arising from a literary critique of Torah and with the replies offered to them by Higher Biblical Criticism, one example of how minutely scholars scrutinized a single chapter may serve as an illustration. A fuller exposition may be found in any Biblical encyclopaedia[6] or, better, in one of the many Introductions to Biblical literature.[7]

The example is taken from the well-known story of how Joseph was sold into Egypt by his brothers (Gen. 37:1-36). The following analysis is H. Holzinger's.[8]

If ch. 37 is read with sufficient care, its two sources may be separated, although the editor is credited by the critic with having here achieved his best: the casual reader remains quite unaware of the two-fold nature of the story's origin. One "track" (*J*) relates that the brothers shepherded their flocks near Dotan; that they hated Joseph because of one of his dreams which did not indicate knowledge of his mother Rachel's death (hence "the moon" beside "the sun"); that his father's name was Israel; and that it was Judah (for whom the Judaean *J* had a preference) who suggested to the brothers not to kill, but rather to sell the lad to the Ishmaelites, which they did. In the parallel "track" (*E*), the brothers still sojourned in the "wilderness". Joseph's other dream implicitly assumes Rachel to have died; the brothers did not hate him, they envied him; his father's name was Jacob; and not Judah, but Ruben, one of the *heroi eponymoi* of the Northern Tribes, tried to save the boy by proposing to throw him, for the time being, into an empty pit. From there, he was not bought, but stolen (cf. 40:15) by Midianites. The plurality of sources thus being firmly established, Holzinger distributes the thirty-six verses among *J, E* and *P* as follows:

*P*: vv. 1-2 (because of the geographical and chronological details);

*J*: vv. 3-4, 9-10, 12-13a, 14b-17, 19-21, 23b. 25b, 26-27, 28b, 29a, 32, 34-35;

*E*: vv. 5-8, 11, 13b, 14a, 22-23a, 24-25a, 28a, 29b, 31, 33, 36.

---

[6] E.g., *Encyclopaedia Judaica* (Jerusalem: MacMillan, 1971), s.v. "Genesis".

[7] E.g., S. R. Driver, *An Introduction to the Literature of the Old Testament* (1897, repr. New York: Meridian, 1956), esp. pp. 14-21.

[8] H. Holzinger, "Das erste Buch Mose oder die Genesis" in *Die Heilige Schrift des Alten Testaments*[4], übers. E. F. Kautzsch, herausg. A. Bertholet (Tübingen: Mohr, 1922), *ad loc.*

Why the analysis of ch. 37 is such a good example of the Documentarians' skill is that this opening of the Joseph Cycle, as it stands, makes such smooth reading that *prima facie* no one would suspect it to be a medley of contradictory elements. Critics are of one opinion that in weaving these elements together into one fabric the editor (*Redaktor*) has accomplished a masterpiece. Conversely, one must acknowledge that unravelling them was also a masterpiece — this time, on the part of the analyst. In numerous instances his task was of course much easier, since Pentateuchal storytelling is rich in overlapping, inconsequential and, to the mind of the modern, logic-trained reader, of unsound arrangement of details.

It is therefore quite understandable why the Documentary Hypothesis had conquered the world of Biblical scholarship by 1875 — had taken it by storm, as a matter of fact. Its rational, unemotional and for all purposes unprejudiced approach, ready as it was to sacrifice time-honoured taboos for the sake of expansion of knowledge and perhaps similar to vivisection in medical research, all this appealed to the humanist — and very many Bible scholars had by the end of the century shaken off the fetters of theistic thought and turned humanists.

For an exhaustive description of the fortunes of the Documentary Hypothesis after Wellhausen there is no room in a necessarily brief résumé.[9] It was modified, recast, sharpened, mitigated and qualified. One way or the other, it had provided an answer to the question of how the Five Books of Moses had come into existence. So convincing this answer was that, in the thirties of this century, a British orientalist confided to a friend that he intended to turn his attention in future to studies outside the Old Testament, since there was nothing more to be done in this field. All problems had been studied and stable conclusions reached, so that all that remained for scholars to do was to go on repeating what had already been sufficiently said before.[10]

## 1.1.3. OPPOSITION TO THE DOCUMENTARY HYPOTHESIS

As may be expected, Wellhausen's theory did not go uncontested. Right from the beginning, Christian fundamentalists and literalists treated it with scorn and disdain, and Jewish orthodox rabbis hardly ever deemed it worth discussing, much less refuting. Yet, after recovering from the early shock, a small group of scholars rose in opposition, challenging the Documentarians

---

[9] Wellhausen's congeners, disciples and revisers number many hundreds. Post-Wellhausen development is briefly described in *Encyclopaedia Judaica* (see note 6), s.v. "Bible, Exegesis of", vol. 4, col. 905-10.

[10] Quoted from H. H. Rowley, *The Old Testament and Modern Study* (Oxford: Clarendon, 1951), XV.

not, as the latter had foretold, because of being blinded by religious prejudice, but on the Documentarians' own ground. Foremost among the Jewish scholars were Benno Jacob,[11] Umberto Cassuto [12] and Yehezkel Kaufmann.[13] The earliest gentile rejectionists were J. Dahse [14] and, still sharper, W. Möller,[15] later joined by P. Volz and W. Rudolph.[16] A recent attempt to re-evaluate the problem of the sources is an enquiry by R. Rendtorff into the *Überlieferungsgeschichte* of the Pentateuch.[17] To be sure, not all of these disagree with Wellhausen in every detail or in the same details. Some accept *J* and *P* and doubt the existence of *E*, others combine *J* and *E*, a third group draws the very method in question and refuses to endorse the *Quellenkritik* in principle.

Of the many, often highly complex methodological reasons for repudiating the validity of Wellhausen's theories, only the most essential ones can be enumerated here.

Firstly, Wellhausen's opponents claim that ascribing two text blocks to two different sources because each uses a different name for the Deity rests on a fatal misunderstanding of classical Hebrew and on poor knowledge of ancient Semitic thinking. The two names are anything but interchangeable: on the contrary, they stress two different aspects of the same Deity. One, *YHWH*, is a sort of personal name, in place whenever the intimate relationship between Him and Man is alluded to; the other, *Elohim*, is appellative and properly employed whenever God is conceived of as a supranatural authority. The same idea had already been suggested in early Rabbinic thought where the first name is identified with God's abundant grace, the second with His stern judgment. Furthermore, analysts are accused of bending the evidence. Thus, if *Elohim* is found in a passage declared to belong to the *J*-source, they call this

---

[11] B. Jacob, *Das erste Buch der Tora: Genesis* (Berlin: Schocken, 1934). This highly original work of over 1000 pages has for decades remained almost unnoticed,the more so as it had become a rarity, the Nazis having destroyed the plates. It has recently been translated by E. I. and W. Jacob and been published in an abridged form as *The First Book of the Bible: Genesis* (New York: Ktav, 1974).

[12] U. Cassuto, *A Commentary on the Book of Genesis,* 2 vols. (unfinished) (Jerusalem: Magnes, 1961). Cassuto first dealt with the problem in *La questione della Genesi* (Firenze: F. de Monnier, 1934). His strongest onslought, however, on Wellhausen's approach is *Torat ha-Teʾudot* (Jerusalem: Hebrew University Press, 1941), transl. I. Abrahams, *The Documentary Hypothesis* (Jerusalem: Magnes, 1961).

[13] In his monumental seven volumes of *Toledot ha-Emuna ha-Yisreʾelit,* condensed and transl. M. Greenberg, *The Religion of Israel* (London: Allen and Unwin, 1960).

[14] J. Dahse wrote several short essays, e.g., "Naht ein Umschwung?" *Neue kirchliche Zeitschrift* (1912), 748-56.

[15] W. Möller, *Die Einheit und Echtheit der fünf Bücher Mosis* (Solzuflen; Selbstverlag, 1931).

[16] P. Volz und W. Rudolph, "Der Elohist als Erzähler — ein Irrweg der Pentateuchkritik", *BZAW* 63 (Giessen: Töpelmann, 1933).

[17] R. Rendtorff, "Das überlieferungsgeschichtliche Problem des Pentateuch", *Beihefte zur Zeitschrift für die alttestamentliche Wissenschaft* 147 (Berlin-New York: de Gruyter, 1977).

unpleasant occurrence $R$'s doing or a scribal error: a classic example of the scholar who clings to his theory and asks not to be confused with facts.

Secondly, if Documentarians differ among themselves in attributing a passage to a certain source, how can one take their assertions seriously? Volz tabulates such disagreements in Gen. 27:27-29: [18]

| | Kautzsch [19] | Kautzsch-Socin [20] | Ball [21] | Gunkel [22] | Procksch [23] | Smend [24] |
|---|---|---|---|---|---|---|
| v. 27b | E | J | J | J | J | E |
| v. 28a | E | E | E | E | E | E |
| v. 28b | E | J | E | E | E | E |
| v. 29a | E | E | J | J | E | J |
| v. 29a | J | J | J | E | J | E |
| v. 29b | J | J | J | J | J | J |

Thirdly, what is labelled as doublets and contradictions must not be mechanically solved by dissecting, nay atomizing the text, but should be explained by semantics, hermeneutics and genuine instead of sham literary criticism. Why may one method and one yardstick apply in Herodotus and Josephus (where similar lapses can be found) and another method and yardstick in the Hebrew Bible? In no other literary work, not even in the New Testament, have critics so diligently and avidly searched for lack of total agreement between two halves of the same sentence.

Fourthly, what the editor $R$ did is altogether unintelligible. At one place, he is said to have included in his work two parallel, though mutually exclusive versions of the same incident because he revered his two sources so much that he was loth to renounce either. At another, he allegedly felt no compunction to cut the very same sources to pieces and to bluepencil what he regarded as redundant or unfitting. One may also ask why he did not go one step further and use the same Divine name throughout. In addition, how can Wellhausen's followers explain the astonishing fact that the editor worked in one passage so shrewdly that the sources can no longer be untwined, while at another place so slovenly that a German professor, living three millennia later, has no difficulty in discovering the glue that holds the conglomerate together?

---

[18] Volz, op. cit. (see note 16), 65.

[19] Kautzsch, op. cit. see note 8), ad loc.

[20] E. F. Kautzsch – A. Socin, Die Genesis mit äusserer Unterscheidung der Quellenschriften (Giessen: Töpelmann, 1888), ad loc.

[21] C. J. Ball, The Book of Genesis in Hebrew (Leipzig: Hinrichs, 1896), ad loc.

[22] H. Gunkel, Genesis[3] in Der Göttinger Handkommentar zum Alten Testament (Göttingen: Vandenhoeck, 1910), ad loc.

[23] O. Procksch, Genesis (Leipzig: Deichert, 1924), ad loc.

[24] R. Smend, Die Erzählung des Hexateuch auf ihre Quellen untersucht (Berlin: Reimer, 1912), ad loc.

Moreover, has any book in world literature been compiled in this manner, and if so, could it still have preserved its unquestionable beauty and vitality? Their lack of artistic appreciation, and, what is even worse, lack of understanding of how a writer works led Staerk to name the Documentarians' approach *Stubengelehrsamkeit*.[25]

Fifthly, arguing from vocabulary and style is ludicrous. Followers of Wellhausen find themselves enmeshed in an *argumentum in circulo*: they maintain, for instance, that *P* was written by priests, that priests are officials, that officials are pedants, that pedants love to enumerate and to date — hence all lists, legal niceties, chronological information and whatever a nineteen-century professor was bored with must have been written by priests. But even arid stretches like tables of people's ages may be fascinating when their true import is understood. And if lengthy genealogies are *a priori* set apart and titled "priestly writings", then one must not argue that such writings are easily recognized as "priestly" by being long-winded — except by *petitio principii*. Schoolmasterly marks like those given to *J, E* and *P* by Pfeiffer and his colleagues are subjective and overlook the interdependence between subject matter and diction.

The sixth objection is only rarely voiced, perhaps because it is the most scathing. Those who took pride in not being shackled by religious dogma such as the Mosaic origin of the entire Torah are blamed for being inaccessible to new evidence and having become dogmatic themselves. This reproach is the weightier when it comes from scholars to whom the unity of Torah and the integrity of the text are by no means unimpeachable tenets of a creed which regulates their actions and dominates their intellectual activities.

## 1.1.4.  SUBJECTIVITY INEVITABLE

It is only natural that in such a controversy the initial attitudes of either side must be reflected for it touches the intimate and innate sentiments of men in Western civilization. Deep-seated belief in the teachings of Christianity or Judaism must somehow motivate the anti-documentarian stance taken by the unitarians, while repudiation of either, on the one hand, and, on the other, be-lief in the power of man's analytical reason must inevitably tint the opinions held by the critical school.

The allegation, though, that both sides are prejudice-ridden is less preju-dice-ridden than it sounds, if only we are honest. We must not delude oursel-ves that it is in our power to seek in matters of literature for what Burckhardt called in his field of learning the "Archimedean point outside events" which would enable us to make truly impartial judgments. We must acknowledge we cannot find it in full. Also, to be *engagé* may even be a precondition and

---

[25] Volz, *op. cit.* (see note 16), 7.

an asset in the study of literature.  If, however, a tool offers itself for maximizing objectivity, it should be welcomed enthusiastically and made use of.  That such a tool is available nowadays is the contention of Section 1.1.6. below.

One more remark on the subject of possible *parti pris*.  Not only unitarians and Documentarians hold their inceptive (and perhaps deceptive) beliefs when they defend or attack the homogeneity of Genesis, but also the researchers who participated in this project.  All the same I wish to state that all of us never discussed among ourselves our attitudes toward the "ideological" side of the problem which we banded together to investigate, if for no other reason than that of lack of opportunity: living in different countries, we hardly ever met in the flesh.  Our religious allegiances and our personal convictions differ widely, from deep commitment to the teachings of the book under review, to indifference vis-à-vis them and to mere scientific interest in an interdisciplinary scientific undertaking.  Thus, our personal stances could not have influenced the results obtained since the very strength of the method which we employed and which will be expounded in what follows lies in disallowing subjectivity, as will be shown.  I also hope that the way the problem has been presented here does not reveal my own bias which, I admit, exists.

## 1.1.5.  THE STATE OF THE CONTROVERSY

Before continuing, it may be beneficial to summarize and update the present state of the controversy.  At a late stage of his work on the Hexateuch, i.e., the Pentateuch plus the Book of Joshua, Wellhausen himself confessed that "freilich ist es mir nicht gelungen, den Faden von *J* and *E* durch das Ganze zu verfolgen".  This task his successors tried to accomplish.  But they too encountered difficulties.  The foremost was that, when *J* and *P* were eliminated, what was left, namely *E,* seemed hardly to be an integrated conception nor "das Werk *eines* Geistes".  Reluctant, though, to abandon the formidable mental end-product of three generations of scholars and faced with inexplicable repetitions and flat contradictions in the book, one of their spokesmen, Rudolph, suggested his *Ergänzungshypothese* as the best working one: whatever can not be placed within *J* or *P* must be supplementary and subsequent.[26]

It did not take long before Rudolph's theory, too, became suspect.  In a recent work, Weinfeld states that the Documentary Hypothesis is allegedly "based on bias, foregone conclusions, argument from silence, and misunderstanding, and therefore cannot be considered successful", although he dissociates himself from this view.[27]

---

[26] W. Rudolph, *Der "Elohist" von Exodus bis Josua* (Berlin: Töpelmann, 1938), 263.

[27] M. Weinfeld, *Getting at the Roots of Wellhausen's Understanding of the Law of Israel on the 100th Anniversary of the Prolegomena* (Jerusalem: Hebrew University Institute for Advanced Studies, Report No. 14, 1979).

To call today's situation a crisis may be too melodramatic, but it cannot be denied that the historical-critical method, in various forms the *modus operandi* since the Enlightenment, is under fire from many directions. From without, there is new life from old enemies of critical inquiry into the Bible: traditional, conservative and fundamentalist theology. More decisive, however, for the future of Biblical scholarship are the rumblings within the ranks. These are perhaps more audible among Christian than Jewish exegetes (except, of course, those who are *Torah-treu* and who anyhow never showed the slightest interest in Wellhausen's theories). What lies behind this curious phenomenon is a matter for sociologists to ponder.

At any rate, there is talk of a paradigm shift from the historical to the linguistic. Walter Wink's *The Bible in Human Transformation* created a minor flap with its assertion that historical Biblical criticism is bankrupt.[28] While not many have rallied to his flag, evidence that talk of a paradigm shift is more than idle chatter or wishful thinking can be seen in numerous publications calling themselves, to name just two, structuralism and rhetorical criticism.

This is where the matter stands today. Obviously, an issue like the present, because of the deep convictions involved, must lead, at best, to heated dispute, and, at worst, to cessation of any dialogue between the two camps. But to insulate one's belief and preconceptions against all possibility of refutation is surely a desperate strategy and the very antithesis of rational and scholarly enquiry — and this holds true for those who doubt the unity of Genesis and those who defend it alike.

## 1.1.6.  A NEW APPROACH

One thing is clear: a problem like the one described here must not be decided by majority vote or by the number of arguments advanced by either party to it. If only these arguments could be weighed — but they cannot, to the chagrin of many researchers, particularly in the humanities. Yet if in scholarship and science, as often in fields of intellectual enquiry, the truth is not to be counted by heads or arguments, it might be, instead, a good idea to try to discover it by counting words. This points to the new approach proposed here.

1.1.6.1.  **Philology or Linguistics?** The problem of the unity of Genesis belongs to the realm of philology. This discipline deals with, a certain language (or with a group or family of languages) at one time (which in our case are Hebrew and other Semitic languages), with its history, with its

---

[28] This quotation stems from a note which I made when I read it. Unfortunately, I am unable to reconstruct the bibliographical details.

literature, with the history and artistic development of this literature and with cognate issues.

Not so linguistics. Its domain is, in short, the mechanism of language: with how language works, irrespective of which specific language is being investigated. To examplify: in German, there are Grimm's Laws of *Lautverschiebung* which obviously refer solely to German or, at most, to other Teutonic languages, and which are a great help in reading, deciphering and understanding ancient German texts, but, clearly, they are irrelevant in Romance languages and literatures. Grimm's laws are therefore philological. In contrast, Zipf's famous law, that multiplying the rank number of a word in the frequency list of any language by the frequency of that word ($r \times f$) will result in the same product, i.e., remain constant, describes the mechanism of language *per se*. It is either valid or not, but in any case is not restricted to English: it is a linguistic law. Lack of space disallows any further juxtaposition of philology and linguistics.

From what has been said so far of linguistics it follows that this discipline is totally disinterested in the world of ideas as mirrored in the literature of a given language but rather concentrates on formal aspects. Thus, while philology is a branch of humanistic scholarship, linguistics is a science in the narrow sense of the term, and as such admirably suited to providing the tools for the new approach so urgently called for here.

In order to neutralize preconceived ideas, this new approach will completely disregard the book's spiritual message and equally leave aside all semantics, matters governed by interpretation, not to mention personal taste. How perilous it is to allow the latter to play any part is plain from the way Pfeiffer lavishes praise on *J* and blame on *P*: whether the content of a given work of literature is "interesting" or "indifferent" may vary from reader to reader, should be left to him to decide and is surely beyond the terms of reference of the scholar.

It may not be impossible, though, to detect in a text such characteristics as are really objective and, to quote Karl Popper, communicable and enforcing assent. These must then be clearly defined, precisely countable and measurable. "Counting", said Dr. Johnson, "brings everything to a certainty which before floated in the mind indefinitely". Characteristics of this kind do indeed exist, and, paradoxically, exactly where the greatest weakness of the Documentarians' argument lies, namely in what they call stylistic expression.

Ways and means of linguistic expression are not to be confused with what is generally named *style*. Lacking exactitude and all too often loosely used, this term is preferably left out in a scientific discussion. Nor should the case for or against single authorship be based on style as long as the word means two different things to any two different critics. More on this point below.

It follows, and cannot be repeated often enough, that investigations into allegedly multiple authorship make sense only on the condition that, in terms of information theory, no «noise» is caused by the intrusion of variables such as change of literary type. Comparing, for example, in Genesis the language behavior — let this term be used henceforth instead of style as long as the latter is not defined — of the Paradise story with the ordinances concerning circumcision in ch. 17, and inferring heterogenous authorship from the difference between the two is futile and methodologically wrong. Nobody would surmise, because of the difference in "style" between *Dichtung und Wahrheit,* as the title indicates, a miscellany of memoirs and notes on literary topics, and the anti-Newton treatise *Farbenlehre,* that there was one Proto-and one Deutero-Goethe. For this telling example see Section 2.2.5.

These remarks already. delineate the course of the present enquiry. It will try to quantify the case of homogeneity vs. heterogeneity in Genesis by means of statistical linguistics, and take the "text as it stands" as the only unquestionable data one can be certain of. It aims at arriving at calculating the probability that one section, hypothetically originating in, say, *J* was written by the same person to whom an *E*- or *P*-section is ascribed.

1.1.6.2. **Statistical Linguistics.** Statistics and linguistics are two comparatively young sciences, the application of the former to the study of the latter being even younger. Combining the two in order to solve authorship problems on a large scale has become feasible only with the advent of the computer. That conservative philologists should still regard this approach with suspicion will consequently not cause astonishment. To adduce an example of how powerful the new tool is may therefore not be superfluous. Lauter and Wickmann demonstrated its potency in a test case of texts the authors of which were known.[29] They drew two samples, each of 10,000 words, from the prose writings of Herder, Goethe and Kant, compared the six with each other and computed the probability of each pair having originated in the same language population. The comparison between Herder A and B resulted in the homogeneity probability of 70.5%, between Goethe A and B in 21.5% and between Kant A and B in 8.7%. When, however, the samples were compared "across" writers, probability values fluctuated between $10^{-20}$ p.c., at the highest, and $10^{-135}$ p.c., at the lowest. Since $10^{-10}$ is a conventional way of writing 0.000 000 000 1, values obtained for crosswise comparisons were without exception practically nil, which should suffice to convince the sceptic.

In books belonging to the Hebrew Biblical canon, the same method has also proved itself in three extensive studies and in a considerable number of limited ones, the results of which were published by several of the contributors to the present volume.[30] Here, too, statistical linguistics was capable of

---

[29] J. Lauter and D. Wickmann, "Méthodes d'analyse des différences chez un ou plusieurs auteurs", *Cahiers du Centre de Recherche et d'Applications Linguistiques,* 1ère série, 2 (1967), 16-34.

[30] Their more comprehensive publications are: Y. T. Radday, *The Unity of Isaiah in the Light of Statistical Linguistics,* with a contribution by D. Wickmann (Hildesheim: Gerstenberg, 1973); *id.* and D. Wickmann, "The Unity of Zechariah in the Light of Statistical Linguistics", *ZAW* 87 (1975), 30-55; *id., id.,* G. Leb and S. Talmon, "The Book of Judges Examined by

detecting the seams in heterogeneous texts. For example, it located the *caesura* in Isaiah between chs. 39 and 40, the one in Zechariah between chs. 11 and 12, and established what had long ago been sensed by critics in Judges, namely that the Samson Cycle there is a foreign body. Contrariwise, chs. 13 and 14 in Isaiah, regarded by almost all recent commentators as two of the Second Isaiah's oracles interpolated into the First's, emerged, by virtue of the said method, as linguistically not incongruent with the latter. For the reason stated, good care was taken in all these cases that only *pares cum paribus comparabuntur*: the narrative chs. 36-39 in Isaiah and the poetic ch. 5 in Judges were left out of the counts because they are of a literary genre atypical in these two books.

The three major studies mentioned may actually be seen, to some extent, as exercises in method and techniques designed to prepare the way for the present one. True, their results did perhaps not matter either way to the public at large, whether they supported the views of divisionists or unitarians, because they concerned prophetic books which, at least to the Jewish mind, rank lower in the hierarchy of the Biblical canon. But those studies were needed before approaching the text of the Torah the issues of whose integrity and authenticity are more portentous by far.


## 1.2. Language Aspects

### 1.2.1. ON STYLE

Let us once more go back to the thorny problem of style. The equivocal use of the term by critics of the Scriptures has already been mentioned: they hardly bother to define the term, but very many still base their cases for or against single authorship, as the case may be, on stylistic similarity or dissimilarity. One cannot but wonder whether any one among them has ever given much thought, for instance, to the very simple questions, To what measure does a person's style remain constant within his lifetime, and, How does a given audience influence a speaker's or writer's style? Other points, equally not sufficiently explored, are, What is the correlation between content and genre on the one hand and "style" on the other, and, How far do the former two dictate certain traits in the latter? Roman authors already conformed to what is known as *lex ordinis,* not a statutory law, of course, but a literary edict insisting on clear distinctions of style and content between one form and another. These ancient rules not only of taste but also of common sense appear to have fallen into oblivion and only lately have Biblical scholars begun to turn to them again and to examine the relationship between *Gattung*

---

Statistical Linguistics", *Biblica* 58 (1977), 469-99. These three are in the following called, for short, *Isaiah, Zechariah* and *Judges*.

and form.[31]   In short, any enquiry into the linguistic aspects of a problem in Biblical philology must first of all clarify how language functions at all, and then, more specifically, what actually is meant by style.

This is not the occasion for a discussion of stylistics for the subject is treated in full elsewhere.[32]   Here, a very concise summary should suffice.

When talking of style, we are not concerned with what is written, but with how something is expressed.   Hence, various options of how to tell what he has to tell are open to the writer, and that on several levels such as the lexical, the syntactical, etc.   The first point, then, to note is that whereever style is spoken of there must be a choice for the writer between alternative ways of expression.

The second supposition is that some varieties are typical of the communicational needs of society in certain situations.   The variations employed by a person for fulfilling given needs in given circumstances may be called his style while Halliday calls them "registers".[33]   There are very many (and often little crystallized) registers in all living languages, each representing a linguistic variation within which unmistakable norms have developed.   A person's style thus finds its expression in his deviations from a societally conventionalized norm.   Moreover, it appears that the linguistic properties of a register and extra-linguistic factors such as audience and subject matter are correlated as if diatypical laws existed.[34]   This sort of reasoning naturally leads to what has been posited above, i.e., the close nexus between the style of a piece of writing and its contents, on the one hand, and the reader for whom it is intended, on the other.   These facts alone should put critics on guard before they compare different types of Biblical literature with each other.


## 1.2.2.   ON THE THEORETICAL BACKGROUND

Another angle worth considering is to what extent a person's ways of expressing himself in writing remains the same within the limits set by registers.

A person's language behavior or, using Saussure's terminology,[35] what and how his *parole* realizes in practice what potentially exists in *la langue,* is

---

[31] A concise introduction to form criticism is G. M. Tucker, *Form Criticism of the Old Testament* (Philadelphia: Fortress Press, 1971).

[32] E.g., *Isaiah,* 23-48, not to mention the many works dealing specifically with stylistics, cf. S. Chatman and S. R. Levin, *Essays on the Language of Literature* (Boston: Houghton Mifflin, 1967).

[33] M. A. K. Halliday *et al., The Linguistic Sciences and Language Teaching* (London: Longmans, 1966).

[34] Cf. M. Gregory, "Aspects of Variety Differentiation", *Journal of Linguistics* 3 (1967), 177-274.

[35] Cf. F. de Saussure, *Cours de linguistique générale,* originally published in 1916 (repr. Paris: Payot, 1972).

the sediment of his lifelong experience and the residue of the traces left upon him expressed as a series of routings and junctions in the neural pathways of his brain. These form within his memory a repository of interrelated patterns which provide him with impulses and controls. His utterances are therefore samples drawn from a vast and probably infinite population, a fact constituting the link between language and statistics. For the time being it is enough to state that statistics deals with deviations from a norm and that a person's *parole* finds its expression in his deviations in the frequencies of certain language phenomena from those norms.

It follows that, theoretically at least, each person's language behavior is unique, i.e., an "idiolect". It also follows that the characteristics of a given language behavior must recur and, hence, be countable. Let style then be exhaustively defined by the totality of all quantitatively tangible data concerning the formal structure of a text.[36] And let it be understood that, except for exact statements on these characteristics, nothing else must be implied in the term "analysis of style" as it is used here — if the term is used at all.


## 1.3. The Material

### 1.3.1. GENESIS LINGUISTICALLY ANALYZED

The Book of Genesis consists of 20504 words when this term is defined as a cluster of characters between two blank spaces. Two exceptions to this rule are composite toponyms such as Bet-El and numerals from 11 through 19: *composita* of these two kinds were taken as one word each. The *Ketiv* was throughout given precedence over the *Qere* and no attention was paid to textual variants and conjectural emendations. The entire investigation was based on the Masoretic *textus receptus* of the popular edition supervised by M.L. Letteris and printed by the British and Foreign Bible Society, Vienna 1852. A more exact edition is not needed in a statistical enquiry: it would only unnecessarily burden it with unwarranted details.

Each word was analyzed and the following information on it was registered on magnetic tape:

> (a) its *lemma*, i.e., for nouns (and adjectives, because they cannot unambiguously be distinguished from nouns), the absolute state in singular (except for *pluralia tantum*); for verbs, the third person masculine in singular with each *binyan* taken as a distinct verb; for

---

[36] Quoted from W. Fucks and J. Lauter, "Mathematische Analyse des literarischen Stils", in *Mathematik und Dichtung,* ed. R. Gunzenhäuser and H. Kreuzer (München: Nymphenburger Verlag, 1965/1967), 109.

the inflected forms of the prepositional affixes *bet, kaf* and *lamed,* the third person masculine in singular; and for the rest (numerals, prepositions, conjunctions, pronouns, etc.) as they appear as entries in a conventional dictionary;

(b) word length in terms of phonemes;

(c) number and gender wherever necessary;

(d) bound prepositional prefixes, the definite article (also when elided) and the *waw coniunctivum* and *consecutivum;*

(e) bound possessive and objective pronominal or other suffixes to nouns, verbs, prepositions and numerals;

(f) a detailed numerical code indicating the part of speech, i.e., for nouns the absolute, construct or inflected state, and for verbs the *binyan,* root, tense or mode;

(g) a siglum indicating to which of the three Documents *J, E* and *P* the word is attributed;

(h) a siglum indicating whether the word occurs in the narrator's (*N*) description, in human (*H*) or in Divine (*D*) direct speech;

(i) chapter and verse, and the number of the word within the verse.

Printouts were several times painstakingly checked by means of a key-word-in-context concordance, a sample of which is shown in Figure 1.1. (p. 18).[37]

## 1.3.2. WHICH DOCUMENTARY HYPOTHESIS?

A serious difficulty arose with regard to (g). As mentioned before in passing, while followers of the critical school are of one opinion that different Documents may be distinguished in Genesis, they are far from unanimous as to the specific Document to which a given passage is assigned (see Section 1.1.3.). Obviously, it is beyond the scope of a project like the present to test simultaneously several and mutually contradicting variations of the same hypothesis. After prolonged deliberations and in view of the fact that the extreme and highly fragmentizing analysis has been largely abandoned and that contemporary scholarship somewhat softened in this respect, it was decided to adopt for testing a more moderate version of *Quellenscheidung.*

---

[37] This Key-Word-in-Context Concordance is available in full, as vol. XVIII of the Computer Bible Project directed and edited by J. A. Baird and D. N. Freedman, from Biblical Research Associates, College of Wooster, Wooster OH.

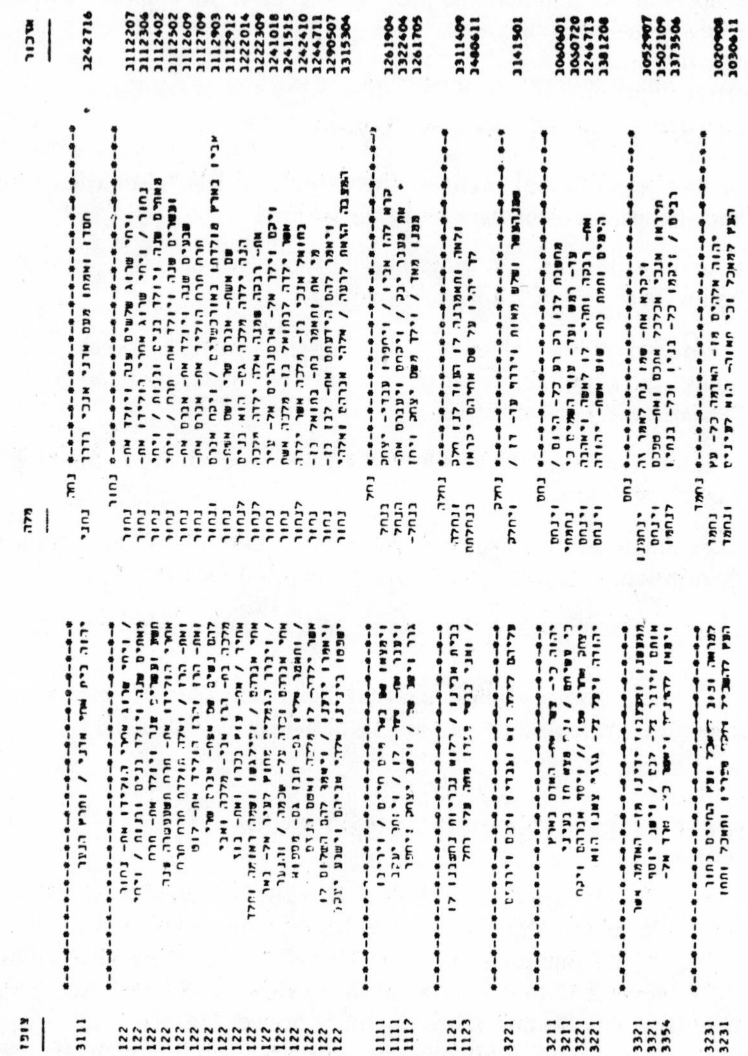

Figure 1.1: Sample Page of the Key-Word-in-Context Concordance of Genesis

The one chosen was originally proposed by Sellin,[38] which is more or less followed in the *Encyclopaedia Judaica*.[39]   There, subdivisions into $J_1$, $J_2$, etc., $E_1$, $E_2$, etc. as well as *R*'s share do not figure, and, therefore, the present analysis acknowledges only *J, E* and *P*.   A special case is ch. 14.   We marked it *P* although it is said to be of an altogether extraneous origin and to defy being apportioned to any of the three sources.[40]   Table 1.1 shows how the entire text of Genesis was divided among these three.   However, since all of Genesis was analyzed and is available on magnetic tape, testing any other variation of the Documentary Hypothesis is of course feasible.   Should, though, a very high degree of similarity or dissimilarity, as the case may be, emerge from examining the one opted for here, it may quite safely be assumed that results would not vary significantly if it were submitted to the same sort of investigation in a somewhat modified form.   See Table 1.1 (p. 20).


## 1.3.3.   TEXT BLOCKS OMITTED

Another question already briefly raised before must be taken up again. It stands to reason, and previous experience has proved, that no purpose is served if different genres of literature are compared with each other, particularly not prose with poetry: the two are mortal enemies, to quote Ronsard.   But, strictly speaking, there is no plain prose in the Torah. Everything is cast in some traditional form possessing a sort of rhythmical diction and obeying certain rules of composition. Genesis, too, is written in this sort of prose but for a small number of very short couplets which were of course included in the counts for they are unlikely to distort the results.   A different case is Jacob's Blessing (49:1-27), a coherent collection of poetic sayings ascribed to *J*.   These had without any doubt to be omitted.   A more problematic instance is ch. 1:1 until 2:3, the so-called First *Schöpfungsbericht,* unless it is declared to be the work of *P*: opinions differ as to whether it should be considered as prose or poetry. Because of its apparent strophic structure, with parallelism of matter and form, its recurring refrain and its corresponding opening and closing formulae which chiastically echo each other, it seemed advisable to take it as a solemn hymnic proemium intended to be a poetic *ouverture* to the whole book.   It was therefore eliminated from the counts.   Nonetheless, since these two poems were analyzed in the same way as the rest of Genesis, nothing prevents their also being statistically examined if so desired.   As to the problematic ch. 14, mentioned above in Section 1.3.2., it is included in the computations of Part Three; Parts Two and Four disregard it.

---

[38] E Sellin und L. Roth, *Einleitung in das Alte Testament*[9] (Heidelberg: Quelle & Meyer, 1959).

[39] See note 6.

[40] Driver (see note 7) states (p. 15) that "the character [of ch. 14] points to its being taken from a special source".

Table 1.1: Attribution to Sources

| Section | J | E | P | Section | J | E | P |
|---|---|---|---|---|---|---|---|
| ch. 1 | | | 1-31 | ch. 25 | 1-6 | | |
| ch. 2 | | | 1-3 | | | | 7-20 |
| | 4-25 | | | | 21-34 | | |
| ch. 3 | 1-24 | | | ch. 26 | 1-35 | | |
| ch. 4 | 1-26 | | | ch. 27 | 1-45 | | |
| ch. 5 | | | 1-28 | ch. 28 | | | 46 |
| | 29 | | | | | | 1-9 |
| | | | 30-32 | | | 10-12 | |
| ch. 6 | 1-8 | | | | | | 13-16 |
| | | | 9-22 | | | 17-22 | |
| ch. 7 | 1-5 | | | ch. 29 | | 1-30 | |
| | | | 6 | | 31-35 | | |
| | | 7-24 | | ch. 30 | | 1-43 | |
| ch. 8 | 1-22 | | | ch. 31 | | 1-54 | |
| ch. 9 | | | 1-17 | ch. 32 | 1-33 | | |
| | 18-27 | | | ch. 33 | 1-20 | | |
| | | | 28-29 | ch. 34 | 1-31 | | |
| ch. 10 | | | 1-7 | ch. 35 | | 1-8 | |
| | 8-19 | | | | | | 9-13 |
| | | | 20-23 | | 14 | | |
| | 24-30 | | | | | | 15 |
| | | | 31-32 | | | 16-22 | |
| ch. 11 | 1-9 | | | | | | 23-29 |
| | | | 10-32 | ch. 36 | | | 1-43 |
| ch. 12 | 1-20 | | | ch. 37 | 1-36 | | |
| ch. 13 | 1-5 | | | ch. 38 | 1-30 | | |
| | | | 6 | ch. 39 | | 1-23 | |
| | 7-18 | | | ch. 40 | | 1-23 | |
| ch. 14 | ? | ? | 1-24 | ch. 41 | | 1-57 | |
| ch. 15 | 1-21 | | | ch. 42 | | 1-38 | |
| ch. 16 | 1-2 | | | ch. 43 | | 1-34 | |
| | | | 3 | ch. 44 | | 1-34 | |
| | 4-14 | | | ch. 45 | | 1-28 | |
| | | | 15-16 | ch. 46 | | 1-5 | |
| ch. 17 | | | 1-27 | | | | 6-27 |
| ch. 18 | 1-33 | | | | 28-34 | | |
| ch. 19 | 1-38 | | | ch. 47 | 1-31 | | |
| ch. 20 | | 1-18 | | ch. 48 | | 1-2 | |
| ch. 21 | | 1-34 | | | | | 3-6 |
| ch. 22 | 1-18 | | | | | 7-22 | |
| | | | 19 | ch. 49 | 1-27 | | |
| | 20-24 | | | | | | 28-33 |
| ch. 23 | | | 1-20 | ch. 50 | 1-11 | | |
| ch. 24 | 1-67 | | | | | | 12-13 |
| | | | | | 14 | | |
| | | | | | | 15-26 | |

## 1.4.  The Three-Dimensional Dissection of Genesis

### 1.4.1. DOCUMENTS, SORTS-OF-DISCOURSE, DIVISIONS

It has already been mentioned in Section 1.3.1. that, in addition to grammatical details into which it was analyzed, each word was given one of the sigla *J, E,* or *P,* denoting the hypothetical Documents, and that, *pari passu* and on afterthought, another set of three sigla was also registered, namely *N,* whenever the word occurs in the mouth of the narrator, *H,* if in human, or *D,* if in Divine direct speech ("Sorts-of-Discourse").

A third way of partitioning the book is sequential.  Genesis may conveniently be divided into three major divisions: (a) the Prologue, i.e., the *Urgeschichte* (chs. 1-11); (b) the Main Body, i.e., the patriarchal history (chs. 12-36), and (c) the Epilogue, i.e., the Joseph Cycle (chs. 37-50).

Of those three ways of dissecting Genesis, the second, i.e., the Sorts-of-Discourse, is inherent without question in the book itself, whereas the first, i.e., the Documents, is speculative.  As to the three Divisions, granted that other segmentations have been proposed in professional literature, it remains to be seen whether the one suggested here is borne out by analysis.  Whether or not there is any interaction between these three dimensions is one of the problems to be tackled in this enquiry.

The proportional sizes of the three divisions within the book are approximately:

> *I.*    "*Urgeschichte*":         19 p.c.
> *II.*   The Patriarchs History: 52 p.c.
> *III.*  The Joseph Cycle:      31 p.c.

Within these, the shares of *J, E, P* and *N, H, D* are most unequal.  This will hardly cause surprise to anybody familiar with the contents of Genesis, but has so far nowhere been precisely measured.  These shares are given in percentages in Figure 1.2 (p. 22).

### 1.4.2.  THE TWO-DIMENSION MATRIX

In many of the following discussions, the dissections of Genesis into the first two dimensions, i.e., into Documents and Sorts-of-Discourse, are dealt with together.  For an easier overview of this procedure, the matrix in Table 1.2 will help.  Its columns represent Documents and its rows Sorts-of-Discourse. Thus, nine "cells" result, each containing a certain number of words.  The cells are of course unequally populated, ranging from more than 5500 to less than 200 words.  In order to examine not only the possible similarity between cells, but also their own inner homogeneity, the total number of words in each

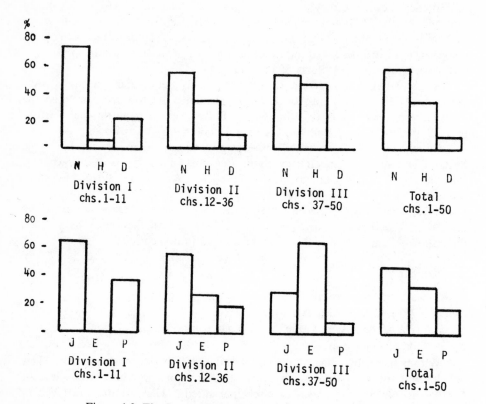

Figure 1.2: The Proportional Shares of *J, E, P,* and *N, H, D,*
in the Three Divisions of Genesis

cell was divided into samples of the same size each, i.e., roughly of 200 words. The matrix is shown in Table 1.2 and indicates the number of samples per cell. (See Table 1.2 (p. 24).

In each cell, the number of the pertaining words are pooled together, as if they constituted a continuous text, with complete disregard to chapter and verse partitions.

These samples were numbered consecutively, so that

| | | | | |
|---|---|---|---|---|
| $NP$ | comprises | sample | nos. | 1-12 |
| $NE$ | ” | ” | ” | 13-28 |
| $NJ$ | ” | ” | ” | 29-55 |
| $HP$ | ” | ” | ” | 56-57 |
| $HE$ | ” | ” | ” | 58-73 |
| $HJ$ | ” | ” | ” | 74-87 |
| $DP$ | ” | ” | ” | 88-90 |
| $DE$ | ” | ” | ” | 91 |
| $DJ$ | ” | ” | ” | 92-96 |

Some of these samples extent over almost half the book, while others cover less than one chapter. A complete list of the limits of each sample in the text is given in Table 1.3. Four-digit numbers in this table refer to chapter and verse, e.g., 2609 means ch. 26, v. 9. The partition between one sample and the following one may of course fall right in the middle of a verse. (See Table 1.3 (p. 25).

As mentioned before, a few samples had to be stretched over half the book so that the size of 200 words be reached (e.g., nos. 90, 91,96), whereas in others (e.g., nos. 17, 18, 24, 42, 43, 67-71, 81) half a chapter was enough for attaining the same length. This fact is easier to survey in Figure 1.3. As it is the rule in schematic presentation, this figure is less accurate than Table 1.3. On the other hand, it offers a better view of where one of the two main presumed authors, $J$ or $E,$ is most active, namely, where there are clusters of several adjacent samples which look shorter in the diagram, although in fact they are not. (See Figure 1.3 (p. 26).

## 1.5. The Criteria

### 1.5.1. CRITERIA REQUIREMENTS

The quantitatively tangible data available for comparing language behavior in parts of Genesis are certain text characteristics that may be expected to be author-specifying criteria. In order to qualify as such, they must meet a number of requirements. They must be countable and accurately counted, preferably by the computer. They must be so minute and unobtrusive that the author himself cannot have been aware of whether he employed a certain linguistic phenomenon or not. They must not depend

Table 1.2: Categories, Subcategories and Numbers of Samples

| Sorts-of-Discourse | DOCUMENTS | | | |
|---|---|---|---|---|
| | *P* | *E* | *J* | Total |
| *N* | *NP* : 12 | *NE* : 16 | *NJ* : 27 | *N* : 55 |
| *H* | *HP* : 2 | *HE* : 16 | *HJ* : 14 | *H* : 32 |
| *D* | *DP* : 3 | *DE* : 1 | *DJ* : 5 | *D* : 9 |
| Total | *P* : 17 | *E* : 33 | *J* : 46 | 96 |

Table 1.3: Limits of Samples

| Sample no. | Cell | Division | Limits | Sample no. | Cell | Division | Limits |
|---|---|---|---|---|---|---|---|
| 1. | NP | I | 0501-0519 | 51. | NJ | III | 3703-3729 |
| 2. | NP | I | 0519-0622 | 52. | NJ | III | 3729-3814 |
| 3. | NP | I | 0622-1113 | 53. | NJ | III | 3814-4707 |
| 4. | NP | I | 1113-1131 | 54. | NJ | III | 4707-4727 |
| 5. | NP | II* | 1131-1603 | 55. | NJ | III | 4727-5026 |
| 6. | NP | II | 1603-2303 | | | | |
| 7. | NP | II | 2303-2512 | 56. | HP | II | 1211-2746 |
| 8. | NP | II | 2512-3513 | 57. | HP | III* | 2746-5026 |
| 9. | NP | II | 3513-3614 | | | | |
| 10. | NP | II | 3614-3632 | 58. | HE | II | 2002-2126 |
| 11. | NP | III* | 3632-4615 | 59. | HE | II | 2126-2927 |
| 12. | NP | III | 4615-5026 | 60. | HE | II | 2927-3032 |
| | | | | 61. | HE | II | 3032-3126 |
| 13. | NE | II | 2001-2114 | 62. | HE | II | 3126-3143 |
| 14. | NE | II | 2114-2812 | 63. | HE | II* | 3143-3915 |
| 15. | NE | II | 2812-2917 | 64. | HE | III | 3915-4111 |
| 16. | NE | II | 2917-3014 | 65. | HE | III | 4111-4128 |
| 17. | NE | II | 3014-3041 | 66. | HE | III | 4128-4207 |
| 18. | NE | II | 3041-3133 | 67. | HE | III | 4207-4233 |
| 19. | NE | II | 3133-3518 | 68. | HE | III | 4233-4311 |
| 20. | NE | II* | 3518-3907 | 69. | HE | III | 4311-4405 |
| 21. | NE | III | 3907-4005 | 70. | HE | III | 4405-4424 |
| 22. | NE | III | 4005-4108 | 71. | HE | III | 4424-4508 |
| 23. | NE | III | 4108-4152 | 72. | HE | III | 4508-4811 |
| 24. | NE | III | 4152-4225 | 73. | HE | III | 4811-5026 |
| 25. | NE | III | 4225-4326 | | | | |
| 26. | NE | III | 4326-4503 | 74. | HJ | I* | 0223-1503 |
| 27. | NE | III | 4503-4802 | 75. | HJ | II | 1503-1832 |
| 28. | NE | III | 4802-5026 | 76. | HJ | II | 1832-2221 |
| | | | | 77. | HJ | II | 2221-2424 |
| 29. | NJ | I | 0205-0219 | 78. | HJ | II | 2424-2445 |
| 30. | NJ | I | 0220-0324 | 79. | HJ | II | 2445-2610 |
| 31. | NJ | I | 0324-0423 | 80. | HJ | II | 2610-2719 |
| 32. | NJ | I | 0423-0711 | 81. | HJ | II | 2719-2743 |
| 33. | NJ | I | 0711-0802 | 82. | HJ | II | 2743-3218 |
| 34. | NJ | I | 0802-0820 | 83. | HJ | II | 3218-3404 |
| 35. | NJ | I | 0820-1015 | 84. | HJ | II* | 3404-3708 |
| 36. | NJ | I* | 1016-1302 | 85. | HJ | III | 3708-3818 |
| 37. | NJ | II | 1302-1512 | 86. | HJ | III | 3818-4706 |
| 38. | NJ | II | 1512-1808 | 87. | HJ | III | 4706-5026 |
| 39. | NJ | II | 1808-1915 | | | | |
| 40. | NJ | II | 1915-1935 | 88. | DP | I | 0613-0906 |
| 41. | NJ | II | 1935-2402 | 89. | DP | II* | 0906-1707 |
| 42. | NJ | II | 2402-2432 | 90. | DP | II* | 1707-5026 |
| 43. | NJ | II | 2432-2505 | | | | |
| 44. | NJ | II | 2506-2609 | 91. | DE | II* | 2003-5026 |
| 45. | NJ | II | 2609-2633 | | | | |
| 46. | NJ | II | 2633-2732 | 92. | DJ | I | 0309-0603 |
| 47. | NJ | II | 2732-3215 | 93. | DJ | I* | 0603-1316 |
| 48. | NJ | II | 3215-3304 | 94. | DJ | II | 1316-1817 |
| 49. | NJ | II | 3304-3413 | 95. | DJ | II | 1817-2212 |
| 50. | NJ | II* | 3413-3703 | 96. | DJ | III* | 2212-5026 |

Remarks: 0501 = ch. 5, v. 1. Samples, the Roman numerals of which carry an asterisk, are apportioned to the Division as indicated although they extend over two.

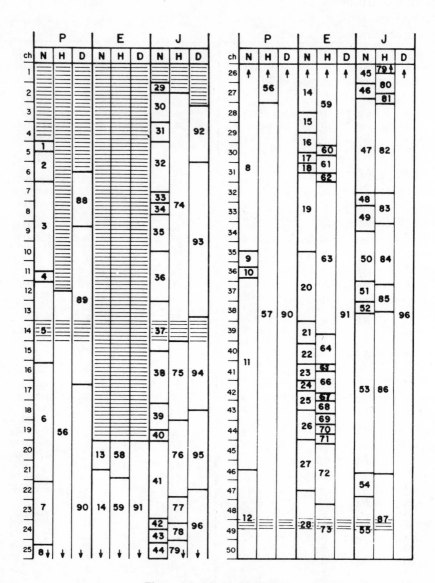

Figure 1.3: Limits of Samples

on subject matter, i.e., be content-free, nor depend on each other. They must not be dictated by inescapable and mandatory rules of grammar but rather be optional and facultative. They should have previously been tested in writings of unquestioned homogeneity as to their consistent use "within" a writer before qualifying as discriminants between writers in order to avoid unnecessary labor by the analyst. If, however, a criterion happens to be taken into account which is not sufficiently discriminating, no harm is done. Simply, non-discriminants do not add to the information gained nor do they detract from it. As Goethe put it, we just remain "*so klug als wie zuvor*".

Finally, these criteria should not be confused with stylistic devices such as figures of speech and the like since these may intentionally be controlled by a writer.

Obviously, the greater the number of these criteria and the greater their discriminative power, the better. An entire battery of such parameters has been proposed in the past and used as a yardstick for measuring affinities between written works, especially in English. If satisfactory results were obtained from them, there are grounds to expect even better results from more sophisticated attributive models and procedures such as those employed in the following parts of this study. It is noteworthy that there are a few *causes célèbres* in which stylometry — an unfortunate term — was practised and its evidence accepted in court.[41]

## 1.5.2.  THE CRITERIA SET

The fifty-four criteria selected to serve in this study and detailed below do indeed meet the conditions set. For the data per text sample of these 54 variables, expressed in relative frequencies, i.e., the percentages of their incidence (multiplied, for convenience's sake, by $10^4$), see the sample page in Appendix 1.A.

Nos. 1-10: word length in terms of phonemes. That word length characterizes an author's writing habits is extensively acknowledged in professional literature where it is mostly measured in terms of syllables.[42] Although the count is much more laborious, it was done here in terms of phonemes because then the range between minimum and maximum values is much wider and the measurement more accurate.[43]

---

[41] A list of characteristics, their description and evaluation may be found in G.T. Carpenter, *The Interrelationship among Various Statistical Measures of Written Language and their Relative Importance in Discriminating between the Works of Two Authors* (Diss. York University, Toronto, 1968). For the use of stylometry in court, see A.Q. Morton, *Literary Detection* (London: Bowker, 1978).

[42] See *Isaiah*, 93-128, *Zechariah*, 35-5, and *Judges*, 482. They are based on W. Fucks, "On Mathematical Analysis of Style", *Biometrika* 39 (1952), 122-29.

[43] See *Isaiah*, 128-34, and *Zechariah*, 35.

Nos. 11-12: nouns in construct and absolute state, respectively, within the total number of nouns. These data are expected to show a writer's propensity to use or not to use *composita*. Inflected nouns must not be taken into account since their occurrence is implied in nos. 11 and 12 combined.[44]

No. 13: verbs in *pa'al*, and no. 14, in *hif'il* within the total number of verbs. These two criteria have previously not been tried out and were here employed on an experimental basis for the first time. If they do not discriminate, much the worse, but the results of calculations will not be distorted, as mentioned in Section 1.5.1.

Nos. 15 and 16: verbs in passive, i.e., in *nif'al* and *pu'al*. *Hof'al* is too rare and *hitpa'el* too dubiously passive for inclusion.[45]

No. 17: subordinative conjunctions. Their number in Biblical Hebrew is less than half a dozen of which three (*ki*, *'im* and *'ašer*) are by far the most frequent. Their occurences reveal to what extent a writer prefers hypotaxis to parataxis.[46]

No. 18: the definite article. Its "intra-writer" and "inter-writers" usage has been examined to some length.[47] Percentages are calculated per potential carriers of the article (which is facultative in Hebrew), i.e., nouns in absolute state, numerals and participles. The rest of potential carriers, namely *gentilicia*, patronyms and several toponyms, are so few that they could be omitted. When the article occurs elided in the proleptic prepositional letters *bet*, *kaf* and *lamed* and may be recognized there only by their vocalization, it was included in the count, for, while the vowel signs may have been inserted late in the consonantal text, they still go back to very old tradition.

No. 19: *waw coniunctivum*. This proleptic bound morpheme may, as is well known, fulfil a great number of functions other than conjunction the foremost of which is consecutivity. As the *waw consecutivum* may be identified with certainty only when it occurs before verbs in imperfect and as in the remaining cases the conjunctive or consecutive function of the *waw* is a matter of interpretation, fine distinctions had to be neglected and all *waws* were counted as if they were conjunctive which they are after all. The inclusion of this criterion in the set relies on previous thorough experiments.[48]

---

[44] See *Zechariah*, 38 (Table 9), and *Judges*, 480.

[45] See *Isaiah*, 155-57, *Zechariah*, 38, and *Judges*, 480-81.

[46] See *Isaiah*, 192-200, *Zechariah*, 36, and *Judges*, 478.

[47] By Y.T. Radday and H. Shore, "The Definite Article — An Author and/or Type-Specifying Discriminant in the Hebrew Bible", *Bulletin of the Association for Literary and Linguistic Computing* 3 (1977), 23-31; cf. also *Judges*, 479.

[48] It was included in the criteria set in *Zechariah*, 36-37, and *Judges*, 478, mainly on grounds of its promising discriminant power as demonstrated in Y.T. Radday and H. Shore, "*Waw* coniunctivum — an Author- and/or Type-Specifying Criterion in Biblical Literature", *Proceedings of the Sixth World Congress of Jewish Studies 1973* (Jerusalem: World Union for Jewish Studies, 1977), 197-206 (in Hebrew), and in their "*And* in Isaiah", *Revue de l'organisation internationale pour l'étude des langues anciennes par l'ordinateur* 2 (1974), 25-41.

Nos. 20-54: transitions between word categories within the sum of all words. The frequencies of these transitions bring to light the *Feinstruktur* of a text. Plainly, the more numerous they are, the finer this analysis is. Only a few categories though, may be unambiguously defined in Hebrew: nouns together with adjectives (*N*), proper names (*L*) (in most counts added to *N*), finite (*F*) and non-finite (*V*) verbs, prepositions and pronouns (*P*) and coordinative conjunctions, adverbs and the rest (*C*). Were not the Masoretic text devoid of all interpunctions, these too could have been considered word categories as it was done in an analogous study in German literature.[49]   The only similar sign in the Hebrew Bible the reader can be relatively sure of is where a verse ends. These stops were therefore added as a sixth category (*S*). Thus, a matrix of 6 × 6 = 36 results. Since the transition *SS* is impossible, thirty-five transitions result.

A complete and detailed list of all criteria, numbered consecutively as they are referréd to as variables in statistical procedures throughout this research, is given in Table 1.4. It will be the task, among others, of these procedures to assign to each variable a coefficient denoting its discriminant potency. See Table 1.4 (p. 30).

Of these, nos. 24, 30, 36, 42-49 and 54, altogether eleven, are not realized at all in Genesis. The investigation will therefore operate not with 54, but 43 variables. These, it is hoped, describe if not in full, then at least to the satisfaction of our present needs, the language behavior of any sufficiently long text sample. What the optimal length of such a sample is, is for the statistician to decide.

## 1.6.  The Outline of the Enquiry

This, then, is the approach chosen, the material prepared and these are the criteria defined for probing, with maximum objectivity, into the problem of the unity of the Book of Genesis. Upon terminating the preparatory stage, a group was formed to pursue this enquiry; the group was made of members representing Biblical and Hebrew scholarship, linguistics, statistics, operations research and computer science. It split into small teams, each undertaking one specific assignment, a division of labor which evolved as follows.

Part Two, the one after the present introductory essay, offers, first of all, a general exposition of statistical theory and the specific mode of thinking upon which the investigation is based. This is mainly intended for the layman in

---

[49] Relative frequencies of transitions between word categories proved to be an efficient tool in author authentication in *Isaiah*, 158-91, *Zechariah*, 39, and *Judges*, 482-83. This criterion was first introduced by D. Wickmann, *Eine mathematisch-statistische Methode zur Untersuchung der Verfasserfrage literarischer Texte, durchgeführt am Beispiel der* Nachtwachen. *Von Bonaventura mit Hilfe der Wortartübergänge* (Opladen: Forschungsberichte des Landes Nordrhein-Westfalen, 1969).

## Table 1.4: The Criteria Set

| No. | Criterion | No. | Criterion |
|---|---|---|---|
| | *Word length* | 29. | finite verb forms/prepositions + pronouns |
| 1. | 2-phoneme words | 30. | finite verb forms/subordinative conjunctions |
| 2. | 3-phoneme words | 31. | finite verb forms/ends of verses |
| 3. | 4-phoneme words | 32. | non-finite verb forms/nouns |
| 4. | 5-phoneme words | 33. | non-finite verb forms/finite verb forms |
| 5. | 6-phoneme words | 34. | non-finite verb forms/non-finite verb forms |
| 6. | 7-phoneme words | 35. | non-finite verb forms/prepositions + pronouns |
| 7. | 8-phoneme words | 36. | non-finite verb forms/subordinative conjunctions |
| 8. | 9-phoneme words | 37. | non-finite verb forms/ends of verses |
| 9. | 10-phoneme words | 38. | prepositions + pronouns/nouns |
| 10. | >10-phoneme words | 39. | prepositions + pronouns/finite-verb forms |
| | | 40. | prepositions + pronouns/non-finite verb forms |
| | *Morphological* | 41. | prepositions + pronouns/prepositions + pronouns |
| 11. | construct nouns per all nouns | 42. | prepositions + pronouns/subordinative conjunctions |
| 12. | absolute nouns per all nouns | 43. | prepositions + pronouns/ends of verses |
| 13. | verbs in *pa'al* per all verbs | 44. | subordinative conjunctions/nouns |
| 14. | verbs in *hif'il* per all verbs | 45. | subordinative conjunctions/finite verb forms |
| 15. | verbs in *nif'al* per all verbs | 46. | subordinative conjunctions/non-finite verb forms |
| 16. | verbs in *pu'al* per all verbs | 47. | subordinative conjunctions/prepositions + pronouns |
| | | 48. | subordinative conjunctions/subordinative conjunctions |
| | *Syntactical* | 49. | subordinative conjunctions/ends of verses |
| 17. | subordinative conjunctions | 50. | ends of verses/nouns |
| 18. | definite article per nouns, numerals and participles | 51. | ends of verses/finite verb forms |
| 19. | *waw* conjunctive + consecutive | 52. | ends of verses/non-finite verb forms |
| | | 53. | ends of verses/prepositions + pronouns |
| | *Transition Frequencies* | 54. | ends of verses/subordinative conjunctions |
| 20. | nouns/nouns | | |
| 21. | nouns/finite verb forms | | |
| 22. | nouns/non-finite verb forms | | |
| 23. | nouns/prepositions + pronouns | | |
| 24. | nouns/subordinative conjunctions | | |
| 25. | nouns/ends of verses | | |
| 26. | finite verb forms/nouns | | |
| 27. | finite verb forms/finite verb forms | | |
| 28. | finite verb forms/non-finite verb forms | | |

Remark: For the realizations (in relative frequencies) of these criteria see Appendix 1.A. They refer there to sample size except, as indicated above, for nos. 11-16, 18.

statistics.   Later, this part approaches the problem of Genesis in the same way as it has already been done, and proved itself, in analogous investigations in other books of the Hebrew Bible.

Part Three continues the same task, using, however, other techniques which, the authors believe, have hitherto served rather rarely in literary criticism and even less often in regard to Scripture.   These recently developed techniques are so sophisticated that their verbal demonstration is inevitably highly technical and demands a certain familiarity, on the part of the reader, with statistical terminology and procedure.   Those lacking in this field may concentrate on the resumés which summarize, at the end of each technique employed, its aim and results.

In contrast to Part Two and Part Three, both of which focus on formal linguistic criteria, Part Four deals with vocabulary and thus completes the two foregoing ones.

No attempt was made by the editors to integrate Parts Two, Three and Four into one whole, the less so as they confirm each other's conclusions to no small extent.

Parts Five and Six are overall appraisals of these conclusions.   They reflect a linguist's and a Biblical scholar's views of what was submitted to them by the statisticians.[50]

---

[50] The present research project could have been completed a full year earlier, had it not been for a regrettable mishap, a good example of the pitfalls hidden on the way of using a computer.   At a certain stage, after the book of Genesis was linguistically analyzed and each word marked by *J*, *E* or *P*, as the case may be, as well as by *N*, *H* and *D*, as prescribed by the text, the material was divided into 96 samples (shown in Tab. 1.3).   These were then numbered in such a way that the *NP*-samples carried nos. 1-12, the *NE*-samples nos. 13-28 and so forth.   Henceforth, for the sake of expediency, the origin of a sample in *NP, NE* etc. was disregarded and its running number only used until results of the statistical calculations came in for interpretation.   While most did indeed make very good sense in general, some were quite puzzling.   The most uncomfortable one was that the Joseph Cycle, the overall homogeneity of which is acknowledged even by the severest of critics, turned out to consist of two unambiguously dissimilar halves (approximately chs. 37-41 and 42-50).   Consultations with prominent colleagues in Israel and the United States did not bear any fruits so that the entire project was almost given up.   At this point, and upon a thorough check of every detail, it turned out to the horror of the participants in the research that somehow the numbering of the samples had been garbled: The five samples made up by chs. 42-50 and ascribed to *NE,* carried nos. 1-5 as if they belonged to *NP*!   Consequently, all computations without exception had to be repeated — a labour of over one year.   The incident is worth reporting not in order to evoke the pity of the reader, but rather for two reasons; it shows how a comparatively small human error jams the most sophisticated computer technique and, what is more, it proves the sensitivity of the method and thus its reliability.

PART TWO

# On Statistics: In General and in Genesis

DIETER WICKMANN

> Statistics is a body of methods for making wise decisions in the face of uncertainty.
>
> (Roberts and Wallis)

## 2.1. Basic Concepts and Problems in Statistical Decision Making

It is curious how antithetically statistics is regarded by the non-statistician. Some hold it to be such an irreproachable authority in decision making that the mere mention of the term suffices to evoke respect bordering on awe, to allay any doubt and to silence all further dispute. But more often than not, it is treated with suspicion as a body of pliable methods from which almost any desired conclusion may ensue. All that the statistician does, it is averred, is collect enough data and then present, or, worse, manipulate, them in a purposefully designed fashion so that they conform to his pet theory. These widespread attitudes are both affective, unlike those toward other scientific disciplines. Both, and the obvious contradiction between them, are worth speculating about where they come from. A tentative explanation of what lies at the bottom of these phenomena may be that the first, the reverent stance, has its cause in the formidable array and impressive variety of statistics' almost arcane techniques, bound to arouse uncritical admiration on part of the layman, whereas the second flows from the fact that statistical decision making is fundamentally surprisingly similar to common sense reasoning.

## 2.1.1. PROBABILITIES IN EVERYDAY LIFE

Toying with this idea, let us consider the case of a person who daily drives his car from home to office. Taking the usual route, he finds it, one day, blocked because of road works. Had he heard of the obstacle before, he would have chosen an alternative route, but, as it is, he has obviously made a wrong decision. However, being unaware of the change which had occurred overnight, and in face of this uncertainty at the beginning of his drive, it was nonetheless a "wise" one, because, relying on his past experience, the hope that the road would be free was justified.

In this rather common situation nobody would think of statistical methods to help him to decide which route to take. But this decision, without the use of statistics, has already a quantitative background. Road works on that drive are a rare event, apt to happen, say, once in every five years. Assuming 220 work days per year, they could be expected to occur once in 1100 days. Deciding for the usual route, therefore, implicates an error risk with the probability of 0.11 p.c. Actually, we need not even calculate this probability, for, the rather fuzzy notion of a "rare event" works just as well: we need not exactly know how rare it is since its rareness is beyond any discussion.

Although this simple example illustrates that decision making involves latent probabilities, it does not yet reveal, as presented, the general features of the decision-making pattern. It does not show that behind a decision, essentially at least, two valuable, but competitive and indeed incompatible aims exist. This is why decisions are so often hard to make when probabilities do not have extreme values.

It seems important that the reader not acquainted with statistical procedures understand the basic concept of their logic and its relation to pre-scientific judgments which everybody is used to, especially since the very subject we are about to deal with here, namely, the doubted unity of the Book of Genesis, is momentous to so many people. A closer look at statistical judgments is therefore apposite.

A statistical judgment, in other words, a statistical test, consists basically of two steps: the objective, or better, the inter-subjective, and the subjective.

The first is the application of mathematical-statistical methods and techniques of analysis, the statistician's tools in the proper sense. This step is inter-subjective insofar as everybody who feels inclined to check the formal series of the procedures can, at least theoretically, do this. In practice, a non-statistician, even the statistician's colleague, will trust the results, without, however, being obliged to do so.

Then, there is the subjective step. Every decision maker has to account for the risks he is ready to undergo in choosing one of the given alternatives. The risks can be expressed quantitatively, and are, in statistical terms, of two kinds: error probability of type I and of type II, their symbols being $\alpha$ and $1-\beta$,[1] respectively. An individual's decision for giving the error probabilities certain values has to be distinguished from the proper decision to be made. The latter depends on the values of the former. The subjective account for the risks and, hence, for fixing the values for $\alpha$ and $1-\beta$, must precede the main statistical investigation. Even if the reader is ready to have confidence in the results of the present and the subsequent contributions to this volume, he still may change the error probabilities according to his own most personal attitudes, that is, according to what the Book of Genesis means to him.

---

[1] For a reason which need not be discussed here, it is common in statistical literature to use, as the error probability of type II, the complement $1-\beta$ instead of $\beta$.

## 2.1.2.  POPULATIONS, DISTRIBUTIONS, SAMPLES AND DECISIONS

With this in mind, let us modify the example of the driver.  He has the choice of two routes on his way to his office: one leads through the center of town and is the shortest, the other circumvents the city.  The latter, and longer in mileage, is almost surely free from traffic jams, contrary to the former. Having calculated the mean running times for either route to be equal and preferring easy to nerve-racking driving, he decides, from now on, to take the highway which outflanks the city.  In any case, when setting out, every morning, on his way to work, he acts on grounds of the hypothesis that the running time distribution has not altered.

And then, one day, he is told that traffic conditions in the city have so much improved that the city route may be quicker.  Among five successive trials on this route, he finds one to last longer and four to be shorter than the out-of-town road.  He now decides to assume a systematic and persisting change in the traffic situation and, in consequence, to choose the city route in the future.  The question is, Was this a "wise" decision?

This we cannot say yet, but the example enables us to reveal the general decision making pattern.  Specifically, it is the following.

The driver makes a decision on the grounds of a sample consisting of five consecutive running times drawn from a hypothetical infinite population of all the times his daily drives through the city would take.  Such a population is a mere product of the mind: it does not exist in reality.  Its real counterparts are the sample elements, namely, the limited number of running times of his actual experience.  We shall come across several more constructs of this kind later on.  Such a theoretical population may be described by a distribution with certain parameters, e.g., the mean value and the variance.  It may be symmetrical in regard to the mean.  How to get the characteristics of the distribution need not be elaborated here.

## 2.1.3.  THE DECISION-MAKING PATTERN

In fact, the driver has to deal with two such populations.  He does not know what effect the aforesaid traffic improvements are actually having on his mean running time $\tau$: either it did not change its old value $\tau_1$ (e.g., $\tau_1 = 20$ min.), and then he would prefer to continue using the by-pass, or it decreased to a new value $\tau_2 < \tau_1$ (e.g., $\tau_2 = 15$ min.), in which case he would take the city route.  Put differently, he does not know whether the running time is distributed with mean $\tau_1$ or $\tau_2$, and whether his sample was drawn from the one population or the other.

On account of some properties in the sample he decides either for $\tau_1$ or $\tau_2$, so that necessarily one of the following possibilities occurs:

    (a)   $\tau_1$ is true and he decides for $\tau_1$;
    (b)   $\tau_1$ is true and he decides for $\tau_2$;
    (c)   $\tau_2$ is true and he decides for $\tau_2$;
    (d)   $\tau_2$ is true and he decides for $\tau_1$;

He, and any decision maker, finds himself fundamentally in a dilemma: by deciding for $\tau_1$, he risks error (d), and by deciding for $\tau_2$ he risks error (b). The lower the one risk, the higher the other.

This is the pattern no decision maker can escape. One could go so far as to say that the term "decision" is meaningful only on the condition that this dilemma exists. The risks are not merely formal ones deduced from logical deliberations: they also do have an emotional aspect since one has to pay for the consequences of one's wrong decision. If there were no detrimental consequences in committing error (d), one would doubtless decide for $\tau_1$, and, likewise, if there were no detrimental consequences in committing error (b), one would doubtless decide for $\tau_2$.

Having delineated the general scheme of a decision maker's dilemma, let us now call a decision "wise" if the expected losses due to errors (b) and (d) are minimized. To quote Fieldmarshal Montgomery, "Victory goes to the side that makes fewer blunders". And this is where statistics and probability theory start.

## 2.1.4.  CALCULABLE AND NON-CALCULABLE RISKS

Our driver does in effect not run a high risk and would therefore never turn to a statistician. By deciding for $\tau_2$, he may have committed error (b) because, unfortunately, he happened to get an untypical sample from the population with $\tau = \tau_1$. All that ensues from this error is that he arrived at his office later than he should have and that he burned a little more fuel, which in his case is the only "fine" he must pay for making a wrong decision. But what happens if an error of this sort is committed in deciding the Genesis problem? What would then be the price to pay if we decide in favor of the Documentary Hypothesis although it was, say, Moses who in reality penned the book? Or, conversely, if we decided that Moses was the author of the book although it cannot in fact be ascribed to him or, for that matter, to any other single writer?

Whereas in the driver's example it is relatively easy to see that the costs of committing either of the two errors are the same, this is obviously not the case in the Genesis problem. Since "time is money", the consequences of the driver's errors can easily be converted into currency units and his risks thus be quantified: with certain parameters given, one would be able to calculate the probabilities $\alpha$ and $1-\beta$ of committing one of the two possible errors. And when the probabilities are deducible from some optimized (financial) criteria, they have a definite, concrete meaning. But what if their import cannot be expressed in monetary terms, for instance, when a wrong decision in the

Genesis problem is at stake? This question brings us right to the crucial point of the present investigation: it is *the* essential question. But before trying to reply to it we must first discuss some features of the underlying statistical model.

## 2.1.5.  FEATURES OF THE STATISTICAL MODEL

The gravamen of the Genesis problem under examination is whether the book was written by one author — whether he was Moses or someone else is beside the point — or by several. Let us call the assumption of single authorship the null hypothesis, $H_O$, and the assumption that the book is composed of several sources or Documents the alternative hypotheses, $H_{Al}$. Hypothesis $H_{Al}$ is actually a whole set of hypotheses unless the sources are exactly specified. After analyzing the text, a verdict is pronounced in favour of $H_O$, risking error (d), or in favour of $H_{Al}$, risking error (b).

But what exactly is the sample? What are the properties of the sample elements, on the grounds of which the verdict is pronounced? And what is the population the sample is drawn from?

2.1.5.1.  **Author-Specific Differences.**  First of all, we have to recall the rather trivial fact that any analysis — statistical, philological or whatever — must hope for marked differences in different writers' writing habits: if everybody wrote in the same fashion, such analyses would of course be in vain. To concretize this with an example: an excavation brought to light an ancient manuscript. The archeologist conjectures, by virtue of some indications and, in addition, of the Latin he has acquired at school, the manuscript to be written by Caesar. It is being submitted to an expert in Latin who maintains that Caesar could never have written this text. The Latinist must clearly have detected certain differences between some data in the manuscript, on the one side, and some corresponding data in the set of Caesar's uncontestedly genuine texts known to the expert, on the other.

The very suspicion alone that Caesar might have written the newly found text shows that there is a hypothetical population behind the Latinist's reasoning. For instance, there may more of Caesar's texts be extant, but still hidden in the ground, or Caesar may have written many other texts, but destroyed them for an unknown reason. In this way, we return to the notion of an infinite population, similar to the one mentioned apropos of the driver's problem: the population of all texts Caesar's brain might have produced of which the texts, nowadays at our disposal, are sample elements. We can now reformulate the archeologist's enquiry in statistical terms: "Here are two samples: one has only one element, that is, the recently discovered manuscript, the other consists of all other texts known to be written by Caesar. Are the two samples drawn from the same population?" The Latinist thinks not.

2.1.5.2. **Genesis: Three Problems in One.** In Genesis, matters are somewhat more complex. First, we are dealing with one single text only. The unitarian school assumes the book to be homogeneous, whereas Wellhausen and his followers claim certain passages to stem from different sources. Confining ourselves to the source documents $E$, $J$ and $P$, let us denote the ensembles of text passages attributed to one of the three sources by $T_E$, $T_J$ and $T_P$. Therefore, there are three samples to be compared instead of the two in the example above. But what are the sample elements? While we shall have more to say on this delicate point later on, we can make do with text sections of a certain length to be the sample elements. To adapt the archeologist's enquiry to our case: "Here are three samples, $T_E$, $T_J$, and $T_P$, with $n_E$, $n_J$ and $n_P$ text sections respectively. Are the three samples drawn from one and the same infinite population consisting of all imaginable text sections of the kind which, say, Moses could have conceived?" Wellhausen thinks not.

Moreover, Wellhausen even disputes that any two documents were drawn from the same population. Consequently, we are faced with three problems in one: (a) Is $E = J$? (b) Is $E = P$? Is $J = P$? Wellhausen negates all three questions. Denoting the members of the pairs by the indices $A$ and $B$, we are called upon to investigate for each pair whether or not $T_A$ and $T_B$, with sample sizes $n_A$ and $n_B$, are drawn from the same population. Thus the above mentioned, tentatively stated hypotheses are $H_O$: $A = B$; $H_{AI}$: $A \neq B$ (where, for instance, $A$ is the Elohist, $B$ is the Jahwist).

2.1.5.3. **The Variables.** Prior to returning to the *essential question,* i.e., the interpretation of the error risks, we have to ask ourselves what the aforesaid "certain differences" are that are supposed to exist between the data of the samples to be compared.

There are a host of linguistic, syntactic, semantic and other criteria available for comparison, but not always easily manageable. The simplest are the ones either present or not in the text. Our Latinist could have argued that the manuscript shown to him contained certain phenomena which do not at all occur in Caesar's genuine texts, just as Wellhausen asserts that the Jahwist would never call his Deity by the name *Elohim,* nor the Elohist call his by the name *YHWH* — to put Wellhausen's theory in a nutshell. In a similar, but slightly different vein from the yes-or-no data is the more-or-less concept. Let $X$ denote a (linguistic) variable which takes on values $x$. Thus, $X$ may stand for the number of nouns per text section (which is the not yet defined sample element). In a given text section, $X$ takes on, for instance, the value $x = 35$. $X$ is not confined to integer numbers: it may represent, to give an example, the mean sentence length per text section.

2.1.5.4. **Concentrating on One Single Variable.** Altogether, $K$ such variables were defined so that $X_k$ is one of them, with $1 \leq k \leq K$. If $i$ denotes the running index of the sample elements with $1 \leq i \leq n_A$ in $T_A$ and $1 \leq i \leq n_B$ in $T_B$, then $x_{kAi}$ ($x_{kBi}$) is called the realization of variable $X_k$ in the $i$-th sample element of sample $T_A$ ($T_B$). Let $T_A$ consist of $n_A = 4$ and $T_B$ of $n_B = 5$ text sections. In the following Figure 2.1, the realizations of an arbitrary variable $X_k$ are indicated by circles for $T_A$ and by crosses for $T_B$, and the vertical bars represent the corresponding mean values. See Figure 2.1 (p. 39).

The two samples in (1) are likely to be drawn from two different populations, whereas those in (2) are not, although the differences between the means, $\bar{x}_{kA} - \bar{x}_{kB}$, be equal. In order to obtain a measure of dissimilarity of the samples, one has therefore to relate the differences of the means to the scattering of the values around their respective means.

2.1.5.5.   **The Generalized Distance and Its Distribution.**   We need not carry out the task alluded to at the end of the foregoing paragraph since the well-known $t$-statistic offers its solution.   Moreover, the same statistic contains additional information: the sample sizes, $n_A$ and $n_B$, which are integrated, though not *expressis verbis,* in the intuitive judgment, too.   In other words, the $t$-statistic as a measure of dissimilarity is a kind of a generalized distance: the farther apart the samples lie, the greater $t$ is.   The rather impressive algebraic formula of $t$ is here omitted lest the reader be deterred from continuing.

The most important point is that the theoretical distribution of $t$ has been derived mathematically (in 1908, by one of the pioneers in modern statistics, W. Gosset, an English brewer, better known under his pseudonym, Student). To know the theoretical distribution is tantamount to knowing the probability of $t$ to fall into a given interval with lower and upper boundaries, $t_l$ and $t_u$. This piece of information, much welcome as it is, however, evokes a new question: what exactly does it mean that the probability $p$ of such an event is, say, 0.15?

If the null hypothesis, $A = B$, is true, $T_A$ and $T_B$ are samples drawn from the same population.   From $n_A = 4$ plus $n_B = 5$ sample elements we calculate the generalized distance $t_k$, in respect to the variable $X_k$, to be $t_k^*$ which is to say that the variable $t_k$ takes on the value $t_k^*$.   Now, imagine that this experiment of drawing 4 plus 5 sample elements from the (infinite) population is repeated $N$ times.   It will result in $N$ different $t_k^*$-values being the generalized distances of the $N$ pairs of samples.   Among the $N$ are $N'$ values falling into the specified interval $[t_l, t_u]$; $N'/N = f$ is the relative frequency of the event in question.   Now, with increasing $N$, $f$ converges against $p$.   Thus, $p = 0.15$ means that, in the long run, 15 p.c. of the $t_k^*$-values would fall into the specified interval.

2.1.5.6.   **Error Risk of Type I; the Critical Value.**   If we let $t_u$ increase to infinity, we get an open interval with lower boundary $t_l$, and we may then search for the probability of drawing two samples, the generalized distance of which is greater than $t_l$.   Or, inversely, the probability is the given $\alpha$ and $t_l$ is sought.   In this manner, $t_l$ turns out playing a central role in statistical decision making.   It is called the critical value and denoted by $c$.

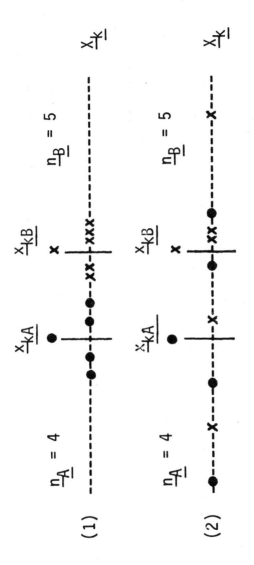

Figure 2.1: Measuring the Dissimilarity of Two Samples, $T_A$ and $T_B$, for One Single Variable

If, on the other hand, $H_O$ is not true, i.e., $A = B$, the generalized distance between $T_A$ and $T_B$ is expected to be the greater, the more the two populations lie apart.

2.1.5.7. **If We Knew More about the Documents.** Suppose for a while that we knew a little more about $A$ and $B$, that is, any two of our three Documents, than we actually do, for instance, that we knew their stylistic habits and, in particular, their respective mean values. If so, we would know how far their populations are apart from each other with regard to the linguistic variable $X_k$, and we could then deal with a definite alternative hypothesis, say $H_1$, out of the set $H_{Al}$. It would then be possible to calculate the corresponding probability distribution of $t_k$ and, therefore, the probability $1 - \beta$ of drawing two samples (one from $A$ with size $n_A$, the other from $B$ with the size $n_B$), the generalized distance between the two being smaller than $c$.

2.1.5.8. **The Decision-Making Pattern in Genesis.** Faced, contrary to the above hypothetical case, with an unknown reality, i.e., not knowing which of the two hypotheses, $H_O$ or $H_{Al}$, is true, the decision maker is bound to follow the general pattern previously discussed. If $t_k{}^*$, the actual value of $t_k$ between the two given samples $T_A$ and $T_B$, is greater than $c$, he opts for $H_1$, otherwise for $H_O$. In this fashion, the situation of the driver as described before is repeated here, as four alternatives offer themselves:

(a)   $H_O$ is true and $t_k{}^* < c$;
(b)   $H_O$ is true, but $t_k{}^* > c$;
(c)   $H_1$ is true and $t_k{}^* > c$;
(d)   $H_1$ is true, but $t_k{}^* < c$.

What must be decided at this juncture is of course which value should be attached to the limit $c$.

Recall that $\alpha$ is the probability of committing error (b), and $1 - \beta$ the probability of committing error (d). According to what has been said about probability distributions, $c$ is known with $\alpha$ given, and $1 - \beta$ is known with $c$ given, the two error probabilities being countercurrent.

## 2.1.6.   THE ESSENTIAL QUESTION AGAIN

Finally, we are coming back to the essential question, giving it a formal interpretation. Let $c$ be defined as such a value that $\alpha = 0.10$ and $1 - \beta = 0.20$. This means (if we imagine repeating the experiment many times, i.e., the experiment of drawing two samples $T_A$ and $T_B$ of sizes $n_A$ and $n_B$, respectively, under the condition of $H_O$) 10 p.c. of our decisions will be wrong — viz. (b) — and 90 p.c. will be correct — viz. (a) —, and when we do the same under the condition of $H_1$, 20 p.c. of them will be wrong — viz. (d) — and 80 p.c. will be correct — viz. (c).

Now, at last, it will be understood how difficult the choice of $\alpha$ and $1 - \beta$ is, since there is no objective criterion for evaluating the error probabilities, contrary to the driver's case. Everybody has to assess the matter for himself and to weigh the risks and consequences of his possibly wrong decisions. One person, less inclined to rely on religious tradition, will tend to attach to the error probabilities completely different values than another who is closely and dutifully committed to what the Bible and its pre-critical commentators have to say on the authorship of Torah in general and of Genesis in particular. Plainly, a reader of the latter type will keep the risk of wrongly rejecting the null hypothesis, i.e., that Genesis is homogeneous, extremely low. For that matter, he may just as well refuse to undergo any risk at all.

Should he come to the conclusion that wrongly rejecting $H_O$ would be catastrophe and, on the other hand, wrongly accepting it would not cause any detriment, he would be wise indeed not to run any risk whatsoever and to accept $H_O$ at all events. This, in turn, renders totally useless any investigation, statistical or not.

If, however, he is only slightly affected by the (supposed) truth of $H_1$, then, if $H_{Al}$ produces a trifling change in his outlook and, indeed, his life, he cannot, this time, help taking a risk to accept $H_O$, though it may be false. He will, nevertheless, ponder on the significances which the four possible outcomes of a decision may have for him. Eventually, he has to transform the results of his thorough deliberations into values of $\alpha$ and $1 - \beta$, a most hard pre-statistical task left to him as an individual. He must do this by means of the concept of probability, that is, by means of an imaginary, infinite repetition of the experiment, effectuated in reality so far but once.

Having acquainted the reader with the decision pattern and its inherent conflicts, I may well have bewildered him, especially the one who has previously perused one or two introductions into statistics. There, he may have found a somewhat awkward convention which camouflages the real problem by attaching certain values — 5 or 1 p.c. are quite common — to $\alpha$, without, as far as I can see, discussing their meaning. These values are meaningless unless the significances of the four possible outcomes of a decision and their mutual dependences have individually been taken into account. But is this altogether feasible? I doubt it.

Still worse is to come.

2.1.6.1. **No Optimal Path to Follow.** The dilemma has the traits of a twofold classical tragedy. The greater the endeavour to achieve the one good, the greater the risk of missing the other, and vice versa. The critical value $c$ represents the optimal path in this hazardous game against nature, balancing the expected winnings and losings. It is clear, however, while disregarding all the difficulties mentioned in estimating the error risks, that $c$ can be defined only if the two kinds of good to gain can be located. The one good is $H_O$, if it is true, the other $H_{Al}$, if it is true. Locating $H_1$ entails assuming knowledge of the differences between the Documents' mean values in employing the linguistic variable $X_k$. Since, as the matter stands, we do not know the Elohist, the Jahwist and the Priestly Writer, nor their stylistic habits, no alternative hypothesis can be stated and, hence, no location of their parameters is possible. Whence, there exists no optimal path to follow and no critical value $c$, balancing the expected winnings and losings, to find.

2.1.6.2. **Solving Half the Problem?** The probability $\beta$ of (c), i.e., $1 - \beta$ of (d), cannot be assigned any meaningful value, owing to the lack of $H_{Al}$. At a quick glance, this seems to make things rather easier for we have got rid, willy-nilly, of this part of the problem. But the case is quite the reverse: the problem cannot be separated into two because of the basic interdependences between the four possible outcomes (a) through (d). To illuminate this point, let us say that a person fixes $\alpha$ at the value of 10 p.c. and calculates, on the basis of $H_O$, the corresponding $c$. It is then formally correct to state that, if the experiment of this kind is repeated again and again, 10 p.c. of these repetitions will result in wrongly rejecting $H_O$. Yet it does not make much sense to do so since there is not the faintest clue to the probability of that event occurring for the sake of which one is taking the risk. There appears to be little point in risking ever so little without having any notion about the chance of winning.

It is nonetheless, as I said before, common practice to perform statistical tests although concrete alternative hypotheses cannot be formulated. Furthermore, the idea is obviously common not only in statistics, but also in non-statistical reasoning: the Latinist rejected the archeologist's conjecture without having an $H_{Al}$ at hand. It follows that he did not have any notion of his chance of winning either. Yet could not his conclusion be meaningful all the same?

We can put the matter this way. It is true that there is no quantitative access to $\beta$; it is, at the same time, also true that $H_O$ may be wrong. In order to reject $H_O$, when it is wrong, the decision maker risks no more than accepting it with the relative small probability $\alpha$, no matter what the chance of winning might be. For lack of an optimal path, he might lose in the long run, but not very much because of the small $\alpha$: he is simply prepared to risk that much.

Thus, if I wish to give a certain purport to the 10 p.c., I cannot help giving $\alpha = 10$ p.c. the same meaning as found in everyday life. When asked, "How sure are you?", a person may reply, "Up to ninety percent". When, in this sense, he is asked, "How great an error are you ready to risk in the Genesis problem?", he may answer, "Ten percent". We can not trace what exactly happened in his mind, and probably he, for that matter, could not either, as he weighed the pros and cons before he arrived, for himself, at this value of $\alpha$. On top, I am positive that he would give it another value after a while if he is scrupulous enough.

It may look as if all that I, although a statistician myself, have been elaborating in the foregoing discussion were nothing but disparaging my own art. The accusation is unwarranted. I have been simply trying to prevent the reader from interpreting a statistical test as an authorative battery of high-level mathematics which usurps the genuine domain of his individual judgmental freedom to choose his own risks and benefits. In short, I have argued against formalistic ideology.

If so, what are we left with?

## 2.1.7.  THE MATHEMATICIAN'S TASK

So far the ontological background of statistics — the decision-making pattern and its inherent dilemma. It may be called pre-statistics. The next step to take is to ask, What does the statistician do with all the powerful mathematical tools available to him? While refraining from going deeply into mathematics and rather staying within the confines of our specific problem, namely, the statistical analysis of the Book of Genesis, I propose the following answer.

In our pre-statistical discussion, the decision problem was elucidated by means of a single linguistic variable, $X_k$, and its realizations $x_k$ in the sample elements, i.e., text sections of a certain length. The dissimilarity of two samples, $T_A$ and $T_B$, was measured by the generalized distance, $t_k$, having the realizations $t_k{}^*$ from a particular, given pair of samples. Why are we not satisfied with this neat measure, comprising, as it does, a rich number of detailed aspects of dissimilarity — the difference of the sample means, the scattering within samples, and the sample sizes? Why reject the null hypothesis if the actual $t_k{}^*$ has too small a probability to occur instead of rejecting it simply when $t_k{}^*$ is too great?

The answer is that a human being harbours a somewhat intrinsic scale of probabilities, whereas for generalized distances or other measures, instead, there is no gauge as a basis for judgment. Whence a mathematician's task in this areas is to connect the two scales in such a way that the one is mapped onto the other. Sometimes, he is lucky enough to find the solution, as for instance in the generalized distances provided for by Student's distribution. Solely by virtue of Student's distribution, the statement "$t_k{}^*$ is too great" becomes meaningful when exceeding the critical value $c$.

## 2.1.8.  THE MULTIVARIATE CASE AND THE REAL GENERALIZED DISTANCE

We are now prepared for a more realistic view of our problem. No one would be so bold as to pronounce a judgment on the homogeneity or heterogeneity of Genesis on the grounds of one single linguistic variable, but rather demand as many as possible. Assume, then, that $K$ variables have been defined. Still, it would not help very much to perform $t$-tests separately for every single variable $X_k$: what would then have to be done if some tests show significance and others do not?

There is still another problem in the multivariate case, i.e., when a number of variables are taken into account. I am referring to the possibility of interdependence between them. Take, for instance, the two variables "word length in terms of syllables" $(X_k)$ and "word length in terms of phonemes" $(X_{k'})$. With an assumed significance of a test on $X_k$, it stands to reason to deem an additional significance of a separate test on $X_{k'}$ of less importance because of the manifestly strong correlation between the two variables, and vice versa. In general, each variable has to be assessed in the context of the others. To put it differently: the configurations of the realizations of the various variables within the text sections given must not be isolated. They sum up to an integral set of information as a whole.

We must strive, therefore, to construct a global statistic comprising all that was said about the single values of $t_k$, as well as the mutual relations between the $K$ variables. This aim is achievable in the multidimensional generalized distance, more briefly referred to as the Generalized Distance or the Mahalanobis-Distance, in honour of the Indian mathematician who established it. Moreover, under conditions that are fulfilled in most cases, even its probability distribution is known, and called the $F$-distribution, in honour of the English mathematician R. A. Fisher who was the first to calculate it.

2.1.8.1. **Section Length.** The above mentioned conditions, however, are not easily met in the present case. The first of these is that each of the linguistic variables must be normally distributed; and the second, that $n_A + n_B - 1 > K$, which means that the number $K$ of variables must be smaller than the sum of the two sample sizes minus one.

Now, in accordance with the Documentary Hypothesis in its form as investigated here (and detailed in Part One of this volume), there were three *Quellenschriften*, P, E and J, of which the book is woven together. Again, let us consider two and call them $A$ and $B$. The text passages ascribed to $A$ and $B$ consist of $w$ words, the sum of $w_A$ words of $A$ and $w_B$ words of $B$. We divide the two texts into sections of equal length $l$, measured in terms of words per section. These sections are, as stated before, the sample elements. There are $n_A$ sections in $A$ and $n_B$ in $B$. The greater the length $l$ chosen, the smaller the number of sample elements, $n_A$ and $n_B$, since the numbers $w_A$ and $w_B$ of words is limited. For identification of the $K = 54$ variables, consult Table 1.4 in Part One.

These 54 variables are essentially binomially distributed. The binomial distribution, however, is sufficiently approximated by the normal distribution, if the mean occurrence of the respective event per section is at least 7.

2.1.8.2. **The Quandary.** The frequencies of the 54 linguistic properties vary considerably, and it may be just the rare ones among them that are of particular interest. In order to expect at least seven occurrences of a certain variable in a section one would have to fix $l$ at such high a value that the sample sizes, $n_A$ and $n_B$, would be too small to fulfil the inequality which is the second of the two conditions. Or, conversely, $K$ would have to be limited to such a small number that most of the linguistic information available would get lost.

Two ways are open to extricate us from this quandary.

One is the possibility of transforming binomially distributed variables into normally distributed ones by means of the *arcsin*-transformation. Following this avenue, a rather short section length could be chosen in order to obtain a sufficient number of sample elements, $n_A$ and $n_B$, to fulfil the unequality condition: rather rare occurrences would then be transformed into appropriate realizations of normal distribution, thus causing no more trouble. This device is being used by the authors of Part Three.

The other means, described in detail elsewhere,[2] is the one to be employed below. Its basic idea is the following. The unequality, $n_A + n_B - 1 > K$, is a result of the variables' possible correlations integrated in the concept of the Generalized Distance. One may well ask to what extent eventual correlations could have a noticeable effect on a dissimilarity measure at all. It turns out that variables, except strongly correlated ones, can be treated as if they were independent. By consequence, a *t*-test can be performed for each variable separately, and the single results be combined in a global distance statistic, $\Xi$, which is normally distributed. This seems to be useful in getting around the nasty unequality. We cannot ignore, though, that we have to pay for this benefit, but not too high a price: several variables will have to be excluded owing to strong correlation. This is not a real loss, for, after eliminating one of two strongly correlated variables, the discriminating information is still found in the other, and that exactly because of their strong interdependence.

## 2.1.9. HOW TO INTERPRET RESULTS — A PERSONAL DECISION

An attempt has been made in the foregoing paragraphs to verbalize the pre-statistical and mathematical-statistical implications in the quantitative approach to the Documentary Hypothesis. This was done so as to give the reader who is not too familiar with statistics the opportunity to inspect the main features of decision making which involve weighing the chances of winning and the risks of losing. The inter-subjective, mathematical part consists of measuring the dissimilarity between the given samples in terms of some global Generalized Distance on grounds of numerous configurations of

---

[2] A detailed description of the statistical method referred to here may be found in my *Eine mathematisch-statistische Methode zur Untersuchung der Verfasserfrage literarischer Texte. Durchgeführt am Beispiel* Nachtwachen. Von Bonaventura *mit Hilfe der Wortübergänge* (Opladen: Forschungsbericht des Landes Nordrhein-Westfalen 2019, 1969), and in my contribution to Y. T. Radday, *The Unity of Isaiah in the Light of Statistical Linguistics* (Hildesheim: Verlag Gerstenberg, 1973), 251-72. The method is furthermore defended in my "Eine mathematisch-statistische Überprüfung der Klingemann-Hypothese", *Lili-Zeitschrift für Literaturwissenschaft und Linguistik* 4 (1974), Heft 16. It was also applied, with comparative success, by Y. T. Radday and myself in "The Unity of Zechariah in the Light of Statistical Linguistics", *Zeitschrift für die alttestamentliche Wissenschaft* 87 (1975), 30-55, and by Radday and me, in cooperation with S. Talmon and G. Leb, in "The Book of Judges Examined by Statistical Linguistics", *Biblica* 58 (1977), 469-99.

linguistic observations, and in mapping this measure onto a probability scale. The results are listed in Section 2.2. below. There, $P(\Xi > \Xi^*)$ means the probability of occurrence of the distance measure to be greater than the actual value $\Xi^*$, under the null hypothesis of the two respective samples being drawn from the same population.

The subjective part, however, must precede the intersubjective. This means to say that before looking at the results, the reader has to make up his mind as to what risk he is ready to wrongly rejecting the null hypothesis of homogeneity. The answer depends on his own, individual and rather intimate attitude to the problem of Genesis. Is he prepared to take no more than a very low risk — say, $\alpha = 1$ p.c.? Or perhaps a little more because he would gladly decide in favour of the Documentary Hypothesis if it is true — say, $\alpha = 10$ p.c.? Be it as it may, if $P$ is smaller than $\alpha$, he will decide to reject the null hypothesis, $A = B$.

If, on the other hand, $P$ is not smaller than $\alpha$, he will not be much wiser than before because of the lack of an alternative hypothesis: could not $A$ and $B$ actually be written by two different authors who nevertheless wrote in the same 'style'? In terms of the present enquiry this would mean that the relative frequencies of the various linguistic properties are almost equal in both cases. In view of this eventuality, we are compelled to conclude that the observations do not contradict the null hypothesis. Hence, the result of the test ($P > \alpha$) may not be interpreted as evidence in favour of the null hypothesis. Of course, there is no evidence for an alternative either; and thus, the question of the authorship remains unanswered when $P > \alpha$.

With regard to the mathematics upon which the following calculations are based, and to all the remaining details about to be submitted, the reader may, and must, trust the statistician. But with regard to the risks of judgment he had better choose them himself. Left, thus, to his own devices, so to say, he may, upon the conclusion of this long preliminary excursus, be still confused to some degree, but then, I hope, at least confused at a higher level than at the beginning.

## 2.2.  Procedures and Results

### 2.2.1.  FIRST STEPS

All steps described in this paragraph were carried out by means of a PASCAL-program.

The incoherent passages attributed to $E$, $J$ and $P$ were first pooled respectively and then divided up into text blocks of about 200 words. The realizations of the variables are counted per text blocks. This is the original data set. The variables are binomially distributed, as mentioned in Section 2.1.8.1. Most of them cannot be approximated by a normal distribution because of the short text block length. Thus, the text blocks are partially combined into *sections*, the shortest of which number 618 words. This is a compromise between section length and the number of sections. Thus, we have 4 sections (each of 824 words) in $E$, 9 sections (each of 618 words) in $J$ and 3 sections (each of 804 words) in $P$. The sections are our sample elements, whereas the variables are the relative frequencies of the linguistic observations per section.

## 2.2.2. ELIMINATED VARIABLES

The samples of the whole text are pooled and the total frequencies of the 54 defined variables are counted. By means of a simple proportion calculus one obtains the mean frequency $\bar{f}_k$ of each variable $k$ per sample as an approximation of the corresponding "mathematical expectation". If $\bar{f}_k < 7$, $k$ is eliminated from the variable list. The following variables (cf. Table 1.4.) are eliminated after this check:

nos.  16   24   28   30   31   32   33   34   36   37   42
      43   44   45   46   47   48   49   50   52   53   54

The distributions of the remaining 32 variables are sufficiently normal.

## 2.2.3. CORRELATION CHECK

Pearson's correlation coefficient is calculated for each pair $(k, k')$ of the 32 variables, thus obtaining $\binom{32}{2} = 496$ values. A significance test of the null hypothesis $\rho = 0$ is performed and all pairs $(k, k')$ significant on the $\alpha = 0.01$ level are output. The output shows 23 of such pairs. Several variables appear more than once, in particular variables nos. 8 and 19 five times each and no. 15 six times. After ejecting these three from the list of variables, seven pairs still show strong correlation. It has, however, to be considered that, with the chosen $\alpha$, five correlation values are expected to be significant even if $\rho = 0$ (because $0.01 \cdot 496 \approx 5$). Therefore, only the three variables nos. 8, 15 and 19 are removed from the list, which finally comprises the following 29 variables:

nos.   1    2    3    4    5    6    7    9   10   11
      12   13   14   17   18   20   21   22   23   25
      26   27   29   35   38   39   40   41   51

## 2.2.4. THE MAIN TESTS

Three comparisons are carried out, i.e., three null hypotheses are tested: $E = J$, $E = P$ and $J = P$.

Table 2.1 contains the absolute $t_k$-values of the 29 variables for the three null hypotheses. The sample sizes are: $n_E = 4$, $n_J = 9$ and $n_P = 3$. (See Table 2.1, p. 49).

Although this Table may not be of great interest to the reader keen only to learn the final results, it is shown here in order to demonstrate the "all-over behavior" of the variables in regard to the following global statistic $\Xi$. Skimming through the Table, we easily recognize a certain homogeneity: the clearly smaller values are found in the first column and almost all values in the two adjacent columns are relatively great. In other words, the significance of the two last tests (see below) does not depend on a "run-away effect" of a few erratic variables — a rather gratifying observation.

Now, $\Xi$ is calculated as follows:

$$\chi^{2*} = -2 \cdot \sum_{k=1}^{K} \log P(|t| > |t_k|)$$

$$\Xi^* = \frac{\chi^{2*} - 2 \cdot K}{\sqrt{4 \cdot K}}$$

where $K = 29$, the number of variables, and $P$ the probability of "drawing" an absolute $t$-value greater than the actual absolute value $t_k$. $\chi^{2*}$ is distributed as $\chi^2$ with $2 \cdot K$ degrees of freedom. Because of the great number of degrees of freedom ($2 \cdot K = 58$), $\chi^{2*}$ may be approximated by the normal distribution: $\Xi^*$ is a realization of a standardized normal distribution.

The following table contains the final results. $P(\Xi > \Xi^*)$ is the probability of "drawing" a $\Xi$ greater than the actual $\Xi^*$.

| $H_0$ | $\Xi^*$ | $P(\Xi > \Xi^*)$ |
|-------|---------|------------------|
| $E = J$ | −0.94 | 0.82 |
| $E = P$ | 6.02 | 0.0000000 |
| $J = P$ | 9.06 | 0.0000000 |

Although the formal test is herewith terminated and the reader is left with the (subjective) rest, I think that little disagreement can arise about the meaning of these clear-cut results.

Table 2.1: Absolute $t_k$-Values of 29 Variables

| K | $E = J$ | $E = P$ | $J = P$ |
|---|---------|---------|---------|
| 1 | 0.530 | 3.190 | 2.484 |
| 2 | 0.703 | 1.702 | 1.631 |
| 3 | 0.846 | 2.979 | 3.641 |
| 4 | 0.416 | 1.115 | 2.355 |
| 5 | 2.094 | 3.205 | 3.016 |
| 6 | 0.705 | 0.062 | 0.582 |
| 7 | 0.034 | 1.889 | 1.869 |
| 9 | 0.961 | 2.228 | 1.342 |
| 10 | 0.195 | 2.057 | 2.163 |
| 11 | 1.476 | 1.488 | 2.850 |
| 12 | 0.846 | 0.740 | 1.464 |
| 13 | 0.844 | 2.855 | 3.974 |
| 14 | 0.000 | 0.650 | 1.020 |
| 17 | 1.742 | 2.012 | 1.271 |
| 18 | 0.722 | 2.956 | 3.394 |
| 20 | 0.323 | 1.398 | 1.803 |
| 21 | 1.504 | 1.275 | 2.742 |
| 22 | 0.217 | 1.055 | 1.404 |
| 23 | 0.179 | 0.946 | 0.935 |
| 25 | 0.215 | 0.978 | 1.120 |
| 26 | 0.483 | 3.765 | 6.036 |
| 27 | 0.846 | 3.614 | 2.526 |
| 29 | 0.439 | 4.187 | 2.956 |
| 35 | 0.205 | 0.418 | 0.741 |
| 38 | 0.353 | 0.548 | 0.152 |
| 39 | 0.002 | 4.668 | 2.893 |
| 40 | 0.188 | 0.187 | 0.161 |
| 41 | 1.399 | 1.607 | 0.414 |
| 51 | 2.563 | 1.115 | 0.431 |

The 82 p.c. of the first test is far from any reasonable significance. In view of the previously discussed asymmetry of the null hypothesis against all possible alternatives we could verbalize the result as follows: "The test does not contradict the null hypothesis that the E-samples, on the one hand, and the J-samples, on the other, stem from the same population".

Quite the reverse is true of the other two tests: "Both are significant to such an extent that nobody would think of accepting the null hypotheses that the E-samples and the J-samples, respectively, stem from the same population as the P-samples".


## 2.2.5. CONCLUDING DISCUSSION

Do the above results lend support to the defenders of the Documentary Hypothesis or to its opponents?

E and J may, but need not, stem from the same population; P, though, has its origin neither in the population where E, nor in the one where J came from. These three facts cannot be disputed. What, however, constitutes this population referred to here and which has been mentioned before over and over again?

This question opens up a ticklish problem for, what this population really is, defies being accurately formalized and delimited.

In Sections 2.1.5.1. and 2.1.5.2., it was defined as the imaginable (and imaginary) totality of all those texts that could have been conceived by the brain of a given author. The actually available text sections are merely samples drawn from it at random. Yet, this conception is not satisfying, a point elaborated by me at another place.[3] The population, thus defined, may after all be composed of various constituents, for instance other sub-populations. One could with ease envisage a number of such, all authored by one and the same writer, but differing from each other in some respect, particularly in their literary *Gattung*. If so, the eventuality can hardly be excluded that this difference might heavily influence their linguistic nature and character. That this may happen I have myself been able to demonstrate in an investigation of Goethe's works. There, not the slightest uncertainty, of course, exists about Goethe's authorship. Yet, when I applied a test as structured and performed as the one described here, to his *Dichtung und Wahrheit* and *Farbenlehre,* I found that the latter, a scientific treatise, was significantly at variance with the former, a medley of reminiscences, meditations, reflections and diary-like records. It follows that, since in that case the investigation dealt with samples gleaned from two different sub-populations of all (hypothesized) texts written by Goethe, the test must not be interpreted as a proof of author inhomogeneity.

---

[3] See note 2.

That experiment is of trenchant import in our study and should serve as a *caveat* not to interpret the significant results of the comparisons $E$ vs. $P$ and $J$ vs. $P$ as stringent proofs of $P$'s heterogeneity in relation to $E$ and $J$. The $P$ Document is by the Documentarians' own definition and admission — actually, *ipso facto* — of a *Gattung* apart: it contains lengthy enumerations of proper names, family trees and cultic instructions whereas the $E$- and $J$-Documents are almost without exception stories told. That the subject matters treated by $E + J$ and $P$, respectively, have so little in common cannot but affect the variables which were used in our enterprise. It was for this reason that I was of the opinion, right in the beginning, that any comparisons between $E$ and $J$ with $P$ are meaningless because an eventual (and indeed revealed) significance may always be attributed to the fundamental variety between the two literary types. At most, such tests may serve for control purposes and no more. One may even go one step farther and argue that, had the comparisons of $E$ and $J$ with $P$ resulted in non-significance, one would feel compelled to infer from it that unsuitable variables were chosen, that is, criteria lying on such a common level of linguistic formulation that they are lacking any discriminatory power whatsoever.

The main thrust of the present enquiry is the non-significance between the $E$- and $J$-Documents: they may well have been written by the same person.

PART THREE

# Statistical Analysis of Formal Criteria

HAIM SHORE and YEHUDA T. RADDAY

## 3.1. Introduction

### 3.1.1. GENERAL

The English language, as has been recently remarked by Beatie, an American linguist,[1] utterly lacks a general word for the activity of studying literature in the sense that "chemistry" is a word for the activity of studying the nature of elements. The French *belles lettres* and the German *Literaturwissenschaft* are awkward or clumsy in comparison with *Chemie*. The discipline called "philology" offers little help: it means "love of words", and objectivity is implicitly denied. But this objectivity is central in any science, and there is no reason why it should not be within reach when the object of study is a piece of literature. "Nous possédons", said Roland Barthes, "une histoire de la littérature, mais non une science de la littérature, parce que, sans doute, nous n'avons pu encore reconnaître pleinement la nature de l'objet littéraire, qui est un objet écrit... une *certaine* science de la littérature est possible".[2]

The italics are Barthes' for he seems to have reservations vis-à-vis the feasibility of his desideratum, among other reasons perhaps because he could not imagine how the literary object, extending over myriads, if not millions of words, could be scrutinized. This "state of the art" has undergone a radical change with the advent of the computer, still in its infancy when Barthes wrote that passage. Since then, a *certain* exact analysis of literature has become fairly certain, and, to boot, an established branch of study, conscious, however, of its limitations. One must distinguish carefully between three provinces: the activity of enjoying literature, the activity of describing one's mode of appreciation and the activity of investigating literature as a phenomenon. It is in the last one, and only there, that are we scientists.

---

[1] B. Beatie, "Measurement and the Study of Literature", *Computers and the Humanities* 13 (1979), 3, 185ff. The next few paragraphs follow this article closely.
[2] R. Barthes, *Critique et vérité* (Paris: Seuil, 1966), 56-7.

It may not be superfluous to state here *in expressis verbis* what the "scientific" approach to literary study implies, and what the ground-rules are upon the totality of which such an approach must be based. A scientific study (1) begins with observing a phenomenon and (2) develops hypotheses to explain or interpret the data observed. It then (3) sets up experiments of analytical procedures, and, (4) using measuring devices or standards which are widely accepted, it (5) tests the validity of the hypotheses, and (6) reports the results in such a way that (7) the experiment or analysis may be easily repeated by others. Only when (8) a hypothesis is confirmed by repeated experiments is it (9) provisionally accepted as a valid interpretation of the observed data.

This rather simplistic formulation is adequate to delineate the steps to be taken in examining the unity of the Book of Genesis.

Beatie correctly predicts that it will not be easy for the traditional scholar to follow these steps if he is not a scientist in the narrower sense of the term. Recalling C. P. Snow's "Two Cultures", one may diagnose this syndrome as a problem in communication. The computer-assisted literary researcher employing statistical techniques usually fails to convince his more conservative-minded colleagues, mainly because they find his work incomprehensible. Only when literary critics learn to understand the language of measurement, and when computer scientists and statisticians learn how to write readable prose, can what Beatie calls the computer revolution in literary studies really begin. Both are tall tasks, to be sure. The present writers will try their best, hoping to be met halfway by their reader.[3] We start with a short introduction into the underlying philosophy of our research design.

Any appropriately conducted empirical research is essentially composed of two phases: the inductive phase and the deductive phase.

The first comprises the fact-finding stage. This is where exploration is carried out and, without adherence to a theoretical nomological network, the data in hand are probed, their basic structure and features examined and relations between variables sought. This stage is, in a way, "preconception-free", inasmuch as its function is to expand our intuitive knowledge about the information retained in the data, while theoretical views and attitudes which may prevail at the time are ignored.

The deduction phase is the statistical testing stage, where hypotheses are formulated and tested for validity by means of statistical analysis. Although formally and technically inductive in nature, this stage is nevertheless deductive in that the features and relations, which have emerged intuitively from the data, are hypothesized to be true, and statistical tests are applied in order to assess these hypotheses, i.e., to validate or invalidate them.

---

[3] Conscious of the difficulty of this assignment and anticipating our failure to fulfil it when dealing with nothing else except statistical techniques, we shall interrupt the discussion with short resumés and advise readers who find the going too heavy, to concentrate on them, figures and tables.

To cite an example. Suppose that by means of some of the descriptive clustering methods employed in this research two sets of samples emerge, each clustered about its own centroid. The mere fact that such clustering has occurred is in itself almost meaningless, since it may be the effect of coincidence alone. Whether the configuration of samples is indicatory of a similar structure in the population from which the samples have been drawn and may thus be taken as evidence of possible different sources of the two clusters, is a question to be answered only by statistical inference.

Thus, while the inductive phase leads to a formulation of hypotheses about possible source populations, the statistical analysis puts these hypotheses to a critical test, thereby concluding whether empirical evidence is sufficient to accept them as valid. In our enquiry, though, the deductive phase to follow the inductive one may turn out to be redundant, since there already exist, in current Biblical scholarship, some prevailing hypotheses with regard to the composition of Genesis (see introduction of the hypotheses set in Part One of this volume). Therefore, a statistical evaluation of these hypotheses, one which has not yet been executed, precedes the two aforementioned phases. Thence, the inductive phase is carried out, and, according to its results, a decision is taken as to whether new hypotheses are suggested, which necessitate a further deductive phase. Order of presentation of the quantitative analyses that follow adheres to the outline sketched above.

In Section 3.2, a statistical evaluation of current hypotheses is carried out — irrespective of whether or not these are upheld by the majority of Biblical researchers. Its aim is to assess evidence, from the point of view of statistical linguistics, as to the validity of the Documentary hypothesis and others, concerning the composition of Genesis. If such evidence is missing or found to be lacking, the next, the inductive, phase is called for.

This phase is presented in Section 3.3., where the inner structure of the data on-hand is explored, and homogeneous clusters are sought in the search for traces of possible plurality of source populations. However, results suggest no new hypotheses, so that Section 3.4. integrates the various analyses and offers some preliminary conclusions.


## 3.1.2.  MULTIVARIATE ANALYSIS AND THE PATTERN RECOGNITION APPROACH

In statistical linguistics we "measure" text samples by means of quantitative and linguistically meaningful variables, and test actual differences occurring between samples (or categories of samples) for statistical significance. The fundamental philosophy is that when such differences are found to be significant, this suggests the existence of different sources from which the samples (or categories of samples) have stemmed.

However, when each of the measures (variables) is tested separately, difficulties arise as soon as the results are statistically interpreted.

Suppose, for the sake of argument, that we have $n$ measures to be tested, and each is statistically independent of all the rest (zero correlation among variables). Allowing for a type I error probability (see this term in Section 2.1.1.) of $100\alpha$ p.c. for each test, namely, a probability of $\alpha$ of incorrectly rejecting the null hypothesis that the samples under study originated in the same population, it can be shown that for the $n$ independent tests the probability of making at least one such error is $1 - (1 - \alpha)^n$. For example: suppose $\alpha = 0.10$ and $n = 10$. Then the probability of at least one test rejecting, on false grounds, the null hypothesis that the study samples originated in the same population, is $1 - (1 - 0.10)^{10} = 0.651$. If our criterion is so formulated as to lead us to reject the null hypothesis when any significant result is found, then of course the probability of 65 p.c. of making a type I error is much too high compared with the $\alpha$ we had in mind. When variables are dependent, this error probability may even be larger.

To resolve this difficulty, two solutions may be pursued:

One is to define a single summary measure which will serve as our orientation variable. It must fulfill three conditions:

(a)   that it be a function of all the relevant original variables;

(b)   that it could be shown meaningful inasmuch as it represents most of the discriminating information retained in the original variables; and

(c)   that its theoretical distribution under the null hypothesis be known.

This solution is adopted in our analysis in order to enable us to apply several univariate statistical methods of analysis for which no analog yet exists or is programmed in the area of multivariate analysis. Factor Analysis is summoned to help in the examination of various definitions of summary measures. The results of this univariate analysis, are shown in Section 3.2.2.

The other solution is to apply multivariate methods where statistical significance is sought between vectors of variables rather than between sample values of a single variable. The main advantage of the extension to the multivariate case is that correlations between variables which constitute the "variables vector" are accounted for, thus limiting the type I and type II error probabilities to acceptable predetermined values. The result of the multivariate analysis is shown in Section 3.2.3.

Yet, multivariate analysis has its own merits which by far transcend the above mentioned reason. First and foremost, the multivariate approach is pursued in our research since it constitutes the main tool by which statistical conclusions are derived in the field of Pattern Recognition. This field has recently been gaining an ever increasing and expanding applicability in various theoretical and applied branches of contemporary science, where the main research issue is detection of patterns, or clusters of patterns, nested in a multitude of data. Since the issue of our enquiry is not dissimilar in character, it is only fitting that the Pattern Recognition approach be adopted and its methodology employed.

The multivariate analysis shown in the following Sections reflects, *au fond,* the Pattern Recognition approach. Hence, a brief digression into its basic philosophy and terms may be in order.

A pattern is a set of measurements carried out on an object to be recognized. Each of the measured elements is supposed to describe one characteristic of the object. The act of Pattern Recognition lies in assigning the pattern to one among $M$ pattern classes to which it most probably belongs.

The set of measurements is arranged in the form of a vector, known as the pattern vector $\vec{x}$:

$$\vec{x} = \begin{pmatrix} x_1 \\ x_2 \\ \vdots \\ x_n \end{pmatrix}$$

This vector is supposed to contain all the available information about the object. When the measurements yield information in the form of real numbers, it is often useful to think of a pattern vector as a point in an $n$-dimensional Euclidean space. The set of all points that occupy the same region in that space constitutes the pattern class.

Three problems may arise in Pattern Recognition:

(a) Presence of correlations between components of the pattern vector may indicate that the same discriminating information, contained in the original input data (the pattern vector), could be represented by a smaller number of variables, thus reducing dimensionality. At times, economic considerations or sheer technical difficulties in measuring demand a reduction of the number of discriminating variables measured. This is known as the Dimensionality Reduction Problem.

(b) If a complete set of discriminating features for each pattern class can be determined from the measured data, recognition and classification of a pattern pose only little difficulty. Unfortunately, such a set is rarely available *a priori*: most frequently it is extracted from the input data by various methods such as Factor Analysis or Discriminant Analysis.

Extraction of characteristic features or factors, while reducing the dimensionality of the pattern vector, is known as the Feature Selection Problem. Its main output is the transformation of points from the original pattern space to a "feature space" of reduced dimensionality. In the majority of cases, the derived features are actually linear combinations of the original variables, hereafter referred to as Discriminant Functions.

Various approaches to achieve optimal feature extraction have been developed.[4] Yet, selecting an appropriate set of features which takes into account the difficulties present in the measuring process, and which, at the same time, results in acceptable performance regarding success in pattern classification and in characterization of pattern classes — selecting such a set in one of the hardest tasks in Pattern Recognition.

(c) The third difficulty in a Pattern Recognition design system involves determining optimum decision procedures, needed in the identification and classification processes. After the observed data, from patterns to be recognized, have been expressed in the form of pattern points or measurement vectors in the pattern space, a classifying mechanism is required to decide to which pattern class these data belong.

The recognition problem can be viewed as one of generating decision boundaries which separate the pattern classes on the basis of observed measurement vectors.

These boundaries are defined by decision functions or classification functions, which are scalar and single-valued functions of the pattern $\vec{x}$. The classification decision, based on the decision function $d_i(\vec{x})$ ($i = 1, 2, \ldots, M$) is commonly carried out as follows: for an unidentified pattern $\vec{x}$, if $d_i(\vec{x}) > d_j(\vec{x})$ for all $i \neq j$ ($j = 1, 2, \ldots, M$), then $\vec{x}$ most probably belongs to pattern class $i$.

Derivation of the decision functions may be based on several concepts. Tou and Gonzalez suggest three possible approaches:[5]

Firstly, when a pattern class is characterized by a roster of its members, the design of a Pattern Recognition system may be based on the membership roster concept: a pattern will be classified as a member of one of the pattern classes, if it matches one of the stored patterns belonging to that pattern class.

Secondly, when a pattern class is characterized by common properties, shared by all its members, the design may be based on the common-property concept.

Thirdly, when a pattern class exhibits clustering properties in the pattern space, the design may be based on the clustering concept.

Since in our enquiry the pattern classes from which samples are drawn are in themselves scientifically debatable it is only the clustering concept that the definition of any pattern class can objectively be based upon. This will immediately be demonstrated.

## 3.1.3. HOMOGENEITY AS A PATTERN RECOGNITION PROBLEM

The problem of the homogeneity of Genesis may now be expressed in terms of Pattern Recognition.

---

[4] For examples, see J. T. Tou and R. C. Gonzalez, *Pattern Recognition Principles* (Massachusetts: Addison-Wesley, 1974), ch. 7.

[5] *Ibid*, p. 17.

Let Genesis be divided into samples of about equal length, each being homogeneous with respect to any of the two main categorizations, namely according to both the Documentary (*P, E, J,* see Section 1.1.2.2.) and the Discourse (*N, H, D,* see Section 1.3.1.h.) hypotheses. We then define *n* linguistic measures and calculate an *n*-dimensional vector for each sample (here, $n = 43$).

In terms of Pattern Recognition, the issues debated among Biblical scholars may now be formulated as follows:

Let $M_1$, $M_2$, $M_3$ be the pattern classes (*P, E, J* or *N, H, D*), and let Discriminant Functions be so constructed as to measure in the best possible way[6] the discriminating features[7] which separate and distinguish between the hypothesized pattern classes. The questions arising here are:

(a)   Is the discriminatory variance, retained in the Discriminant Functions, statistically significant?

(b)   To what extent do the pattern classes overlap in the feature space (the Discriminant Function Space)?

(c)   How successful is the classification by the decision functions of samples of "known" origin with regard to the hypothesized pattern classes?

(d)   Are the features, extracted from the data by any of the dimensionality decreasing methods, meaningful in any linguistic sense?

The same four questions may be asked in regard to all pattern families newly crystallized in the course of this study as results of data analyzed in the exploration phase.

## 3.1.4.   METHODOLOGY

3.1.4.1.   **Input Data and Programs Description.**   The input data for the statistical analyses comprises three matrixes:

— Matrix I, composed of 96 lines and 54 columns, includes the original values of the 54 variables (expressed in percentages) of the 96 samples into which Genesis was subdivided. (For description of samples and list of variables, see Table 1.3. and Table 1.4.). Averages and standard deviations of the variables are shown in Table 3.1. (See Table 3.1, p. 59).

— Matrix II, composed of the same number (96 × 54) of cells, includes the same data, this time expressed in *z*-scores (see Section 3.1.4.4.). For variables which require application of mathematical transformations (see

---

[6] Various methods are available for this "best way" of building Discriminant Functions, e.g., "Select variables for the Discriminant Function which minimize Wilks's Lambda" or "Select variables which maximize Rao's *V*". For a preliminary introduction, see the S.P.S.S. Manual.

[7] In all methods used here, the derived features are expressed as linear combinations of the original variables.

Table 3.1: Means and Standard Deviations of the Forty-Three Original Variables

| Variable | Mean | STD | Variable | Mean | STD |
|---|---|---|---|---|---|
| x1 | 4.719 | 3.085 | x23 | 7.321 | 2.893 |
| x2 | 13.346 | 2.927 | x25 | 3.113 | 1.185 |
| x3 | 7.528 | 3.271 | x26 | 5.491 | 2.383 |
| x4 | 23.879 | 4.565 | x27 | 2.866 | 2.069 |
| x5 | 11.637 | 3.474 | x28 | .662 | .699 |
| x6 | 15.210 | 3.735 | x29 | 8.235 | 2.813 |
| x7 | 12.923 | 4.742 | x31 | .855 | .826 |
| x8 | 5.946 | 2.662 | x32 | 1.064 | .847 |
| x9 | 3.032 | 1.571 | x33 | .698 | .723 |
| x10 | 1.776 | 1.233 | x34 | .393 | .531 |
| x11 | 22.552 | 14.202 | x35 | 1.797 | 1.133 |
| x12 | 48.786 | 15.363 | x37 | .394 | .513 |
| x13 | 75.326 | 12.295 | x38 | 10.952 | 3.357 |
| x14 | 9.874 | 8.168 | x39 | 5.379 | 3.094 |
| x15 | 4.466 | 4.261 | x40 | 1.487 | 1.173 |
| x16 | .719 | 1.600 | x41 | 6.437 | 3.786 |
| x17 | 3.943 | 2.280 | x43 | 1.273 | .973 |
| x18 | 45.670 | 19.728 | x50 | .708 | .925 |
| x19 | 20.019 | 7.226 | x51 | 5.055 | 1.624 |
| x20 | 9.691 | 4.265 | x52 | .062 | .194 |
| x21 | 5.551 | 2.347 | x53 | 1.060 | 1.103 |
| x22 | 1.388 | 1.079 | | | |

Section 3.1.4.3.), the proper columns include values of variables after transformation (also expressed in z-scores).

— Matrix III, the transposed Matrix II, is composed of 54 lines and 96 columns. It is constructed to enable application of programs capable of analyzing relations between variables (see Section 3.1.4.5.).

However, out of the original 54 variables, eleven were found to have zero value throughout the book (see Section 1.5.2.) and were hence deleted from all following analyses. They are those numbered nos. 24, 30, 36, 42, 44, 45, 46, 47, 48, 49, 54 in Table 1.4. In consequence, 43 variables only are taken into consideration.

For data processing, various programs were used, both from S.P.S.S. and B.M.D.P. packages. Lists of these programs follow, thus providing the reader with references which may aid him to gain further information on symbols appearing in the exhibits of the output to be displayed later on.

(a)   Programs from S.P.S.S. (in alphabetical order)*:

| Name | Analysis |
|---|---|
| ANOVA | Univariate Analysis of Variance |
| Condescriptive | Various statistics; optionally output of z-scores |
| Discriminant | Discriminant Analysis |
| Factor | Factor Analysis |
| Frequencies | Frequency counts, histograms, various statistics |
| MANOVA | Multivariate Analysis of Variance |
| One-way | One-way Univariate Analysis of Variance and allied procedures |
| Reliability | Reliability Analysis |
| SSA1 | Smallest Space Analysis 1 (Guttman's technique) |

* Source: N.H. Nie et al., S.P.S.S. (New York: McGraw Hill, 1975²) and various documents published separately for some of the more recent programs.

(b)   Programs from B.M.D.P.*:

| Name | Analysis |
|---|---|
| B.M.D.P.-2M | Cluster Analysis of cases |
| B.M.D.P.-5D | Descriptive statistics, histograms, normal probability curves |

* Source: W.J. Dixon and M.B. Brown, B.M.D.P.-79 (Los Angeles: P-Series, University of California, 1979).

3.1.4.2. **Determining Sample Size.** The raw data for this enquiry was derived from an aggregate of 96 samples, each composed of about 200 words, which constituted the strata for calculating pattern vector values.

Now, the use of the word *sample* in this context is somewhat misleading. The term is commonly used to denote a collection of observations by which various statistics are calculated for purposes of statistical inference. In our case, though, the variables, as defined above, are not directly observable, since they are all based on a count of their occurrence in a *group* of words. It is this group which has been referred to as a *sample*. This "sample" is, in fact, one item on which a single multivariate observation has been carried out. Consequently, it is only the collection of all 96 pattern vectors, derived from what we called samples, which constitutes the real sample of our investigation.

Determining sample size, therefore, is concerned here with the number of "samples" rather than with the number of words in each. Obviously, these two issues are not independent since the whole population, from which samples could be drawn, is itself limited to the roughly 20,000 words of Genesis.

Different and contradicting considerations are relevant in this respect.

In the first place, how large should the number of samples be so as to keep down the type I and type II error probabilities to acceptable limits when statistical tests are performed?

To illustrate the problem, suppose that we calculate the average proportion of occurrence of a certain variable, e.g., the definite article, in a group of $k$ samples, assumed to originate, according to the null hypothesis, in the same population. If the total available text is composed of $N$ words (which may potentially carry the tested variable, i.e., in Hebrew, mainly nouns, participles and numerals), and if the "samples" are all of the same length (namely, $N/k$), then the standard deviation of the average proportion, calculated from observed proportions in the $k$ samples, will, according to the Binomial Model, be: $\sqrt{p(1 - p)/(N)}$, where $p$ is the true proportion in the population and where the samples are assumed to be statistically independent. Since the standard deviation determines the error probabilities, $k$ may be chosen arbitrarily.

Hence, in the ideal case, i.e., when the Binomial Model holds, any division of the source text into samples will result in the same type I and type II error probabilities, including samples of one word each.

This argument, though, ceases to be valid as soon as $p$ itself is not stable. That such is the common case is a well known phenomenon which is attributable to the intrusive and disruptive effect of "background" noise caused by local differences in the text, e.g., its content. Other, less unequivocally definable factors may also play their role, such as an author's emotional state that imposes on him, at a certain point, an affective manner of writing which again has its correlate in various linguistic variables.

To cancel out such local disturbances, text segments are used as sample elements. Obviously, as their size increases, $p$ stabilizes and its author-specifying character, as observed in actual sections, becomes more prominent.

Yet this increase of segment length comes at the price of reducing the number of sample elements, i.e., the number of text segments, and, consequently, of a decreased discriminating power of the statistical tests employed.

A second consideration refers to the assumption that the sample observations (in our study, the 96 samples) are independent. This assumption is fundamental in the majority of methods used for statistical inference. If, however, samples drawn consecutively from the available text are too small, a serial correlation, i.e., a correlation between adjacent samples, should be expected due to local influence. If this is the case, the whole statistical analysis may be invalidated.

It is therefore highly desirable that the number of words which constitute each sample, should be enlarged as much as possible. Yet, the ensuing decrease in the number of samples raises, as noted above, the probability of erroneous statistical decisions.

How to overcome this quandary? A successful way of doing this is setting the criterion that no fewer than three samples be available for any of the nine cells (see Table 1.2.). This decision determines sample size at approximately 200 words — as already stated at the beginning of Section 1.4.2. We abandoned this decision in one case only: cell *DE* was found so sparsely populated (161 words) that it allows for no more than one sample. As it turned out, information on the within-variance of variables in *DE* is of minor importance in the light of the results of analyses performed.

3.1.4.3. **Normality and Outliers.** One of the basic assumptions in most current multivariate parametric statistical methods of analysis is that the vector of dependent variables follows a multidimensional normal distribution. Although sensitivity to deviations from normality differs from one statistical analysis to another, one feels inclined to state that such normality is most expedient if conclusions are to be well founded.

However, when it comes to the distribution of statistics based on counts of linguistic variables, this distribution is known to be quite often skewed to the left, i.e., a large proportion of its mass is concentrated near the origin (zero), and to be long-tailed to the right. This deviation from normality constitutes a shortcoming which frequently renders the application of statistical methods invalid. One solution, commonly encountered in statistical literature, is to apply mathematical transformations to the "mal-behaved" variables in order to normalize them.

Four of the most commonly used transformations are:

— $y = 2 \, arcsin \, x$ and $y = \sqrt{x}$, two moderate transformations in the sense that they tend to distort the original data only slightly;

— $y = \log x$ and $y = 1/x$ which in an increasing order tend to distort the original data.

The most suitable transformation in our case is the first ($y = 2 \, arcsin \, x$), since all the well-known test procedures, based on the decomposition of the total variance in the "linear model", e.g., Analysis of Variance, Discriminant Analysis and related procedures, can be applied to $y$, even when $n$, the number of words in a sample, is rather small.

To check the original 43 variables for normality, we sketch each on a normal probability curve by means of program B.M.D.P.-5D (see Section 3.1.4.1.). Variables manifesting deviations from normality as judged by the normal probability curve and by various statistics (such as skewness, kurtosis, mean minus median) are then subjected to trial transformations until the proper transformation is· established for each variable that showed non-normality.

The problem of outliers poses still another obstacle on the way to statistical analysis. When those observations are defined as outliers that deviate more than 3.5 standard deviations from the mean, the probability of an outlier occurring under the normality assumption is 0.0004. Obviously, the occurrence of such an outlier defies the normality assumption, and it is, therefore, discarded from any *parametric* statistical analysis, performed in this investigation.

A table to be shown later (Table 3.27.) details variables having outlying values, and the samples where these values occur. An explication of that table may be found in Section 3.3.3.

3.1.4.4. **Standardized Scores.** Presence of large differences in the order of magnitude of the values which the various variables assume, is disposed to obscure the true significance of variation between samples. Clearly, the meaning of a difference in the occurrence frequency of a variable in two different samples depends on the mean value of this variable and its standard deviation. A discrepancy of, say, 2 p.c. weighs differently when its mean value is 5 p.c. and its standard deviation 1 p.c.; when its mean value is 5 p.c. and the standard deviation 3 p.c.; and when its mean value is 70 p.c. and the standard deviation 15 p.c. In each of these three cases, another range of natural variation may be expected: whereas in the first, the 2 p.c. may prove to be indicatory of a true difference between the populations from which the samples are drawn, they may not be so in the third. Moreover, since variables, of which the mean value is large, are likely to vary to a much greater extent than those of a small mean value, significant differences may be hidden when they occur in the latter kind, e.g., when Euclidean distances between pattern vectors are calculated.

Hence, what is needed is a uniform scale, common to all variables, which, for a given confidence level, manifests the same range of variation for all. Such a requirement is met by the following linear transformation:

$$z_j = \frac{x_j - \bar{x}}{s} \quad (\bar{x} = \text{the average, } s = \text{the standard deviation}).$$

The process of rendering an observation $x_j$ into $z_j$ is called standardization, and $z_j$ is a "standard score".

Clearly, negative as well as positive standard scores may occur, even if $x_j$ is always non-negative.

It can be shown that the average of the standard scores (taken over all scores) is zero and their standard deviation is unity (1).

In the parametrical statistical analyses that follow, standard scores serve as the input data for analysis: both Matrix II and Matrix III (see Section 3.1.4.1.) contain data expressed in $z$-scores where the averages and standard deviations used in the standardizing process are those of the whole book (96 samples).

Table 3.2.a and Table 3.2.b list means and standard deviations of the standardized scores of a selected group of variables (i.e., those found as discriminating), calculated from the transformed values (Matrix II) for each of the nine subcategories of Table 1.2, as well as for Divisions *I, II, III*. A good example of how to read these Tables is provided by criterion no. 19 in Table 3.2.a. The average of the standardized scores of this variable, the use of the particle *and,* taken over all samples of *NJ,* is .830, which means that its incidence in *NJ* is higher than its average in all samples. Conversely, its incidence in direct speech, *HJ* and *DJ,* tends to be rare (-.951 and -.886, respectively). That these diametrically opposed two frequencies are only to be expected does not detract from, but rather proves, the fact that these two Tables are obviously inordinately instructive also with regard to most other variables: there, the differences in frequencies, although of lesser *éclat,* may well be less trivial than the example cited. It now seems that the two tables contain a mine of information for students of Biblical Hebrew, but since this is not the point of issue in our investigation, we are content to leave it for them to exploit. (See Table 3.2.a and Table 3.2.b, pp. 65-72).

Finally, an important characteristic of the $z$-score is that it measures the distance of an observation from the sample mean in terms of the standard deviation, thus indicating how deviant the observation is. Use of this characteristic is made in the exploratory phase (see Section 3.3.3.) to locate samples having variables with exceptional values.

3.1.4.5. **The Transposed Matrix.** Many of the discriminant analysis techniques now available as computer programs aim at achieving clustering of variables or discrimination between groups of variables. For example, Factor Analysis and *SSA1,* as programmed in the S.P.S.S., produce results concerned with relations between variables rather than between observations. This mode of statistical processing suits social and cognate sciences where meaningful interrelations between variables are sought.

However, when questions of homogeneity of texts are examined, it is the interrelations between samples rather than between linguistic variables that are of prime concern. For this reason, a method of accommodating the data on hand is required so that it can be processed by programs primarily searching for relations between variables.

Table 3.2a: Means and Standard Deviations
of the Twenty-Seven Variables Significantly Discriminating in (N, H, D) and (P, E, J)

| | P | | E | | J | | overall | |
|---|---|---|---|---|---|---|---|---|
| **x1** | | | | | | | | |
| N | −1.142 | ( .498) | −.337 | ( .658) | −.441 | ( .604) | −.506 | ( .653) |
| H | .679 | — | .909 | ( .736) | 1.079 | ( .448) | .964 | ( .681) |
| D | −1.039 | ( .669) | — | — | .808 | ( .411) | .255 | (1.082) |
| overall | −.813 | ( .981) | .301 | ( .938) | .115 | ( .893) | .056 | ( .979) |
| **x2** | | | | | | | | |
| N | −.095 | ( .513) | .317 | (1.033) | .113 | ( .849) | .149 | ( .871) |
| H | −.045 | — | −.122 | ( .842) | .092 | ( .922) | −.028 | ( .837) |
| D | .066 | ( .478) | — | — | .466 | ( .613) | .502 | ( .771) |
| overall | −.047 | ( .437) | .163 | ( .998) | .148 | ( .837) | .127 | ( .855) |
| **x3** | | | | | | | | |
| N | 1.490 | ( .878) | −.670 | (1.013) | −.349 | ( .792) | −.194 | (1.111) |
| H | .799 | — | .016 | ( .599) | −.022 | ( .836) | .054 | ( .706) |
| D | .560 | ( .482) | — | — | −.043 | ( .581) | .171 | ( .560) |
| overall | 1.143 | ( .811) | −.325 | ( .884) | −.225 | ( .784) | −.075 | ( .951) |
| **x5** | | | | | | | | |
| N | .105 | (1.106) | −.930 | ( .828) | −.346 | ( .748) | −.469 | ( .884) |
| H | −.016 | — | .404 | ( .963) | .584 | ( .683) | .450 | ( .827) |
| D | .811 | ( .523) | — | — | .251 | ( .557) | .461 | ( .545) |
| overall | .261 | ( .928) | −.261 | (1.101) | −.024 | ( .815) | −.071 | ( .948) |
| **x7** | | | | | | | | |
| N | .039 | ( .777) | .736 | ( .765) | .703 | ( .919) | .620 | ( .870) |
| H | .035 | — | −.683 | ( .671) | −.902 | ( .591) | −.724 | ( .653) |
| D | −.588 | ( .361) | — | — | −.548 | ( .509) | −.550 | ( .405) |
| overall | −.118 | ( .674) | .034 | ( .998) | .123 | (1.086) | .058 | (1.001) |

Table 3.2a: Means and Standard Deviations
of the Twenty-Seven Variables Significantly Discriminating in ($N$, $H$, $D$) and ($P$, $E$, $J$)
*(Continued)*

| | P | | E | | J | | overall | |
|---|---|---|---|---|---|---|---|---|
| **$x8$** | | | | | | | | |
| N | −.374 | (1.375) | .888 | ( .865) | .233 | ( .817) | .358 | ( .996) |
| H | −.156 | — | −.451 | ( .705) | −.077 | ( .968) | −.276 | ( .812) |
| D | −.050 | ( .472) | — | — | −.635 | ( .763) | −.527 | ( .734) |
| overall | −.257 | (1.055) | .188 | (1.060) | .050 | ( .882) | .059 | (.972) |
| **$x9$** | | | | | | | | |
| N | −.171 | (1.251) | .557 | ( .828) | .312 | ( .889) | .323 | ( .935) |
| H | .117 | — | −.412 | ( .996) | −.632 | ( .794) | −.466 | ( .895) |
| D | .181 | (1.062) | — | — | .201 | ( .750) | −.032 | (1.011) |
| overall | −.035 | (1.065) | .028 | (1.063) | .042 | ( .931) | .026 | ( .988) |
| **$x11$** | | | | | | | | |
| N | .860 | (1.270) | .355 | ( .649) | .104 | ( .593) | .290 | ( .761) |
| H | 1.056 | — | −.781 | ( .780) | −.737 | ( .583) | −.636 | ( .820) |
| D | −.084 | ( .230) | — | — | −.704 | ( .222) | −.483 | ( .360) |
| overall | .656 | (1.063) | −.207 | ( .897) | −.217 | ( .687) | −.094 | ( .868) |
| **$x13$** | | | | | | | | |
| N | −.395 | (1.117) | .482 | ( .627) | .323 | ( .500) | .273 | ( .697) |
| H | .481 | — | −.042 | ( .553) | −.067 | ( .549) | −.016 | ( .627) |
| D | −.641 | ( .544) | — | — | −.453 | ( .550) | −.438 | ( .547) |
| overall | −.311 | (1.069) | .229 | ( .630) | .128 | ( .575) | .105 | ( .692) |
| **$x15$** | | | | | | | | |
| N | .311 | (1.135) | −.543 | ( .808) | −.090 | ( .736) | −.179 | ( .853) |
| H | .612 | — | .082 | ( .965) | .376 | ( .968) | .240 | ( .963) |
| D | 1.323 | ( .913) | — | — | .499 | (1.218) | .802 | (1.053) |
| overall | .614 | (1.100) | −.210 | ( .930) | .104 | ( .876) | .059 | ( .954) |

Table 3.2a: Means and Standard Deviations
of the Twenty-Seven Variables Significantly Discriminating in (N, H, D) and (P, E, J)
*(Continued)*

| | P | | E | | J | | overall | |
|---|---|---|---|---|---|---|---|---|
| **x17** | | | | | | | | |
| N | −1.082 | (1.168) | −.167 | ( .586) | −.540 | ( .574) | −.497 | ( .730) |
| H | .643 | — | .778 | ( .625) | .716 | ( .687) | .743 | ( .623) |
| D | .148 | ( .004) | — | — | 1.423 | ( .486) | 1.030 | ( .751) |
| overall | −.487 | (1.152) | .335 | ( .793) | .025 | ( .951) | .068 | ( .953) |
| **x18** | | | | | | | | |
| N | −.831 | (1.429) | .265 | ( .804) | .508 | ( .821) | .243 | (1.005) |
| H | −.338 | — | −.029 | ( .932) | −.031 | ( .537) | −.051 | ( .787) |
| D | −.363 | ( .538) | — | — | .041 | ( .739) | −.106 | ( .620) |
| overall | −.632 | (1.181) | .116 | ( .853) | .308 | ( .773) | .110 | ( .910) |
| **x19** | | | | | | | | |
| N | .524 | ( .699) | .700 | ( .403) | .830 | ( .668) | .745 | ( .598) |
| H | −1.427 | — | −1.009 | ( .479) | −.951 | ( .460) | −1.014 | ( .462) |
| D | −.451 | ( .294) | — | — | −.886 | ( .529) | −.808 | ( .521) |
| overall | −.045 | ( .941) | −.170 | ( .984) | .149 | (1.050) | .007 | (1.012) |
| **x23** | | | | | | | | |
| N | −.163 | ( .476) | −.274 | ( .846) | −.263 | (1.194) | −.253 | (1.002) |
| H | .421 | — | .540 | ( .691) | .338 | ( .431) | .448 | ( .574) |
| D | 1.079 | ( .310) | — | — | .864 | (1.155) | .878 | ( .861) |
| overall | .245 | ( .680) | .127 | ( .854) | .028 | (1.093) | .094 | ( .956) |
| **x26** | | | | | | | | |
| N | −.965 | ( .820) | .284 | ( .977) | .197 | ( .800) | .062 | ( .944) |
| H | −.559 | — | −.067 | ( .531) | .635 | ( .668) | .190 | ( .702) |
| D | −.233 | ( .242) | — | — | .351 | ( .508) | .018 | ( .583) |
| overall | −.714 | ( .726) | .083 | ( .807) | .334 | ( .750) | .100 | ( .834) |

Table 3.2a: Means and Standard Deviations
of the Twenty-Seven Variables Significantly Discriminating in $(N, H, D)$ and $(P, E, J)$

*(Continued)*

|  | P |  | E |  | J |  | overall |  |
|---|---|---|---|---|---|---|---|---|
| **x27** |  |  |  |  |  |  |  |  |
| N | −1.208 | ( .804) | −.168 | ( .543) | .025 | ( .904) | −.209 | ( .881) |
| H | −.089 | — | .242 | ( .884) | .956 | ( .783) | .515 | ( .884) |
| D | −.429 | ( .427) | — | — | .436 | ( .925) | .161 | ( .818) |
| overall | −.827 | ( .788) | .046 | ( .739) | .326 | ( .949) | .067 | ( .928) |
| **x29** |  |  |  |  |  |  |  |  |
| N | −1.343 | ( .787) | .147 | ( .709) | −.044 | ( .935) | −.165 | ( .965) |
| H | .461 | — | .649 | ( .683) | .183 | ( .689) | .443 | ( .699) |
| D | .112 | ( .593) | — | — | .193 | ( .694) | .276 | ( .668) |
| overall | −.679 | (1.065) | .415 | ( .732) | .045 | ( .841) | .081 | ( .897) |
| **x31** |  |  |  |  |  |  |  |  |
| N | −.461 | (1.244) | −.469 | ( .873) | −.134 | ( .932) | −.287 | ( .955) |
| H | −.014 | — | .270 | ( .941) | .656 | ( .700) | .410 | ( .905) |
| D | .891 | ( .768) | — | — | .544 | (1.263) | .674 | ( .987) |
| overall | −.048 | (1.282) | −.087 | ( .961) | .158 | ( .969) | .041 | (1.008) |
| **x32** |  |  |  |  |  |  |  |  |
| N | −.970 | (1.226) | −.297 | (1.050) | .308 | ( .792) | −.065 | (1.033) |
| H | −.690 | — | .172 | ( .939) | .550 | ( .603) | .269 | ( .871) |
| D | −.475 | (1.157) | — | — | −.055 | (1.038) | −.211 | ( .956) |
| overall | −.800 | (1.137) | −.074 | ( .994) | .332 | ( .777) | .030 | ( .980) |
| **x33** |  |  |  |  |  |  |  |  |
| N | −.857 | ( .656) | .048 | ( .905) | −.251 | ( .947) | −.240 | ( .928) |
| H | .766 | — | .634 | ( .855) | .245 | ( .998) | .484 | ( .894) |
| D | −.795 | ( .772) | — | — | .886 | ( .351) | .325 | ( .957) |
| overall | −.571 | ( .857) | .349 | ( .906) | .013 | ( .978) | .056 | ( .972) |

Table 3.2a: Means and Standard Deviations
of the Twenty-Seven Variables Significantly Discriminating in (N, H, D) and (P, E, J)
*(Continued)*

|  | P | | E | | J | | overall | |
|---|---|---|---|---|---|---|---|---|
| **x39** | | | | | | | | |
| N | −1.110 | ( .363) | −.473 | ( .544) | −.478 | ( .564) | −.565 | ( .570) |
| H | .403 | — | .932 | ( .620) | .998 | ( .440) | .923 | ( .594) |
| D | .058 | ( .095) | — | — | 1.123 | ( .573) | .724 | ( .657) |
| overall | −.566 | ( .835) | .223 | ( .905) | .107 | ( .911) | .057 | ( .924) |
| **x40** | | | | | | | | |
| N | −.409 | (1.224) | −.186 | ( .914) | −.265 | ( .920) | −.260 | ( .945) |
| H | 1.069 | — | .263 | ( .699) | .501 | ( .853) | .417 | ( .759) |
| D | −.560 | (1.341) | — | — | .321 | ( .497) | .165 | (1.015) |
| overall | −.200 | (1.225) | .079 | ( .865) | .001 | ( .920) | .007 | ( .939) |
| **x41** | | | | | | | | |
| N | −.427 | ( .726) | −.163 | ( .457) | −.643 | ( .753) | −.459 | ( .691) |
| H | .796 | — | .846 | ( .772) | .688 | ( .574) | .777 | ( .697) |
| D | .884 | ( .878) | — | — | .850 | ( .632) | .841 | ( .630) |
| overall | .105 | ( .996) | .336 | ( .793) | −.110 | ( .963) | .081 | ( .922) |
| **x43** | | | | | | | | |
| N | −1.077 | (1.013) | −.200 | ( .684) | −.478 | ( .878) | −.473 | ( .869) |
| H | .684 | — | .821 | ( .549) | .410 | ( .893) | .642 | ( .726) |
| D | .633 | ( .390) | — | — | .423 | ( .893) | .606 | ( .738) |
| overall | −.356 | (1.200) | .330 | ( .815) | −.133 | ( .968) | .005 | ( .974) |
| **x50** | | | | | | | | |
| N | .393 | (1.303) | −.501 | ( .430) | −.141 | ( .771) | −.182 | ( .813) |
| H | .753 | — | .115 | ( .682) | −.231 | ( .600) | .015 | ( .780) |
| D | .652 | (1.099) | — | — | .291 | (1.291) | .369 | (1.094) |
| overall | .517 | (1.261) | −.200 | ( .628) | −.116 | ( .794) | −.060 | ( .842) |

Table 3.2a: Means and Standard Deviations
of the Twenty-Seven Variables Significantly Discriminating in (*N, H, D*) and (*P, E, J*)
*(Continued)*

| | P | | E | | J | | overall | |
|---|---|---|---|---|---|---|---|---|
| x53 | | | | | | | | |
| N | −.288 | (1.158) | −.738 | ( .775) | −.288 | (1.007) | −.432 | ( .965) |
| H | −.172 | — | .524 | ( .764) | .163 | ( .903) | .327 | ( .814) |
| D | 1.017 | ( .428) | — | — | .459 | ( .319) | .644 | ( .440) |
| overall | .057 | (1.049) | −.109 | ( .981) | −.080 | ( .953) | −.072 | ( .966) |
| DIS | | | | | | | | |
| N | 8.049 | (1.508) | 5.697 | (1.057) | 5.879 | ( .822) | 6.124 | (1.265) |
| H | 5.972 | — | 5.948 | ( .880) | 5.534 | ( .632) | 5.778 | ( .782) |
| D | 6.146 | ( .468) | — | — | 6.247 | ( .416) | 6.187 | ( .385) |
| overall | 7.227 | (1.541) | 5.825 | ( .952) | 5.826 | ( .757) | 6.017 | (1.068) |

Remarks: All values after transformation and standardization (except DIS) and based on 88
observations.
Standard deviations in brackets.
Overall standard deviations in *H* include *HP*.
Overall means and standard deviations in *D* include *DE*.
Overall standard deviations in *P* include *HP*.
Overall means and standard deviations in *E* include *DE*.

Table 3.2b: Means and Standard Deviations
of the Ten Variables Significantly Discriminating in (*I, II, III*) and (*P, E, J*)

| | P | | E | | J | | overall | |
|---|---|---|---|---|---|---|---|---|
| **x6** | | | | | | | | |
| *I* | −1.056 | (1.456) | — | — | 1.339 | ( .954) | .700 | (1.519) |
| *II* | −.082 | ( .907) | −.120 | ( .777) | −.418 | ( .774) | −.277 | ( .789) |
| *III* | −.471 | — | .078 | ( .809) | −.099 | ( .602) | −.001 | ( .728) |
| overall | | | | | | | −.020 | ( .991) |
| **x8** | | | | | | | | |
| *I* | −.585 | (1.289) | — | — | −.616 | ( .513) | −.606 | ( .738) |
| *II* | −.227 | (1.109) | .399 | (1.154) | .318 | ( .898) | .270 | (1.009) |
| *III* | .445 | — | .109 | ( .939) | .150 | ( .836) | .135 | ( .873) |
| overall | | | | | | | .074 | ( .970) |
| **x12** | | | | | | | | |
| *I* | .999 | (1.165) | — | — | .792 | ( .719) | .847 | ( .818) |
| *II* | −.662 | (1.320) | .147 | ( .746) | .158 | ( .564) | .042 | ( .788) |
| *III* | −.480 | — | −.018 | ( .792) | −.303 | ( .428) | −.130 | ( .683) |
| overall | | | | | | | .129 | ( .827) |
| **x20** | | | | | | | | |
| *I* | −.196 | (1.837) | — | — | .716 | ( .797) | .473 | (1.162) |
| *II* | −.092 | ( .911) | −.219 | ( .738) | −.354 | ( .676) | −.276 | ( .717) |
| *III* | 1.008 | — | .380 | (1.203) | .354 | ( .949) | .394 | (1.088) |
| overall | | | | | | | .065 | ( .984) |
| **x25** | | | | | | | | |
| *I* | .415 | ( .729) | — | — | .443 | (1.080) | .435 | ( .973) |
| *II* | −.731 | (1.296) | −.234 | ( .727) | −.112 | ( .776) | −.235 | ( .849) |
| *III* | .297 | — | .452 | ( .882) | .128 | ( .982) | .338 | ( .893) |
| overall | | | | | | | .062 | ( .927) |

Remark: Based on 86 observations.

Table 3.2b: Means and Standard Deviations
of the Ten Variables Significantly Discriminating in (*I, II, III*) and (*P, E, J*)

*(Continued)*

| | P | | E | | J | | overall | |
|---|---|---|---|---|---|---|---|---|
| **x27** | | | | | | | | |
| I | −1.197 | ( .765) | — | — | −.396 | ( .789) | −.609 | ( .840) |
| II | −.847 | ( .804) | .062 | ( .425) | .676 | ( .857) | .273 | ( .895) |
| III | .028 | — | .004 | ( .945) | .273 | ( .927) | .094 | ( .911) |
| overall | | | | | | | .063 | ( .938) |
| **x29** | | | | | | | | |
| I | −.731 | ( .736) | — | — | −.740 | ( .420) | −.738 | ( .492) |
| II | −.991 | (1.247) | .379 | ( .749) | .241 | ( .788) | .117 | ( .941) |
| III | .769 | — | .398 | ( .738) | .482 | ( .788) | .440 | ( .729) |
| overall | | | | | | | .069 | ( .900) |
| **x33** | | | | | | | | |
| I | −1.241 | (0) | — | — | −.228 | ( .994) | −.498 | ( .960) |
| II | −.460 | ( .888) | .067 | ( .808) | −.056 | (1.000) | −.072 | ( .923) |
| III | .096 | — | .550 | ( .965) | .492 | ( .819) | .514 | ( .887) |
| overall | | | | | | | .038 | ( .976) |
| **x38** | | | | | | | | |
| I | 1.351 | ( .652) | — | — | .543 | (1.519) | .760 | (1.371) |
| II | −.007 | ( .884) | −.336 | ( .970) | −.508 | ( .846) | −.385 | ( .887) |
| III | 1.011 | — | .402 | ( .660) | .118 | ( .624) | .330 | ( .652) |
| overall | | | | | | | .039 | (1.024) |
| **x50** | | | | | | | | |
| I | .977 | (1.777) | — | — | .336 | (1.254) | .507 | (1.373) |
| II | −.046 | ( .655) | −.340 | ( .438) | −.236 | ( .494) | −.243 | ( .497) |
| III | .305 | — | −.090 | ( .761) | −.351 | ( .580) | −.162 | ( .696) |
| overall | | | | | | | −.087 | ( .812) |

This goal may be achieved by constructing, out of the original data, a transposed matrix, where the $i$-th column of the original matrix resides in its $i$-th row, and vice versa. In our case, this pivoting culminates in a matrix which now consists of 43 "observations" (formerly variables) and 96 "variables" (formerly observations). This matrix was presented as Matrix III in Section 3.1.4.1.

The distributions of the new "variables" as well as some statistics calculated thereof turned out to reveal valuable information to be analysed in Section 3.3.

## 3.2. Phase I: Statistical Evaluation of Current Hypotheses

### 3.2.1. GENERAL

Evaluation of the hypotheses under investigation will be divided into the subsequent two parts:

(a) Univariate Analysis (Section 3.2.2.), where a single criterion variable (referred to, hereafter, as DIS), is employed to assess the research hypotheses. This variable serves, by definition, as a discriminant for detecting samples, or groups of samples, which lie exceptionally far from the means vector of the population. A further discussion of the variable follows in Section 3.2.2.1.

Two types of Univariate Analysis are performed:

— One-way Analysis of Variance with allied procedures (*a priori* and *a posteriori* contrasts);
— Two-way Analysis of Variance.

(b) Multivariate Analysis (Section 3.2.3.) where statistical processing is carried out on the pattern vector and inferential evaluation is made based on multivariate statistics. Three types of Multivariate Analysis are executed:

— Multivariate Analysis of Variance, including univariate *a priori* contrasts for each of the components of the pattern vector;
— Factor Analysis (orthogonal mode);
— Discriminant Analysis.

Integration of results and interim conclusions are given in Section 3.2.4.

### 3.2.2. UNIVARIATE ANALYSIS

3.2.2.1. **The Variable DIS.** Applying Univariate Analysis to sampled data, arranged initially in the form of a vector of variables, requires a preliminary stage where a single variable is formulated that may extract, to an acceptable degree, the discriminatory power retained in the original variables. Since our main interest lies in the questioned homogeneity of Genesis, that is, in the degree of similarity between samples, an immediate idea coming into mind is to measure the "distance" of each sample from the means vector (the vector the $j$-th component of which is the mean, over all samples, of the $j$-th variable in the pattern vector — see Section 3.1.2.). In the ideal case, i.e., if Genesis were totally homogeneous, one would expect all 96 pattern vectors to coincide exactly with the means vector. Since, however, the existence of chance deviations is unavoidable, we cannot really hope for this to happen. How great the deviations are, or how dissimilar the pattern vector of any sample is compared with the means vector may be measured by the variable:

$$\text{DIS}_i = \sqrt{\sum_{j=1}^{43} z_{ij}^2} \qquad \text{(distance of the $i$-th sample from the means vector)}$$

where $z_{ij}$, the standardized score of variable $j$ in sample $i$, measures the deviation from the mean in terms of standard deviation units. Thus, DIS may be perceived as the Euclidean distance of the sample from the means vector, or, put differently, as a measure of the sample's unique contribution to the heterogeneity of Genesis. Thus, if a group of samples tends to behave, linguistically, in a manner at variance with the rest of the samples, this deviant behavior will manifest itself in exceptionally high values of DIS. For statistical analysis purposes, the distribution of DIS is still in need of investigation. As most of the univariate statistical inference methods assume that the populations, from which samples have been drawn, are normally distributed, normality of DIS has first to be established.

Proof of this normality is based on the fact that each $Z_{ij}$ follows a Standard Normal distribution. According to a well-known theorem, on condition that the $Z_{ij}$ are mutually independent, the random variable

$$\chi^2 = \sum_{j=1}^{m} Z_{ij}^2$$

follows a $\chi^2$ distribution with $m$ degrees of freedom. Lastly, for a sufficiently large $m$, $\sqrt{2\chi^2}$ is known to be approximately normally distributed, which fact completes establishment of the normality of DIS under the null hypothesis.

## 3.2.2.2.  One-Way Analysis of Variance and Allied Procedures.

3.2.2.2.1.  *Description*.   One-way Analysis of Variance is a statistical technique for testing the null hypothesis of equal means for a group of categories.   It is an overall test the aim of which is to detect existence of differences between means.   Following it, various allied methods are carried out in order to test specific hypotheses concerning assumed patterns (*a priori* contrasts) or to form subsets of homogeneous groups of means (*a posteriori* contrasts).

We employed all three types of techniques, i.e., one-way analysis, *a priori* and *a posteriori* contrasts, and shall explain each in due course.

In order to assess the within-homogeneity of each category defined by the research hypotheses, and thence test for differences between means of separate categories, the 96 samples are subdivided into 25 groups of about four samples each, with subcategory *DE* left out as it comprises sample no. 91 only:

| Group no. | Sample nos. | Origin in Subcategory | Group no. | Sample nos. | Origin in Subcategory |
|---|---|---|---|---|---|
| 1 | 1-4 | NP | 15 | 56-57 | HP |
| 2 | 5-8 | NP | 16 | 58-61 | HE |
| 3 | 9-12 | NP | 17 | 62-65 | HE |
| 4 | 13-16 | NE | 18 | 66-69 | HE |
| 5 | 17-20 | NE | 19 | 70-73 | HE |
| 6 | 21-24 | NE | 20 | 74-78 | HJ |
| 7 | 25-28 | NE | 21 | 79-83 | HJ |
| 8 | 29-32 | NJ | 22 | 84-87 | HJ |
| 9 | 33-36 | NJ | 23 | 88-90 | DP |
| 10 | 37-40 | NJ | 24 | 92-94 | DJ |
| 11 | 41-44 | NJ | 25 | 95-96 | DJ |
| 12 | 45-48 | NJ | | | |
| 13 | 49-52 | NJ | | | |
| 14 | 53-55 | NJ | | | |

Let us note, that since the Division hypothesis is not tested here (due to the too low number of samples available), heterogeneity which might be attributed to it may not be detected in this part of the investigation.

The analysis is now carried out in three stages:

(a)  One-way Analysis of Variance.  An overall test of the null hypothesis

$$H_o : \mu_1 = \mu_2 = \ldots = \mu_{25}$$

against the alternative hypothesis

$$H_1 : \mu_i \neq \mu_{j,}$$
for at least one pair $(i \neq j)$,

where $\mu_k$ denotes the mean of the population from which samples of Group $k$ are drawn.

(b)  *A priori* comparisons (contrasts) of averages of group means:

$$H_o : \psi = \sum a_i \mu_i = 0, \quad \text{where } \sum a_i = 0.$$
$$H_1 : \psi \neq 0.$$

For example, to test the hypothesis that the average of *NE* equals the average of *NJ*, the following comparison is tested:

$$H_o = \frac{\mu_4 + \mu_5 + \mu_6 + \mu_7}{4} - \frac{\mu_8 + \mu_9 + \mu_{10} + \mu_{11} + \mu_{12} + \mu_{13} + \mu_{14}}{7} = 0$$

or:

$$H_o : \psi = 7\mu_4 + 7\mu_5 + 7\mu_6 + 7\mu_7 - 4\mu_8 - 4\mu_9 - 4\mu_{10} - 4\mu_{11} - 4\mu_{12} - 4\mu_{13} - 4\mu_{14} = 0$$

against:

$$H_1 : \psi = 0$$

(c)  *A posteriori* comparisons (multiple range tests).   Unlike *a priori* contrasts, where specific linear combinations of the means of groups are tested for significance according to our *a priori* hypotheses, the multiple range tests examine all possible null hypotheses of the type $H_o : \mu_i - \mu_j = 0$ at a single controlled overall significance level $\alpha$.   Thus, these tests divide the means of the $k$ populations into groups so that any two means in a group do not differ significantly.

Two different tests are used here:

— Duncan's multiple range test, and
— Scheffee's test for multiple contrasts,

each at the $\alpha = .10$ as well as at the $\alpha = .01$ significance level.

The reader is again reminded that all statistical analyses in this Section are performed on values of the variable DIS, the definition of which may be looked up in Section 3.2.2.1. above.

### 3.2.2.2.2.   *Results.*

(a)  *One-Way Analysis of Variance*: Results are tabulated in Table 3.3 (p. 77).

Table 3.3: Summary of One-Way Analysis of Variance

| Source | Degrees of Freedom | Sum of Squares | $F$-ratio | Significance |
|---|---|---|---|---|
| Between Groups | 24 | 175.4 | 7.251 | .0000 |
| Within Groups | 70 | 70.6 | | |
| Total | 94 | 246.0 | | |

Table 3.4: Definitions of the Twelve *a-priori* Contrasts

| Contrast no. | Definition | |
|---|---|---|
| 1 | $\mu_1 - 2\mu_2 + \mu_3$ | = 0 |
| 2 | $\mu_4 - \mu_5 + \mu_6 - \mu_7$ | = 0 |
| 3 | $3\mu_8 + 3\mu_9 - 4\mu_{10} - 4\mu_{11} - 4\mu_{12} + 3\mu_{13} + 3\mu_{14}$ | = 0 |
| 4 | $\mu_{16} - \mu_{17} + \mu_{18} - \mu_{19}$ | = 0 |
| 5 | $\mu_{20} - 2\mu_{21} + \mu_{22}$ | = 0 |
| 6 | $\mu_{24} - \mu_{25}$ | = 0 |
| 7 | $(\mu_1 + \mu_2 + \mu_3) / 3 - (\mu_4 + \mu_5 + ... + \mu_{14}) / 11$ | = 0 |
| 8 | $(\mu_4 + \mu_5 + \mu_6 + \mu_7) / 4 - (\mu_8 + \mu_9 + ... + \mu_{14}) / 7$ | = 0 |
| 9 | $\mu_{15} - (\mu_{16} + \mu_{17} + ... + \mu_{22}) / 7$ | = 0 |
| 10 | $(\mu_{16} + \mu_{17} + \mu_{18} + \mu_{19}) / 4 - (\mu_{20} + \mu_{21} + \mu_{22}) / 3$ | = 0 |
| 11 | $(\mu_1 + \mu_2 + ... + \mu_{14}) / 14 - (\mu_{15} + \mu_{16} + ... + \mu_{25}) / 11$ | = 0 |
| 12 | $(\mu_{15} + \mu_{16} + ... + \mu_{22}) / 8 - (\mu_{23} + \mu_{24} + \mu_{25}) / 3$ | = 0 |

The high significance achieved ($p < .0000$) leaves no doubt that there are significant differences between the means of groups defined above.

(b)  *A priori* Contrasts: Table 3.4 displays twelve contrasts.  (See Table 3.4, p. 77).

The first six contrasts are tests for existence of significant differences between means of groups within subcategories *NP, NE, NJ, HE, HJ* and *DJ*. Thus, they actually test for homogeneity within each of the subcategories. Apart from subcategory *DE* being missing here (see Section 3.2.2.2.1.), subcategories *HP* and *DP* are also not included, since each constitutes one group only (see same Section).  Contrasts nos. 7-12 statistically compare averages of the means of groups as follows:

Contrast no.   7: (*NP*)          ←——→          (*NE* + *NJ*)
Contrast no.   8: (*NE*)          ←——→          (*NJ*)
Contrast no.   9: (*HP*)          ←——→          (*HE* + *HJ*)
Contrast no. 10: (*HE*)          ←——→          (*HJ*)
Contrast no. 11: (*N*)            ←——→          (*H* + *D*)
Contrast no. 12: (*H*)            ←——→          (*D*)

The emerging pattern of differences informs us that:

Contrast no. 1, being highly significant ($p < .004$), *NP* is highly non-homogeneous;

Contrast no. 2, being moderately significant ($p < .030$), *NE* is moderately non-homogeneous;

Contrast no. 3, being highly non-significant ($p < .412$), *NJ* is highly homogeneous;

Contrast no. 4, being highly non-significant ($p < .348$), *HE* is highly homogeneous;

Contrast no. 5, being highly non-significant ($p < .293$), *HJ* is highly homogeneous;

Contrast no. 6, being highly non-significant ($p < .151$), *DJ* is highly homogeneous;

Contrast no. 7, being highly significant ($p < .000$), *NP* is significantly different from *NE* and *NJ*, combined;

Contrast no. 8, being highly non-significant ($p < .560$), no significant difference exists between *NE* and *NJ*;

Contrast no. 9, being highly non-significant ($p < .974$), *HP* is not significantly different from *HE* and *HJ*, combined;

Contrast no. 10, being highly non-significant ($p < .705$), *HE* is not significantly different from *HJ*;

Contrast no. 11, being moderately significant ($p < .020$), *N* is significantly different from *H* and *D*, combined;

Contrast no. 12, being highly non-significant ($p < .408$), there is no significant difference between *H* and *D*.

Note that the set of the first six contrasts and any of the three pairs that follow contain mutually orthogonal contrasts [8] and thus test independent components of variation.

How may this roster be interpreted?

Firstly, there is a clear-cut dividing line between $N$, on the one hand, and $H$ and $D$, on the other, and that in two respects:

— The Documentary Hypothesis manifests itself, to a certain degree, only in category $N$ (see nos. 7 and 8), but fails to do so in $H$ (see nos. 9 and 10);

— Insofar as the inner homogeneity of the subcategories is concerned, it is only within $NP$ and $NE$ that some vestige of heterogeneity may be detected, while all the remaining ones demonstrate a high degree of homogeneity.

Secondly, while $P$ appears as a distinct category in $N$, there is as yet no evidence of dissimilarity in language habits between $E$ and $J$, a statement which holds equally true for $N$ (no. 8), $H$ (no. 10), and probably $D$ (no. 12).

Eventually, let us not forget that the number of observations in each group is rather small. This feature of the data on hand cautions us to take a conservative attitude vis-à-vis the rejection of the null hypothesis. In other words: we may not reject it unless the results are very highly significant. Bearing this reservation in mind, the foremost and perhaps somewhat trivial conclusion (see discussion in Section 3.4.) reached by the above analysis is that $NP$ is very heterogeneous and, at the same time, differs significantly from the other subcategories.

No statistical evidence was found, at this stage, for the Documentary Hypothesis as detailed in Section 1.3.2., although there are indications that a modified version of it might be supported by further analyses.

(c)  *A posteriori* Contrasts: On applying Duncan's and Scheffee's tests, the results presented in Figure 3.1 obtained. Means of the 25 groups are arranged here, in an increasing order, and homogeneous subsets can be seen by joining lines. (See Figure 3.1, p. 80).

Several prominent features of these subsets are clearly in view.

One is that there is an unmistakable distinction between $NP$ and $HP +$ $DP$ and that no similar distinction can be noticed within $E$ or $J$.

Another is visible in $J$. Here, groups nos. 8, 9, 21, 24, which comprise all $NJ$-samples from Division $I$ (starting from the beginning of Genesis and terminating with the last verse of ch. 11), behave more like $NP$-samples than like other $J$-samples. That $NJ$ is of a heterogeneous nature was concealed in

---

[8] Two contrasts, namely $\Psi_1 = \Sigma a_i \mu_i$ and $\Psi_2 = \Sigma b_j \mu_j$, are orthogonal if $\Sigma a_i b_j = 0$.

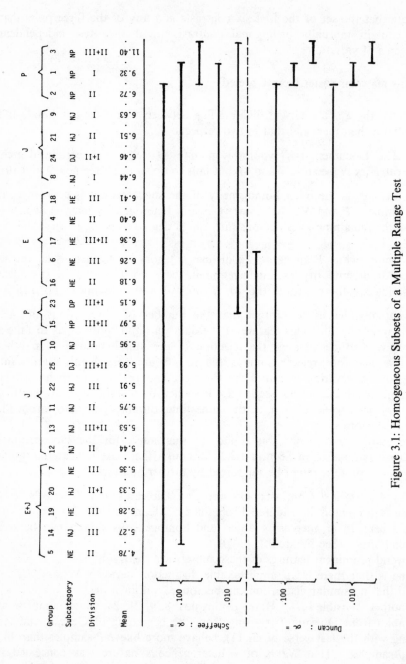

Figure 3.1: Homogeneous Subsets of a Multiple Range Test

the results of Contrast no. 3 owing to the special structure of the coefficients of this contrast: there, the average of groups nos. 8, 9, 13, 14, of which nos. 8 and 9 alone stem from Division *I,* was compared with that of groups nos. 10, 11, 12, none of which stems from that Division. Thus, no separation, due to Divisions, could be detected in this contrast.

Turning to *E,* we observe that group no. 5 (*NE*), on the one hand, and groups nos. 4 (*NE*), 17 (*HE*) and 18 (*HE*), on the other, often belong to separate homogeneous subsets. This particular lends further support to the results of Contrast no. 2 where moderate heterogeneity was located within *NE.*

Yet the most interesting trait of the resulting pattern seems to be the astonishing fact that the groups, arranged in Figure 3.1, as mentioned earlier, in an ascending order of their averages, form clusters in accordance with their assumed Documentary source rather than according to their respective Sort-of-Discourse. In this manner, two repetitive cycles of *E, J, P* are brought to the fore. Moreover, in one of the tests (Scheffee's .01 significance level), the second cycle nearly creates a homogeneous subset of its own, whereas in another test (Duncan's .10 significance level), it is the first cycle which nearly does so. May this not be due — to hazard a guess — to the Divisions of Genesis (see Section 1.4.1.) being at variance with each other in language behavior? We shall have more to say of the meaning of these cycles — if such a meaning may indeed be attached at all — in Section 3.4.

### 3.2.2.3. Two-Way Analysis of Variance

3.2.2.3.1. *Description.* Main effects and interaction effects are examined in several two-way analyses of variance carried out on the dependent variable DIS.

Due to the small number of observations (96), the three hypotheses raised in Section 1.4.1. can not be concurrently analyzed with the aid of three-dimensional analysis of variance. In consequence, multiple Two-way Analyses of Variance (ANOVA) have to be performed separately.

In the following, the three basic designs are displayed, numerals referring to the number of observations in each cell. Certain abbreviations serve in these designs and occasionally also in Tables to follow: DOC = Documents (*P, E, J*), SDS = Sorts-of-Discourse (*N, H, D*), and DIV = Divisions (*I, II, III*) (see Section 1.4.1.).

| Design (a) DIS by DOC and SDS | | | | Design (b) DIS by DIV and SDS | | | | Design (c) DIS by DIV and DOC | | | |
|---|---|---|---|---|---|---|---|---|---|---|---|
| | DOC | | | | | DIV | | | | DIV | | |
| SDS | *P* | *E* | *J* | Total | SDS | *I* | *II* | *III* | Total | DOC | *I* | *II* | *III* | Total |
| *N* | 12 | 16 | 27 | 55 | *N* | 12 | 28 | 15 | 55 | *P* | 5 | 8 | 3 | 16 |
| *H* | 2 | 16 | 14 | 32 | *H* | 1 | 17 | 13 | 31 | *E* | 0 | 14 | 18 | 32 |
| *D* | 3 | 1 | 5 | 9 | *D* | 3 | 3 | 2 | 8 | *J* | 11 | 26 | 9 | 46 |
| Total | 17 | 33 | 46 | 96 | Total | 16 | 48 | 30 | 94 | Total | 16 | 48 | 30 | 94 |

Remark: Designs (b) and (c) do not include samples nos. 57 (*HP*) and 91 (*DE*), because these two cannot be meaningfully attributed to any one Division.


3.2.2.3.2. *Results.* These, for the analyses corresponding to the three designs, are shown in Table 3.5 (p. 83).

Adopting the more conservative significance level of $\alpha = .01$, we find DOC to be significant, DIV to be non-significant either in the main effect or in the interaction effect, and SDS to be significant only through an interaction effect with DOC.

These results clearly suggest a strong evidence for differences between groups classified in the columns *P*, *E* and *J*, as well as for a changing pattern of differences between Documents as one proceeds from one SDS to another. This latter interaction effect is hardly surprising in the light of the high significance of Contrast no. 7 and the high non-significance of Contrast no. 9 (Section 3.2.2.2.2.). The non-significance of the SDS-factor is likewise not unexpected if one is reminded that, apart from *P*, the pattern of grouping of means as revealed in Fig. 3.1 is more in accordance with DOC than with SDS.


**Résumé.** One-way and Two-way Analyses of Variance are carried out on the variable DIS, and *a priori* and *a posteriori* contrasts are performed in order to investigate patterns of differences among subcategories defined by the Documentary and the Discourse hypotheses. Results indicate different language behavior in *N*, on the one hand, and in *H* and *D*, on the other, in two respects: (a) *N* is in general more heterogeneous than *H* and *D*; (b) *NP*, in particular, is exceptionally heterogeneous, and at the same time manifests a significantly deviant language behavior when compared with *NE* and *NJ*, combined. This latter phenomenon is not detectable in *HP*, *HE* and *HJ*. Some traits, though statistically non-significant, may still be philologically meaningful: *J*-samples from Division *I* are grouped together, with their DIS-values closer to those of *NP* than to those of other *J*-samples. When arranged in an ascending order of DIS, samples are grouped according to Documents rather than according to Sorts-of-Discourse.

Table 3.5: Results of the Two-Way Analysis of Variance

| Analysis | Source of Variation | Degrees of Freedom | $F$ | Significance |
|---|---|---|---|---|
| SDS × DOC | Main Effects | 4 | 12.85 | .001 |
|  | SDS | 2 | 1.04 | .356 |
|  | DOC | 2 | 23.67 | .001 |
|  | Interaction | 4 | 5.13 | .001 |
|  | Explained | 8 | 8.99 | .001 |
| SDS × DIV | Main Effects | 4 | 1.44 | .227 |
|  | SDS | 2 | .63 | .534 |
|  | DIV | 2 | 1.81 | .170 |
|  | Interaction | 4 | .48 | .747 |
|  | Explained | 8 | .96 | .469 |
| DOC × DIV | Main Effects | 4 | 12.29 | .001 |
|  | DOC | 2 | 21.23 | .001 |
|  | DIV | 2 | 1.03 | .361 |
|  | Interaction | 4 | .72 | .540 |
|  | Explained | 8 | 7.33 | .001 |

Table 3.6: Coefficients of Eight Contrasts – Control Stage, Design (a)

| Dimension | | Contrast | | | | | | | |
|---|---|---|---|---|---|---|---|---|---|
| SDS | DOC | 1 | 2 | 3 | 4 | 5 | 6 | 7 | 8 |
| 1 | 1 | 1 | 0 | 1 | 0 | 1 | 0 | 0 | 0 |
| 1 | 2 | 1 | 0 | 0 | 1 | 0 | 1 | 0 | 0 |
| 1 | 3 | 1 | 0 | −1 | −1 | −1 | −1 | 0 | 0 |
| 2 | 1 | 0 | 1 | 1 | 0 | 0 | 0 | 1 | 0 |
| 2 | 2 | 0 | 1 | 0 | 1 | 0 | 0 | 0 | 1 |
| 2 | 3 | 0 | 1 | −1 | −1 | 0 | 0 | −1 | −1 |
| 3 | 1 | −1 | −1 | 1 | 0 | −1 | 0 | −1 | 0 |
| 3 | 2 | −1 | −1 | 0 | 1 | 0 | −1 | 0 | −1 |
| 3 | 3 | −1 | −1 | −1 | −1 | 1 | 1 | 1 | 1 |

## 3.2.3.  MULTIVARIATE ANALYSIS

### 3.2.3.1.  **Multivariate Analysis of Variance with Allied Procedures**

3.2.3.1.1.  *Description.*  The use of Multivariate Analysis of Variance (MANOVA) is one of the realizations of the multivariate analysis alternative discussed in Section 3.2.1.

The statistical processing is here divided into two stages.

In the first, MANOVA is applied to the two designs (a) and (c) (see Section 3.2.2.3.1.) which are of prime interest in this study.  Thirty-nine variables,[9] to be analysed by multivariate statistics, Pillai's criterion, Hotelling's trace statistics and Wilks's Lambda, are included in the pattern vector.  In addition, separate Univariate Analysis of Variance is applied to each variable.

This analysis, though, might be of dubious validity, as one may suspect that significant results thereof could be attributed to a low ratio of the number of observations (96) to the number of variables (39) (this suspicion is discussed at some length in Section 3.2.3.3.1.).

A control test is therefore called for, and an additional MANOVA is applied to a restricted group of variables that have been found, through Factor Analysis (see Section 3.2.3.2.), to account for over 50 p.c. of the total variation in the original pattern vector.  One MANOVA, corresponding to design (a) — see Section 3.2.2.3.1. — is carried out.  In addition, contrasts of separate levels are tested for significance.  Specifically, let $\mu_{ij}$ be the population mean in the $(i,j)$ cell, i.e. in the $j$-th column of the $i$-th row of the design table.  Then, the following contrasts are tested:

$$\text{Contrast 1:} \quad \frac{\mu_{11} + \mu_{12} + \mu_{13}}{3} = \frac{\mu_{31} + \mu_{32} + \mu_{33}}{3} \qquad \left\{ \begin{array}{l} \text{Row I (means)} \\ \text{compared with} \\ \text{Row III (means)} \end{array} \right.$$

$$\text{Contrast 2:} \quad \frac{\mu_{21} + \mu_{22} + \mu_{23}}{3} = \frac{\mu_{31} + \mu_{32} + \mu_{33}}{3} \qquad \left\{ \begin{array}{l} \text{Row II (means)} \\ \text{compared with} \\ \text{Row III (means)} \end{array} \right.$$

$$\text{Contrast 3:} \quad \frac{\mu_{11} + \mu_{21} + \mu_{31}}{3} = \frac{\mu_{13} + \mu_{23} + \mu_{33}}{3} \qquad \left\{ \begin{array}{l} \text{Column I (means)} \\ \text{compared with} \\ \text{Column III (means)} \end{array} \right.$$

$$\text{Contrast 4:} \quad \frac{\mu_{12} + \mu_{22} + \mu_{32}}{3} = \frac{\mu_{13} + \mu_{23} + \mu_{33}}{3} \qquad \left\{ \begin{array}{l} \text{Column II (means)} \\ \text{compared with} \\ \text{Column III (means)} \end{array} \right.$$

---

[9] Four of the 43 non-empty variables which proved to be absolutely non-discriminatory were discarded from the analysis.

Interaction contrasts, not made explicit here, are also included, and may be intelligible from Table 3.6, where the coefficients of the complete group of contrasts are shown. (See Table 3.6, p. 83).

In the second stage of the analysis, special orthogonal contrasts are applied to each of the 39 variables of the first stage. These contrasts are so defined as to test specific aspects of the hypotheses set.

3.2.3.1.2. *Results.* For the control stage of the analysis, the following 17 variables are found to have high communalities in Factor Analysis (to identify them, see Table 1.4):

$x1$, $x2$, $x3$, $x4$, $x5$, $x6$, $x7$, $x8$, $x11$, $x17$, $x19$, $x21$, $x23$, $x29$, $x38$, $x39$, $x41$.

Table 3.7 presents the significance levels achieved for Multivariate and for Univariate Two-way Analyses of Variances applied to this group of variables, as well as the significance levels of the contrasts outlined above (sample No. 10 (*NP*), having a deviant value for $x2$, was deleted as an outlier). (See Table 3.7, p. 86).

The most outstanding feature of the pattern of results, as shown in Table 3.7, is the completely different behavior of the three Sorts-of-Discourse. Except for the four variables $x2$, $x3$, $x4$ and $x21$, all the other thirteen are significant ($p < .10$), eleven of which are even highly significant ($p < .01$). Let us recall, that when the variable DIS was analysed under the same design (Section 3.2.2.3.2.) it was found to be non-significant.

When contrasts of separate levels within SDS are examined, $N$ manifests a behavior which is at variance with that of $D$, and, in view of the mostly non-significant results of Contrast No. 2, with that of $H$, too.

Finally, the Documentary hypothesis is also supported here with a very high significance level ($p < .00001$), which remark concludes discussion of the results of the control stage.

For the first of the two stages, outlined in Section 3.2.3.1.1., MANOVA is now expanded to include 39 variables[10], and design (c) is added to the analysis. Outliers, as defined in Section 3.1.4.3., having been removed, and samples Nos. 57(*HP*) and 91(*DE*) eliminated for design (*c*) (these two cannot be meaningfully attributed to any one Division) the following layouts of observations obtain:

| | Design (a) | | | | | Design (c) | | | |
|---|---|---|---|---|---|---|---|---|---|
| SDS | P | DOC E | J | Total | DOC | I | DIV II | III | Total |
| N | 7 | 16 | 27 | 50 | P | 4 | 6 | 1 | 11 |
| H | 2 | 15 | 12 | 29 | E | — | 14 | 17 | 34 |
| D | 3 | 1 | 5 | 9 | J | 11 | 24 | 9 | 44 |
| Total | 12 | 32 | 44 | 88 | Total | 15 | 44 | 27 | 86 |

---

[10] See the preceding note.

Table 3.7: Significance of Results of Multivariate and Univariate ANOVA and of Design (a) Contrasts (Control Stage)

| Statistic | Main Effect | | Interaction SDS × DOC | Contrasts | | | | | | | |
|---|---|---|---|---|---|---|---|---|---|---|---|
| | | | | Between Means | | | | Interactions | | | |
| | SDS | DOC | | (1) N vs. D | (2) H vs. D | (3) P vs. J | (4) E vs. J | (5) | (6) | (7) | (8) |
| Pillai's | .00001 | .00001 | .045 | | | | | | | | |
| Hotteling's | .00001 | .00001 | .020 | | | | | | | | |
| Wilks's | .00001 | .00001 | .031 | | | | | | | | |
| x1 | .00001 | .00002 | .074 | .00000 | .00002 | .00003 | .00933 | | | | .060 |
| x2 | | | | | .081 | .00912 | .065 | | | | |
| x3 | | .00002 | | | | | | | | | |
| x4 | .00007 | .046 | | .00414 | | | | | | | |
| x5 | .096 | .012 | | | | | | .070 | .072 | .106 | |
| x6 | | | | | | | | .022 | | .051 | |
| x7 | .00001 | | .010 | .00001 | .057 | | | .00802 | .00413 | | |
| x8 | .00262 | | | .00610 | | | | | | | |
| x11 | .00001 | .00001 | | .00012 | .070 | .00014 | .040 | | | .087 | |
| x17 | .00001 | .00049 | | .00000 | .00000 | .00513 | | | | .074 | |
| x19 | | | | .00000 | | | | | | | |
| x21 | .00009 | .00267 | .051 | .00054 | | | | .038 | | | |
| x23 | .00082 | .00018 | | .00029 | | | .036 | .044 | | | |
| x29 | .075 | | | | | .042 | | | | | |
| x38 | .00001 | | | .00000 | .00011 | .00101 | | | | | .061 |
| x39 | .00001 | .00004 | | .00000 | .014 | | | | | | |
| x41 | .00001 | .088 | | | | | | | | | |
| No. of Significant Results at (p < .10) | 13 | 10 | 3 | 11 | 7 | 6 | 4 | 5 | 2 | 4 | 2 |
| (p < .01) | 11 | 7 | — | 11 | 3 | 5 | 1 | 1 | 1 | — | — |

Note, that in comparison with the original design (Section 3.2.2.3.1.), the outliers are five samples in *NP,* one sample in *HE,* and two samples in *HJ.*

The significance levels achieved for Univariate and Multivariate Two-way Analyses of Variance are shown in Table 3.8 (pp. 88-89).

Concentrating first on the main effects, we find all three dimensions (i.e., hypotheses), as assessed by the multivariate statistics, to be significant.

Since the magnitude of the significance for design (a) is comparable to that in Table 3.7, it may not be attributed to too low a number of observations, thus defying the invalidity question previously raised.

To arrive at a comprehensive criterion for the significance of results derived from the separate analyses which have been applied to each of the variables, we adopt the Binomial model, and calculate the chance of randomly obtaining, out of 39 independent univariate analyses of variance, *k* or more significant results at the $\alpha = .10$ and at the $\alpha = .01$ levels of significance. These probabilities are given in brackets adjacent to each *k* in Table 3.8. According to this criterion, here after referred to as "the Binomial Criterion," each of the dimensions tested is again significant at the overall 0.01 level of significance. (We should note here, that another widely used criterion for this kind of test is:

$$\chi^2 = -2 \sum_{j=1}^{m} \ln p_j,$$

where $p_j$ is the significance level achieved for the *j*-th of *m* statistically independent tests. This statistic has, under the null hypothesis of no differences between the categories of the dimension under study, a $\chi^2$ distribution with $2m$ degrees of freedom. However, we found the Binomial Criterion to be more appropriate for our study.)

When the interaction effects are reviewed, the only significant one according to both the multivariate statistics and the Binomial Criterion is that between Documents and Divisions. This may well be imputed to the combined effect of the significance of the DOC dimension, and the unequal representation of Documents in the three Divisions.

Considering the separate contrasts, since no multivariate statistic is available, the only overall statistic by which to assess whether the separate tests of each contrast culminate in a meaningful overall significance may be the Binomial Criterion. What conclusions may be drawn from the significance levels achieved by this criterion for the separate contrasts?

With regard to Sort-of-Speech, essential differences in language behaviour between the narrator, on the one hand, and human and Divine speech, on the other, are evidenced. Whether differences of such an order of magnitude might be expected in a literary work of homogeneous origin or,

Table 3.8: Univariate and Multivariate Analyses of Variance of the Three Basic Designs

| Statistic | Main Effects | | | SDS × DOC | DOC × DIV | SDS Contrasts | | DOC Contrasts | | DIV Contrasts | |
|---|---|---|---|---|---|---|---|---|---|---|---|
| | SDS | DOC | DIV | | | N vs. H+D | H vs. D | P vs. E+J | E vs. J | I vs. II+III | II vs. III |
| Pillai's | .00001 | .00040 | .00001 | .240 | .161 | | | | | | |
| Hotelling's | .00001 | .00006 | .00001 | .053 | .020 | | | | | | |
| Wilks's | .00001 | .00015 | .00001 | .126 | .068 | | | | | | |
| x1 | .00001 | .00013 | | .075 | | .00000 | | | | | |
| x2 | | | | | | | .030 | .00084 | | | |
| x3 | | .00001 | | | | | | .00000 | | | |
| x4 | .00001 | | | | .028 | | | | | | .047 |
| x5 | | .049 | .057 | | .040 | .00019 | | | .078 | | .023 |
| x6 | | | .00031 | | .00050 | | | | | .00021 | |
| x7 | .00001 | | | | | .00000 | | | | | |
| x8 | .00146 | | .022 | .022 | | .00107 | | | | .014 | |
| x9 | .00179 | | | .099 | | .00485 | | | | | |
| x10 | .014 | .074 | .024 | | | .041 | | | | .036 | .030 |
| x11 | .00001 | .00073 | | | .047 | .00004 | | | | | |
| x12 | | | .00016 | | | | | .00006 | | .00003 | |
| x13 | .00567 | .081 | .092 | | .00210 | .046 | | | | | |
| x14 | .036 | | .00721 | | .00004 | .055 | | | | .016 | |
| x16 | | | .036 | | | | | | | .024 | |
| x17 | .00001 | .00195 | | | | .00000 | .070 | .00974 | | | |
| x18 | | .00572 | | | | | | .00784 | | | .057 |
| x19 | .00001 | | | | | .00000 | | | | | |
| x20 | .088 | | .00391 | | | | | | | | .00822 |

| | 1 | 2 | 3 | 4 | 5 | 6 | 7 | 8 | 9 | 10 | 11 |
|---|---|---|---|---|---|---|---|---|---|---|---|
| x21 | | | | | .022 | | .045 | | | .043 | .086 |
| x22 | .00021 | .043 | .055 | | .015 | .00083 | | | | | |
| x23 | .019 | | .082 | | | .064 | | .050 | | .092 | .027 |
| x25 | | | .00872 | | | | | | | .014 | .040 |
| x26 | .00103 | .00033 | .015 | | | .00168 | | .00053 | .090 | .00202 | |
| x27 | .00448 | .00017 | .00314 | | | .00187 | | .00085 | .100 | .00062 | |
| x29 | .00211 | .00085 | .00201 | | | .00113 | | .00328 | .061 | | |
| x33 | | .019 | .032 | | .069 | | | | | .046 | .035 |
| x34 | | | | | .013 | .054 | | | | | |
| x35 | | | | .067 | .00613 | | | | | .066 | |
| x37 | | | | | | | .072 | | | | |
| x38 | .099 | | | | | .00000 | | .00130 | | .00871 | .00392 |
| x39 | .00001 | .00077 | .00012 | | | .00115 | | | | .037 | .053 |
| x40 | .00617 | | .066 | | | .00000 | | | | | |
| x41 | .00001 | | | | .011 | .00000 | | | .086 | | |
| x43 | .00001 | .049 | | | | | | | .045 | | |
| x50 | .046 | | .016 | | | | | .011 | | .00773 | |
| x51 | | | | .080 | | | | | | | |
| x52 | | | | .043 | | | | | | | |
| x53 | .00012 | | | | .074 | .00088 | | | | | .00088 |
| No. of Significant Results (p < .10) | 23 (.0000) | 16 (.0000) | 19 (.0000) | 6 (.2150) | 13 (.0000) | 22 (.0000) | 2 (.9124) | 11 (.0012) | 8 (.0366) | 16 (.0000) | 11 (.0012) |
| (p < .01) | 18 (.0000) | 9 (.0000) | 8 (.0000) | — (—) | 4 (.0006) | 17 (.0000) | — (—) | 9 (.0000) | — (—) | 6 (.0000) | 2 (.3243) |

conversely, whether they point to two different authors, each responsible for $N$ and $H + D$ separately, will be discussed in other Parts of this volume.

What role do the Documents play here? That there were indeed three that made up the Book of Genesis is hardly borne out in view of the contrasts' results. The only significant demarcation is that between $P$ and $E + J$. No variable is significant at the $\alpha = .01$ level when $E$ is contrasted with $J$, whereas nine are significant at the same level when $P$ is contrasted with $E + J$. The Binomial Criterion only sums up these findings.

Finally, major differences between the three Divisions are noticeable. Based on the Binomial Criterion, significant differences stand revealed between Division $I$ and $II + III$, and, to a somewhat less pronounced measure, though still significant, between Divisions $II$ and $III$.

In consequence of all the three research hypotheses being strongly sustained, we turn to partial Discriminant Analysis in order to discover which linguistic features differentiate between the categories of a significant dimension (Discriminant Analysis will be presented in full in Section 3.2.3.3.). But before the outcome is shown, the theoretical workings of MANOVA, and the allied Discriminant Analysis procedures, must be briefly outlined.

The multivariate statistical tests in the analysis of variance are based on orthogonal "canonical variates". Each variate is a linear combination of the original variables and, the canonical variates being mutually orthogonal, each accounts for a separate part of the total variation of the source variables. Attached to each canonical variate is its *eigenvalue* (or root), $\lambda_i$, which represents the amount of variation accounted for by the $i$-th linear combination. The multivariate statistics are actually expressed in terms of $\{\lambda_i\}$. For example:

$$\text{Wilks's Lambda} = [(1 + \lambda_1)(1 + \lambda_2)\ldots(1 + \lambda_s)]^{-1}$$

$$(s = \text{number of } eigenvalues)$$

Since significance of the multivariate statistics means that the portion of the total variation, accounted for by the canonical variates, is significantly discriminating between the levels of the dimension under study, examining the relationship between each significant canonical variate and the original variables might yield valuable information about the discriminating features.

Two groups of statistics might be helpful in this respect:

(a)  The correlations between the canonical variates and each individual variable;

(b)  The standardized Discriminant Function coefficients (see Section 3.2.3.3.1.).

Both are bound to deliver an indication of each variable's contribution to the composite score, derived from the Discriminant Function, and thus help in interpreting the canonical variates.

We start by locating the group of variables whose members have the strongest relationship with the canonical variates. To assess the stability of the emerging pattern of either the correlations or the Discriminant Function coefficients, results for design (a), as carried out in the first stage and in the control stage of the analysis, are compared. Findings show that while the pattern of correlations between individual variables and the canonical variates hardly changes from the control stage to the first stage, the pattern of the Discriminant Function coefficients is not stable, due probably to a low ratio between the number of observations and the number of variables taking part in the analysis. Consequently, only correlations should be observed.

These, for the significant canonical variates of SDS, DOC and DIV, are tabulated in Table 3.9 (p. 92).

The implications of this data are primarily linguistic in nature and, therefore, lie beyond the confines of the statistician.

Leading a similar kind of investigation with regard to the results of the contrasts studied in the second stage of the analysis (see Table 3.8), we detect the following variables as being discriminatory at the $\alpha = .10$ level of significance (variables marked by an asterisk are significant also at the .01 level):

SDS:    $N$ vs. $H + D$    :    $*x1$, $*x5$, $*x7$, $*x8$, $*x9$, $x10$, $*x11$, $x13$, $x14$, $*x17$, $*x19$, $*x23$, $x25$, $*x27$, $*x29$, $*x33$, $x35$, $*x39$, $*x40$, $*x41$, $*x43$, $*x53$     (22 variables);

        $H$ vs. $D$    :    $x2$, $x17$     (2 variables);

DOC:    $P$ vs. $E + J$    :    $*x1$, $*x2$, $*x11$, $*x17$, $*x18$, $x25$, $*x26$, $*x27$, $*x29$, $*x39$, $x50$     (11 variables);

        $E$ vs. $J$    :    $x5$, $x21$, $x26$, $x27$, $x29$, $x37$, $x41$, $x43$     (8 variables);

DIV:    $I$ vs. $II + III$    :    $*x6$, $x8$, $x10$, $*x12$, $x14$, $x16$, $x22$, $x25$, $x26$, $*x27$, $*x29$, $x33$, $x37$, $*x38$, $x39$, $*x50$     (16 variables);

        $II$ vs. $III$    :    $x4$, $x5$, $x10$, $x18$, $*x20$, $x22$, $x25$, $x26$, $x33$, $*x38$, $x40$     (11 variables).

Again, it is not for the statistician to form an estimate of the meaning of this list, either in terms of the composition of the groups of discriminatory variables, or by virtue of the remarkably unequal number of variables significantly discriminating in each of the six contrasts.

Table 3.9: Strongest Correlations between Dependent Variables
and Canonical Variates of SDS, DOC and DIV

| SDS Variable Correlation | | DOC Variable Correlation | | DIV | | | |
|---|---|---|---|---|---|---|---|
| | | | | 1st Can. Var. ($p < .00001$) Variable Correlation | | 2nd Can. Var. ($p < .002$) Variable Correlation | |
| $x1$ | −.271 | $x1$ | .269 | $x6$ | −.244 | $x5$ | .178 |
| $x7$ | .223 | $x3$ | −.343 | $x12$ | −.273 | $x20$ | −.226 |
| $x17$ | −.260 | $x11$ | −.238 | $x27$ | .200 | $x25$ | −.194 |
| $x19$ | .407 | $x26$ | .241 | $x29$ | .220 | $x38$ | −.262 |
| $x39$ | −.341 | $x27$ | .241 | | | | |
| $x41$ | −.236 | $x39$ | .238 | | | | |

Table 3.10: *Eigenvalues* and Percentages of Total Variation of the First Four Factors

| *Eigenvalue* | | Percentage of Variation | Cumulative Percentage of Variation |
|---|---|---|---|
| I | 7.07 | 18.6 | 18.6 |
| II | 4.15 | 10.9 | 29.5 |
| III | 3.03 | 8.0 | 37.5 |
| IV | 2.78 | 7.3 | 44.8 |

**Résumé.** Multivariate Analysis of Variance is an extension of the univariate case presented in Section 3.2.2., yet its aim remains the same: to investigate patterns of differences between subcategories defined in our enquiry by the Discourse, the Documentary, and the Division hypotheses. Results tend to support findings of earlier analyses in that there are essential differences in language behavior between the narrator, on the one hand, and human and Divine direct speech, on the other. With regard to the Documentary Hypothesis, multivariate tests do suggest a significant discrimination between Documents. However, on applying tests for the significance of contrasts to individual variables, the Binomial Criterion suggests discrimination between $P$ and $E + J$, but none between $E$ and $J$. Multivariate tests and contrasts, applied to individual variables propound a distinction between the three Divisions, with the one between Division $I$ and the two that follow being even more spectacular.

## 3.2.3.2.  **Factor Analysis.**

3.2.3.2.1.  *Description.* Factor Analysis is a statistical technique aimed at finding a small number of basic factors, which may account for a large portion of the variation inherent in the original variables. Its fundamental philosophy is that covariation of variables as manifested in the existence of groups of highly intra-correlated variables, indicates that there are some basic factors, and that variation in these factors generates the high correlations. Factor Analysis is mainly concerned with the identification of these factors, and there are two modes of analysis: orthogonal and oblique.

In the orthogonal Factor Analysis, which will be used here, we try to define several linear combinations (factors) of the original variables in such a way that each successive factor will account for most of the residual variation, that is not yet accounted for by previously created factors. Put differently: the derived factors are mutually orthogonal, and thus explain separate portions of the total variation.

There are two reasons for employing Factor Analysis here. One is that since correlated variables do exist in our pattern vector, by identifying basic factors which might explain these correlations we might be able to learn a great deal about the language behavior of Genesis. The other reason is related to the application of Discriminant Analysis. In order to derive statistically valid conclusions from this kind of analysis, a certain minimum ratio is required of the number of observations to the number of variables, to be incorporated in the Discriminant Function. In our study, however, the number of observations (samples) is quite limited, thus restricting the number of variables in the Discriminant Function to no more than, say, five to ten variables. Since our pattern vector includes as many as 39 variables, we look for a way to reduce this number, namely: to diminish the dimensionality of the pattern vector, without losing too much discriminatory power that is retained in the original variables. A good way to achieve this is to extract a new, small-sized set of basic variables, i.e., factors, which reflect a large portion of the variation inherent in the original pattern vector.

As a consequence of the above two reasons, orthogonal Factor Analysis is applied, using various methods of principal axis rotation. Such a rotation is needed, after the initial factors have been extracted, in order to facilitate interpretation of the meaning of the derived factors. Varimax, e.g., achieves it by isolating a small number of variables where the contribution of a factor in explaining their variation is decisive. Inspecting the composition of this group of variables helps the investigator in interpreting the factor (See SPSS Manual).

3.2.3.2.2.   *Results.* · Those of the Factor Analysis aimed at reducing the dimensionality of the "pattern vector", will be discussed in Section 3.2.3.3.1. Here, we present results concerning the linguistic behavior of Genesis. The *eigenvalues* and the percentage of the total variation accounted for by the first four factors are shown in Table 3.10. For definition of an *eigenvalue*, see Section 3.2.3.1.2. (See Table 3.10, p. 92).

Variables with the highest coefficients in the Factor Matrix and in the Factor Score Matrix are given in Tables 3.11 and 3.12, respectively (the first matrix contains coefficients, also termed loads, of the equations that express the original variables as linear combinations of factors, while the second contain those that express factors as linear combinations of the original variables). (See Tables 3.11 and 3.12, pp. 95 and 96).

Examination of the results suggests that $x19$, the incidence of the conjunctive *and*, and $x39$, the transition frequency between prepositions + pronouns and finite verbal forms, are the dominant contributors to the first factor, whereas $x1$ through $x8$, i.e., word length, constitute the second. The last two factors do not seem to be meaningful or interpretable.

On the use of the derived factors for Discriminant Analysis — see the coming section.

**Résumé.**   Factor Analysis was carried out in order to locate features that may account for the diversity in linguistic habits found in the samples, and in order to reduce dimensionality of the pattern vector. Two meaningful factors are obtained: the first comprises variables $x19$ and $x39$, while the other represents word length ($x1$ through $x8$).

## 3.2.3.3.   Discriminant Analysis.

3.2.3.3.1.   *Description.* As a final attempt to establish statistical evidence regarding the validity of the Documentary, the Discourse and the Division hypotheses, several Discriminant Analyses are applied to the data.

Discriminant Analysis comprises a group of multivariate statistical methods which strive at constructing Discriminant Functions that best distinguish between sample elements which originate in different populations. Based on a pattern vector which represents measures of their discriminatory characteristics, the aim of Discriminant Analysis is twofold: (a) to assess the statistical significance of discrimination obtained by the derived Discriminant

Table 3.11: Variables with Highest Factor Matrix Coefficients

| Rotation \ Factor | I | II | III | IV |
|---|---|---|---|---|
| Quartimax | x17 (.12)  x19 (−.31)  x39 (.45) | x1 — x8 (⅜ .6)  x11 (−.44)<br>x19 (.43) | x1 (−.37)  x4 (−.36)<br>x11 (−.46)  x38 (.42) | x1 (.37)  x4 (.34)  x6 (.34)<br>x7 (.52)  x8 (.28) |
| Equimax | x1 (.85)  x7 (−.67)<br>x17 (.78)  x19 (−.84)<br>x39 (.91)  x41 (.66)<br>x43 (.55) | x2 (.56)  x13 (−.47)<br>x14 (.47)  x23 (.66)<br>x25 (.59)  x38 (.77) | x4 (−.45)  x11 (−.57)<br>x21 (.62)  x26 (.53)<br>x27 (.50)  x29 (.53)<br>x51 (.51)  x53 (−.49) | x13 (.45)  x22 (.56)  x31 (−.50)<br>x32 (.55) |
| Varimax | x1 (.84)  x5 (.45)<br>x7 (−.68)  x11 (−.49)<br>x17 (.78)  x19 (−.85)<br>x41 (.68)  x43 (.55) | x4 (−.44)  x8 (.41)<br>x11 (−.55)  x21 (.61)<br>x26 (.53)  x27 (.51)<br>x29 (.53)  x51 (.50)<br>x53 (−.50) | x11 (−.41)  x12 (.58)<br>x13 (−.47)  x14 (.49)<br>x20 (.41)  x23 (.63)<br>x25 (.59)  x38 (.77) | x3 (−.49)  x13 (.44)<br>x22 (.56)  x32 (.54) |

Remark: Coefficients in brackets.

Table 3.12: Variables with Highest Factor Score Coefficients

| Rotation \ Factor | I | II | III | IV |
|---|---|---|---|---|
| Quartimax | $x1$ (.15)   $x17$ (.11)<br>$x19$ (−.30)   $x39$ (.45) | $x1 — x8$<br>($\sim$ .6) | $x1$ (−.37)   $x4$ (−.36)<br>$x11$ (−.46)   $x38$ (.42) | $x1$ (.37)   $x4$ (.34)<br>$x6$ (.34)   $x7$ (.52)<br>$x8$ (.28) |
| Equimax | $x1$ (.19)   $x19$ (−.29)<br>$x39$ (.48) | $x1 — x7$ (−.25)<br>$x11$ (−.41)   $x19$ (−.20)<br>$x38$ (.43)   $x39$ (−.26) | $x1 — x8$<br>($\sim$ .50)<br>$x11$ (−.48)   $x19$ (.41) | $x1$ (.40)   $x2$ (.22)<br>$x4$ (.39)   $x5$ (.20)<br>$x6$ (.37)   $x7$ (.57)<br>$x8$ (.30)   $x26$ (.20)<br>$x39$ (−.20) |
| Varimax | $x1$ (.18)   $x17$ (.13)<br>$x19$ (−.30)   $x39$ (.46) | $x1 — x8$ (.50)<br>$x11$ (−.47)   $x19$ (.42) | $x1$ (−.39)   $x4$ (−.39)<br>$x7$ (−.31)   $x11$ (−.43)<br>$x38$ (.42) | $x1$ (.39)   $x4$ (.37)<br>$x6$ (.36)   $x7$ (.55) |

Remark: Coefficients in brackets.

Functions and (b) to assess success of classification by means of the decision functions (see Section 3.1.2.) derived in the process of Discriminant Analysis.

However, before detailing the analyses and the fruit they bore, it must be stressed that these analyses suffer from a number of drawbacks, the primary being the exceedingly small number of observations in hand.

It is a quite established statistical fact that statistical significance of discrimination between populations decreases rapidly as the ratio between the number of observations per class (population) and the number of discriminatory variables becomes smaller. To demonstrate this with an extreme example: one can always achieve a perfect separation between the two subgroups of observations which actually belong to the same population, if the number of observations equals the number of variables in the Discriminant Function. Previous studies have convincingly shown[11] that a ratio of at least 3 to 5 between the number of observations per class and the number of variables is advisable in order to preclude an apparently significant discrimination within an identical distribution.

In the present case, some of the classes contain as few as nine samples, e.g., category $D$. Thus, in certain Discriminant Analyses no more than three discriminating variables should be allowed to enter the Discriminant Function. The number, however, of the potentially discriminating variables is by far larger, and fixing it, for the reason stated, at three to five ensues in a regrettable loss of available discriminatory power. How to solve this predicament?

A possible remedy, already mentioned above, may be to replace the original variables by a small number of extracted factors which still retain the discriminating information contained in the former. For this purpose, orthogonal Factor Analysis is processed and the first ten factors, accounting for over 70 p.c. of the variation inherent in the original variables, are extracted. These factors are incorporated in a Stepwise Discriminant Analysis (SDA) as additional variables. But results are disappointing as far as discriminatory capability of the derived factors is concerned. The factors are, therefore, deleted, and another variable, which has already proved to be discriminating, that is the variable DIS (see Section 3.2.2.1.), is added to the analysis.

Several groups of analyses are run, each allowing for no more than five variables, to be included in any one Discriminant Function. The groups are as follows, with the number of observations (samples) in each category given in brackets. (Outliers, as defined in Section 3.1.4.3., are excluded.)

(a) A set of SDA to test, independently, the three hypotheses under examination, namely:

$P(12)$, $E(32)$, $J(44)$; $N(50)$, $H(29)$, $D(9)$; $I(15)$, $II(44)$, $III(27)$

(b) A set of SDA to test, independently, the Documentary Hypothesis within each of the three Sorts-of-Discourse, namely:

$NP(7)$, $NE(16)$, $NJ(27)$; $HP(2)$, $HE(15)$, $HJ(12)$; $DP(3)$, $DJ(5)$

---

[11] For example, J.D. Sammon, D. Foley and A. Proctor, "Considerations of Dimensionality versus Sample Size", *IEEE Symposium on Adaptive Processes* (Austin, Texas: December 1970).

(c)  A set of SDA to test, independently, the Sort-of-Discourse Hypothesis within each of the three Documents, namely:

$NP(7)$, $HP(2)$, $DP(3)$; $NE(16)$, $HE(15)$, $DE(1)$; $NJ(27)$, $HJ(12)$, $DJ(5)$

3.2.3.3.2.  *Results*.  The first step in the analysis is to calculate Wilks's Lambda (the U-statistic), a measure of discrimination among groups.  This is done separately for each variable in all of the above analyses.  U-statistic is then transformed into a univariate F-ratio in order to assess its significance. The results of these computations are given in Table 3.13 for group (a), in Table 3.14 for group (b) and in Table 3.15 for group (c).  (See Tables 3.13, 3.14, 3.15, pp. 99-101).

Reference to these Tables shows a number of noteworthy particularities.

In the first place, of the 40 variables employed, i.e., the 39 listed in Table 3.8 plus the variable DIS, at least twenty support, at the .10 significance level, all three of the hypotheses studied, i.e., the Documentary, the Discourse and the Division hypotheses.  The actual significance level achieved, as summarized for the various analyses by the Binomial Criterion (see Section 3.2.3.1.2. for its definition), shows the results in their entirety to be highly significant, too.

Then, there is a sharp distinction between $N$, on the one hand, and $H$ and $D$, on the other, in regard to the three Documents (Table 3.14).  Whereas discrimination among Documents in $N$ follows almost the same pattern as revealed in Table 3.13 — nearly the same groups of significant variables are found in either Table — the number of significantly discriminating variables within $H$ and $D$ is by far smaller, and turns out to be non-significant according to the Binomial Criterion.

Table 3.15 displays the striking distinction between $P$ and $E + J$ in regard to the Sorts-of-Discourse.  Whereas discrimination among Sorts-of-Discourse follows, in $E + J$, almost the same pattern as revealed in Table 3.13 — nearly the same groups of significant variables are found in either table — the number of significantly discriminating variables in $P$, though significant by the Binomial Criterion, is by far smaller, both at the .10 and at the .01 level.

The last two observations seem to present $P$ as of a unique character, distinct from $E$ and $J$ in $N$, on the one hand, and relatively uniform across Sorts-of-Discourse, on the other.

To follow up these first-glance clues, we may now proceed to the results of the Stepwise Discriminant Analysis.

Total discriminatory power, retained in the variables prior to deriving any Discriminant Function and after deriving the first one, is presented, for the various analyses, in Table 3.16 (p. 102).

The statistic used there is Wilks's Lambda transformed into a $x^2$ statistic. Due to the small number of observations, a significance level of 1%, at the most, is required for rejecting the null hypothesis of homogeneity. (See Table 3.16).

Table 3.13: Variables Significantly Discriminating among Groups of SDS, DOC and DIV
(*U*-statistic Used)

| SDS<br>(*N*   *H*   *D*)<br>(50 + 29 + 9 = 88)<br>Variable Significance | | DOC<br>(*P*   *E*   *J*)<br>(12 + 32 + 44 = 88)<br>Variable Significance | | DIV<br>(*I*   *II*   *III*)<br>(15 + 44 + 27 = 86)<br>Variable Significance | |
|---|---|---|---|---|---|
| $x1$ | .0000 | $x1$ | .0023 | $x3$ | .0428 |
| $x5$ | .0000 | $x3$ | .0000 | $x5$ | .0308 |
| $x7$ | .0000 | $x10$ | .0516 | $x6$ | .0034 |
| $x8$ | .0025 | $x11$ | .0045 | $x8$ | .0081 |
| $x9$ | .0021 | $x13$ | .0655 | $x10$ | .0692 |
| $x10$ | .0154 | $x15$ | .0331 | $x12$ | .0004 |
| $x11$ | .0000 | $x17$ | .0337 | $x13$ | .0815 |
| $x13$ | .0078 | $x18$ | .0054 | $x14$ | .0216 |
| $x14$ | .0299 | $x21$ | .0542 | $x15$ | .0830 |
| $x15$ | .0069 | $x26$ | .0003 | $x16$ | .0296 |
| $x17$ | .0000 | $x27$ | .0004 | $x20$ | .0034 |
| $x19$ | .0000 | $x28$ | .0156 | $x22$ | .0570 |
| $x20$ | .0898 | $x29$ | .0010 | $x23$ | .0780 |
| $x23$ | .0001 | $x32$ | .0009 | $x25$ | .0079 |
| $x25$ | .0199 | $x33$ | .0168 | $x26$ | .0228 |
| $x27$ | .0028 | $x39$ | .0349 | $x27$ | .0057 |
| $x29$ | .0102 | $x43$ | .0455 | $x29$ | .0001 |
| $x31$ | .0012 | $x50$ | .0326 | $x31$ | .0234 |
| $x33$ | .0034 | $x52$ | .0965 | $x33$ | .0024 |
| $x39$ | .0000 | DIS | .0001 | $x38$ | .0001 |
| $x40$ | .0062 | | | $x39$ | .0242 |
| $x41$ | .0000 | | | $x43$ | .0487 |
| $x43$ | .0000 | | | $x50$ | .0059 |
| $x53$ | .0001 | | | DIS | .0021 |
| No. of Signifi-cances at | (p < .10)   24<br>(p < .01)   19 | 20<br>9 | | 24<br>11 | |

Table 3.14: Variables Significantly Discriminating among DOC within SDS
(*U*-statistic Used)

| Subcategory No. of Observations | (*NP*   *NE*   *NJ*) (7 + 16 + 27 = 50) Variable Significance | | (*HP*   *HE*   *HJ*) (2 + 15 + 12 = 29) Variable Significance | | (*DP*   *DJ*) (3 + 5 = 8) Variable Significance | |
|---|---|---|---|---|---|---|
| | *x*1 | .0154 | *x*11 | .0051 | *x*1 | .0026 |
| | *x*3 | .0000 | *x*25 | .0627 | *x*11 | .0093 |
| | *x*5 | .0168 | *x*26 | .0061 | *x*17 | .0046 |
| | *x*8 | .0099 | *x*27 | .0631 | *x*33 | .0048 |
| | *x*11 | .0561 | *x*38 | .0070 | *x*39 | .0212 |
| | *x*13 | .0151 | | | *x*52 | .0338 |
| | *x*15 | .0601 | | | *x*53 | .0777 |
| | *x*17 | .0163 | | | | |
| | *x*18 | .0050 | | | | |
| | *x*21 | .0216 | | | | |
| | *x*26 | .0055 | | | | |
| | *x*27 | .0027 | | | | |
| | *x*28 | .0676 | | | | |
| | *x*29 | .0010 | | | | |
| | *x*32 | .0056 | | | | |
| | *x*33 | .0968 | | | | |
| | *x*39 | .0209 | | | | |
| | *x*41 | .0855 | | | | |
| | *x*43 | .0811 | | | | |
| | *x*50 | .0457 | | | | |
| | *x*51 | .0775 | | | | |
| | DIS | .0000 | | | | |
| No. of Significances at | (p < .10) | 22 | 5 | | 7 | |
| | (p < .01) | 8 | 3 | | 4 | |

Table 3.15: Variables Significantly Discriminating among SDS within DOC
(*U*-statistic Used)

| Subcategory No. of Observations | (*NP HP DP*) (7 + 2 + 3 = 12) Variable Significance | | (*NE HE DE*) (16 + 15 + 1 = 32) Variable Significance | | (*NJ HJ DJ*) (27 + 12 + 5 = 43) Variable Significance | |
|---|---|---|---|---|---|---|
| | x1 | .0418 | x1 | .0001 | x1 | .0000 |
| | x17 | .0810 | x2 | .0797 | x5 | .0017 |
| | x19 | .0063 | x3 | .0835 | x7 | .0000 |
| | x20 | .0484 | x5 | .0010 | x9 | .0097 |
| | x23 | .0088 | x6 | .0357 | x11 | .0001 |
| | x29 | .0152 | x7 | .0000 | x13 | .0056 |
| | x33 | .0326 | x8 | .0001 | x14 | .0601 |
| | x38 | .0954 | x9 | .0046 | x17 | .0000 |
| | x39 | .0071 | x11 | .0005 | x18 | .0933 |
| | x41 | .0762 | x13 | .0639 | x19 | .0000 |
| | x43 | .0271 | x15 | .0971 | x23 | .0511 |
| | DIS | .0764 | x17 | .0001 | x25 | .0665 |
| | | | x19 | .0000 | x27 | .0140 |
| | | | x23 | .0229 | x31 | .0365 |
| | | | x29 | .0890 | x33 | .0322 |
| | | | x31 | .0690 | x34 | .0921 |
| | | | x38 | .0764 | x39 | .0000 |
| | | | x39 | .0000 | x40 | .0368 |
| | | | x40 | .0730 | x41 | .0000 |
| | | | x41 | .0005 | x43 | .0089 |
| | | | x43 | .0002 | x51 | .0265 |
| | | | x50 | .0183 | | |
| | | | x53 | .0003 | | |
| No. of Significances at | (p < .10) | 12 | 23 | | 21 | |
| | (p < .01) | 3 | 12 | | 11 | |

Table 3.16: Significance of Residual Discriminating Power

| Analysis | Statistics Calculated after Derivation of | | | | | |
|---|---|---|---|---|---|---|
| | No Discriminant Function | | | 1st Discriminant Function | | |
| | $\chi^2$ | Degrees of Freedom | Significance | $\chi^2$ | Degrees of Freedom | Significance |
| *(N, H, D)* | 160.6 | 10 | 0 | 5.2 | 4 | .2702 |
| *(P, E, J)* | 70.3 | 10 | .0000 | 3.4 | 4 | .4854 |
| *(I, II, III)* | 70.9 | 10 | .0000 | 16.9 | 4 | .0021 |
| *(NP, NE, NJ)* | 65.8 | 10 | .0000 | 17.4 | 4 | .0016 |
| *(HP, HE, HJ)* | 38.8 | 10 | .0000 | 14.5 | 4 | .0059 |
| *(DP, DJ)* | 30.2 | 5 | .0000 | | | |
| *(NP, HP, DP)* | 60.5 | 10 | .0000 | 11.7 | 4 | .0194 |
| *(NE, HE, DE)* | 81.1 | 10 | .0000 | 3.4 | 4 | .4980 |
| *(NJ, HJ, DJ)* | 90.3 | 10 | .0000 | 13.9 | 4 | .0077 |

Table 3.17: *Eigenvalues,* Percentages of Trace and Canonical Correlations of the Discriminant Functions

| Analysis | Discriminant Function | | | | | |
|---|---|---|---|---|---|---|
| | First | | | Second | | |
| | *Eigenvalue* | % of Trace | Canonical Correlat. | *Eigenvalue* | % of Trace | Canonical Correlat. |
| *(N, H, D)* | 5.507 | 100 | .920 | | not significant | |
| *(P, E, J)* | 1.237 | 100 | .744 | | not significant | |
| *(I, II, III)* | .948 | 80 | .697 | .231 | 20 | .433 |
| *(NP, NE, NJ)* | 1.931 | 80 | .812 | .472 | 20 | .566 |
| *(HP, HE, HJ)* | 1.750 | 68 | .798 | .828 | 32 | .673 |
| *(NP, HP, DP)* | 1052.389 | 100 | 1.000 | | not significant | |
| *(NE, HE, DE)* | 16.824 | 100 | .971 | | not significant | |
| *(NJ, HJ, DJ)* | 6.099 | 93 | .927 | .428 | 7 | .547 |

The *eigenvalue,* percentage of trace and canonical correlation for each of the significant Discriminant Functions are shown in Table 3.17. (See Table 3.17, p. 102).

What sort of discrimination does each of the derived significant Discriminant Functions represent? To answer this question, it is profitable to examine the configurations of observations in the Discriminant Function space. This is done, separately for each analysis, in Figures 3.2 through 3.10, where the location of each observation and of the centroids (the points which represent the averages) are given, too.

Figure 3.7, unlike the rest of the figures, represents a unidimensional graph, since the number of subcategories, taking part in the respective analysis (*DP, DJ*) allows for only one Discriminant Function to be derived. (See Figures 3.2 to 3.10, p. 104).

Several impressive peculiarities of the language habits of the book are made explicit in these figures.

The first and only significant Discriminant Function in (*N, H, D*) separates *N* from *H + D.*

The first and only significant Discriminant Function in (*P, E, J*) separates *P* from *E + J.* When comparing the spread of points in the Discriminant Function space, one cannot ignore that the spread in (*P, E, J*) by far exceeds that of (*N, H, D*) as may indeed have been foreseen in view of the respective values of $\chi^2$ in Table 3.16.

The first Discriminant Function in (*I, II, III*) separates *I* from *II + III.* The second Discriminant Function (represented by the vertical axis), although significant, suggests no meaningful separation: points of *II* and *III* are interspersed.

The first Discriminant Function in (*NP, NE, NJ*) separates between *NP* and *NE + NJ,* but the second, although again significant, reveals no meaningful discrimination.

Discrimination among subcategories (*HP, HE, HJ*) is much milder when compared to (*NP, NE, NJ*) by the $\chi^2$ statistic, which is quite in line with Table 3.15. Studying the configuration of points in the Discriminant Function space in Figure 3.6, we observe once more the isolation of *P* from *E + J.*

In any of Figures 3.8 through 3.10, a sharp line divides *N* from *H + D.*

To bring about a better understanding of the discrimination emerging from the analyses shown in the figures, it might prove useful to find out, by means of the classification functions, how many samples of a certain category or subcategory are classified into a wrong one. The rates of errors are given in Table 3.18 where samples, rejected as ungrouped in the derivation stage of the Discriminant Functions, are also added. (See Table 3.18, p. 113).

The following Table 3.19 lists the misclassified samples together with the category, or subcategory, they were each misclassified into. (See Table 3.19, p. 114).

Several telling conclusions may be drawn from Table 3.19.

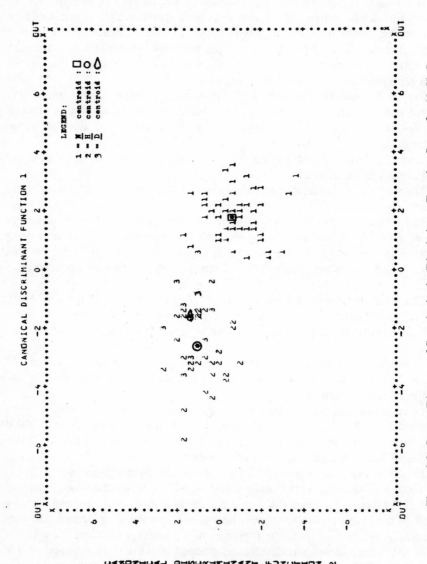

Figure 3.2: Scatter Diagram of Samples in the Discriminant Function Space for *N, H, D*

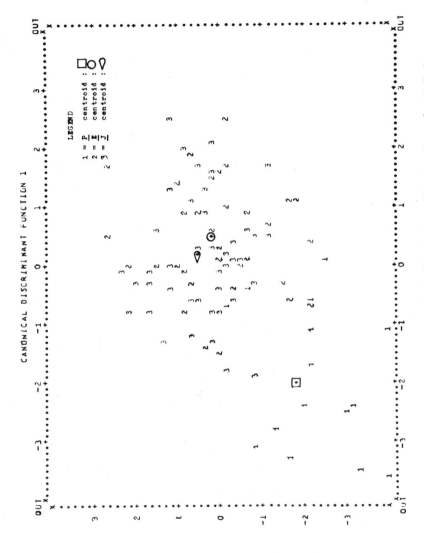

Figure 3.3: Scatter Diagram of Samples in the Discriminant Function Space for *P, E, J*

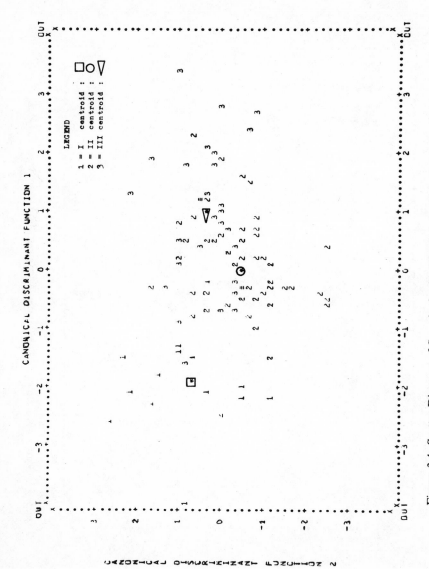

Figure 3.4: Scatter Diagram of Samples in the Discriminant Function Space for *I, II, III*

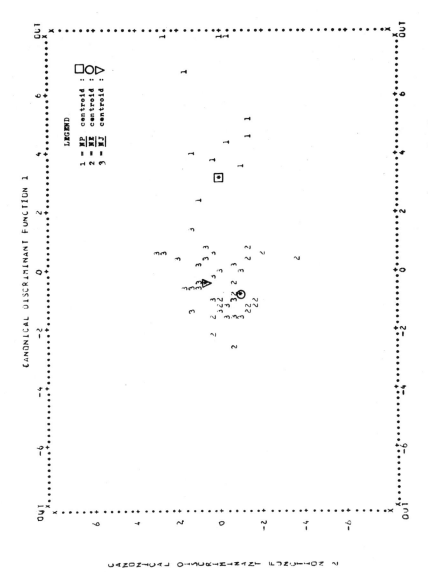

Figure 3.5: Scatter Diagram of Samples in the Discriminant Function Space for *NP, NE, NJ*

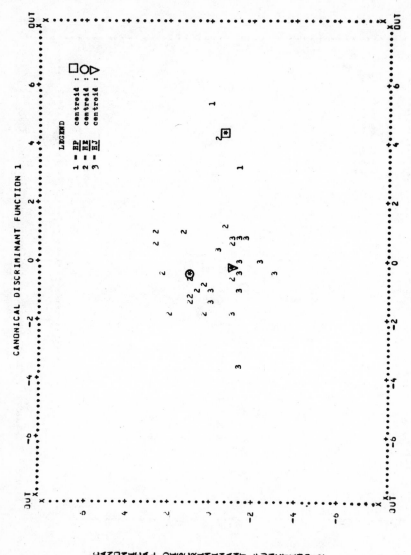

Figure 3.6: Scatter Diagram of Samples in the Discriminant Function Space for *HP, HE, HJ*

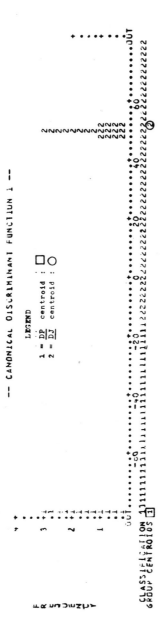

Figure 3.7: Scatter Diagram of Samples in the Discriminant Function Space
for *DP, DJ*

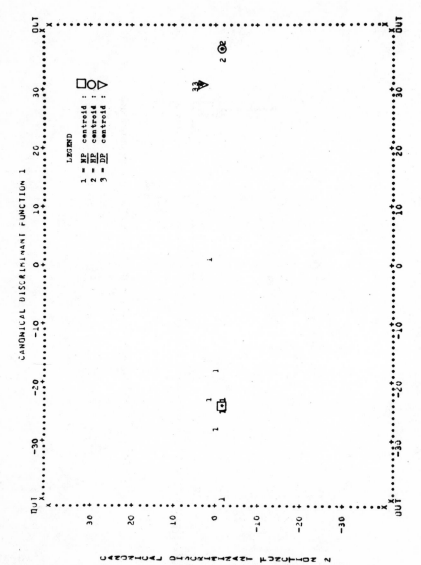

Figure 3.8: Scatter Diagram of Samples in the Discriminant Function Space
for *NP, HP, DP*

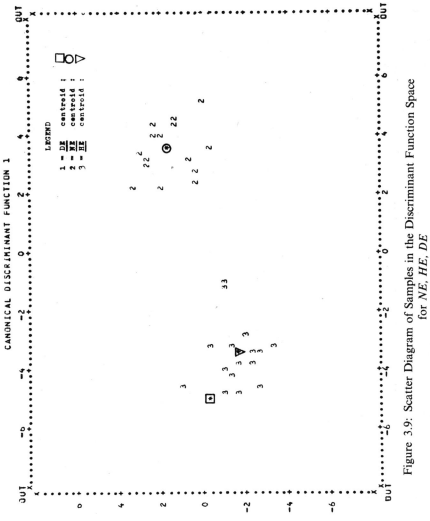

Figure 3.9: Scatter Diagram of Samples in the Discriminant Function Space
for *NE, HE, DE*

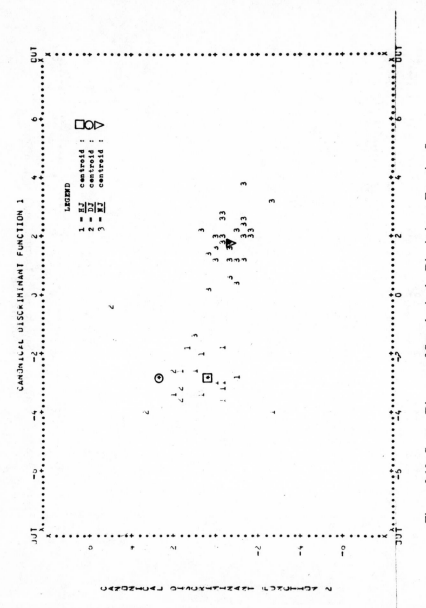

Figure 3.10: Scatter Diagram of Samples in the Discriminant Function Space for *NJ, HJ, DJ*

Table 3.18: Rates of Misclassification

| Analysis | Respective No. of Samples | No. of Misclassified Samples per Category/Subcategory | | | | | |
|---|---|---|---|---|---|---|---|
| (N, H, D) | (54,32,9) | N: 0 | | H: 10 (31 p.c.) | | D: 3 (33 p.c.) | |
| (P, E, J) | (17,33,46) | P: 2 (12 p.c.) | | E: 15 (45 p.c.) | | J: 23 (50 p.c.) | |
| (I, II, III) | (16,48,30) | I: 2 (12 p.c.) | | II: 16 (34 p.c.) | | III: 8 (27 p.c.) | |
| (NP, NE, NJ) | (12,16,27) | NP: 1 (8 p.c.) | | NE: 2 (12 p.c.) | | NJ: 8 (30 p.c.) | |
| (HP, HE, HJ) | (2,16,14) | HP: 0 | | HE: 4 (25 p.c.) | | HJ: 2 (14 p.c.) | |
| (NP, HP, DP) | (11,2,3) | NP: 0 | | HP: 0 | | DP: 0 | |
| (NE, HE, DE) | (16,16,1) | NE: 0 | | HE: 2 (12 p.c.) | | DE: 0 | |
| (NJ, HJ, DJ) | (27,14,5) | NJ: 1 (4 p.c.) | | HJ: 2 (14 p.c.) | | DJ: 0 | |

Table 3.19: Samples Misclassified

| Analysis | Sample no. | Misclassified into | Analysis | Sample no. | Misclassified into |
|---|---|---|---|---|---|
| 1. (N, H, D) | 61,62 (HE, II) | D | 3. (cont.) | 26 (NE, III) | II |
| | 64-66 (HE, III) | D | | 31 (NJ, I) | II |
| | 72 (HE, III) | D | | 41 (NJ, II) | III |
| | 74 (HJ, I) | D | | 46 (NJ, II) | III |
| | 78,79 (HJ, II) | D | | 48 (NJ, II) | III |
| | 82 (HJ, II) | D | | 50 (NJ, II) | III |
| | 92 (DJ, I) | H | | 60-62 (HE, II) | III |
| | 94,95 (DJ, II) | H | | 63 (HE, II) | I |
| | | | | 65,66 (HE, III) | I |
| 2. (P, E, J) | 5 (NP, II) | J | | 67 (HE, III) | II |
| | 8 (NP, II) | E | | 80 (HJ, II) | III |
| | 13 (NE, II) | J | | 84 (HJ, II) | III |
| | 15 (NE, II) | J | | 86,87 (HJ, III) | II |
| | 17-20 (NE, II) | J | | 89 (DP, II) | I |
| | 24 (NE, III) | J | | 92 (DJ, I) | II |
| | 26 (NE, III) | J | | | |
| | 28 (NE, III) | J | 4. (NP, NE, NJ) | 5 (NP, II) | NJ |
| | 29,30 (NJ, I) | E | | 19 (NE, II) | NJ |
| | 42 (NJ, II) | E | | 22 (NE, III) | NJ |
| | 44 (NJ, II) | E | | 31 (NJ, I) | NE |
| | 50 (NJ, II) | E | | 40 (NJ, II) | NE |
| | 54,55 (NJ, III) | E | | 42 (NJ, II) | NE |
| | 61 (HE, II) | J | | 44 (NJ, II) | NE |
| | 63 (HE, II) | J | | 48 (NJ, II) | NE |
| | 66,67 (HE, III) | P | | 51 (NJ, III) | NE |
| | 72 (HE, III) | P | | 54,55 (NJ, III) | NE |
| | 73 (HE, III) | J | | | |
| | 74-80 (HJ, II) | E | | | |
| | 81 (HJ, II) | P | 5. (HP, HE, HJ) | 61,62 (HE, II) | HJ |
| | 82-84 (HJ, II) | E | | 67 (HE, III) | HP |
| | 87 (HJ, III) | E | | 73 (HE, III) | HJ |
| | 92,93 (DJ, I) | E | | 84 (HJ, II) | HE |
| | 94,95 (DJ, II) | E | | 85 (HJ, III) | HE |
| | | | | | |
| 3. (I, II, III) | 6 (NP, II) | III | 6. (NE, HE, DE) | 67,68 (HE, III) | DE |
| | 8,9 (NP, II) | III | | | |
| | 12 (NP, III) | II | 7. (NJ, HJ, DJ) | 32 (NJ, I) | HJ |
| | 15 (NE, II) | III | | 78 (HJ, II) | DJ |
| | 18 (NE, II) | I | | 83 (HJ, II) | DJ |
| | 24 (NE, III) | II | | | |

Regarding the Sort-of-Discourse hypothesis, the Table highlights the fact that almost no misclassification occurs of $N$ samples, either in an overall analysis ($N$, $H$, $D$) or in separate analyses where samples are classified according to Documents, i.e., in the third group of analyses. Further, not even one single $H$-sample or $D$-sample is incorrectly classified as belonging to $N$.

Finally, when misclassification of SDS occurs (see Analysis 1 in Table 3.19), it is never of $P$ samples. This complements data of Table 3.15: all three Sorts-of-Discourse in $P$, as well as $P$ on the whole, are of a distinct *portrait parler*.

Turning now to the Documentary Hypothesis (Analysis 2 in Table 3.19), the above result is reinforced. We see that out of 40 misclassified samples, two only belong to $P$ (nos. 5 and 8), whereas half of all $E$-samples and $J$-samples are mutually misclassified. Moreover, out of 38 misclassifications of $E$ and $J$, only four are wrongly classified as $P$. An additional feature which stands revealed in this analysis is the relatively high incidence of entire groups of consecutive samples which have been misclassified (see for example nos. 17-20($NE$), nos. 74-84($HJ$) and 92-95($DJ$)).

Let us note, finally, that only two, out of the 40 misclassified samples in this analysis, are from Division $I$. This may well be due to $E$ not being represented in that division, and to the distinct character of Division $I$, as may also be realized from the results of the ($I$, $II$, $III$) analysis (Analysis 3 in Table 3.19). Here, out of 26 misclassifications, only two are of samples from Division $I$. Moreover, no misclassification takes place of Division $I$ into Division $III$, and hardly any in the opposite direction: only two, and consecutive, samples of $III$ are allocated to $I$. Thus, language habits seem gradually to change as we move from Division $I$ to Division $II$ and thence to Division $III$. However, the rate of incidence of misclassifications among the three Divisions is rather unequal: they are much more frequent between $II$ and $III$ than between $I$ and $II$ — see Table 3.19. What all this may mean to the Biblical scholar will be discussed in Section 3.4. At the present place, suffice it to note that the partition of Genesis into three parts as proposed, with some reserve, in Section 1.4.1., is strongly corroborated by the findings set out here.

The last four analyses in Table 3.19 (namely: Analyses 4-7) do not seem to suggest any new features, except perhaps Analysis 4, where the majority of misclassifications are of $NJ$-samples, not from Division $I$, into $E$.

The matter of misclassifications leads naturally to that of the probabilities $P(x/G)$ and $P(G)/x)$, as defined in Appendix 3.A. Only the three main analyses ($N$, $H$, $D$), ($P$, $E$, $J$) and ($I$, $II$, $III$) will be considered here. They are the subject of Tables 3.20 through 3.22. (See Tables 3.20, 3.21, 3.22, pp. 116-18).

When these probabilities are divided into three degrees, namely, low ($0.5 < P(G/x) < 0.75$), medium ($0.75 \leq P(G/x) < 0.90$), and high ($P(G/x) \geq 0.90$), samples (not including misclassified ones) group themselves as seen in Table 3.23. (See Table 3.23, p. 119).

| SUBCAT. & SAMPLE NO. | | ACTUAL GROUP | MISCLASS-IFIED | HIGHEST PROBABILITY GROUP | $P(X/G)$ | $P(G/X)$ |
|---|---|---|---|---|---|---|
| NP | 1 | 1. | | 1 | .4787 | 1.0000 |
| NP | 2 | 1. | | 1 | .5246 | 1.0000 |
| NP | 3 | 1. | | 1 | .2290 | 1.0000 |
| NP | 4 | 1. | | 1 | .2783 | 1.0000 |
| NP | 5 | 1. | | 1 | .3071 | .9999 |
| NP | 6 | 1. | | 1 | .9149 | .9985 |
| NP | 7 | 1. | | 1 | .5338 | .9739 |
| NP | 8 | 1. | | 1 | .8121 | .9985 |
| NP | 9 | 1. | | 1 | .6413 | .9996 |
| NP | 10 | 1. | | 1 | .0339 | 1.0000 |
| NP | 11 | 1. | | 1 | .9740 | .9994 |
| NE | 12 | 1. | | 1 | .9610 | .9995 |
| NE | 13 | 1. | | 1 | .4513 | 1.0000 |
| NE | 14 | 1. | | 1 | .7640 | 1.0000 |
| NE | 15 | 1. | | 1 | .7060 | 1.0000 |
| NE | 16 | 1. | | 1 | .5933 | .9996 |
| NE | 17 | 1. | | 1 | .6820 | 1.0000 |
| NE | 18 | 1. | | 1 | .3413 | .9997 |
| NE | 19 | 1. | | 1 | .1137 | .9991 |
| NE | 20 | 1. | | 1 | .4358 | .9930 |
| NE | 21 | 1. | | 1 | .3043 | .9995 |
| NE | 22 | 1. | | 1 | .2657 | .9994 |
| NE | 23 | 1. | | 1 | .2964 | .9880 |
| NE | 24 | 1. | | 1 | .7904 | .9559 |
| NE | 25 | 1. | | 1 | .9031 | .9987 |
| NE | 26 | 1. | | 1 | .6418 | .9958 |
| NE | 27 | 1. | | 1 | .9451 | 1.0000 |
| NJ | 28 | 1. | | 1 | .5026 | .9835 |
| NJ | 29 | 1. | | 1 | .7594 | .9940 |
| NJ | 30 | 1. | | 1 | .9614 | .9998 |
| NJ | 31 | 1. | | 1 | .0642 | .5260 |
| NJ | 32 | 1. | | 1 | .0540 | .7180 |
| NJ | 33 | 1. | | 1 | .3523 | .9849 |
| NJ | 34 | 1. | | 1 | .1135 | .9987 |
| NJ | 35 | 1. | | 1 | .3872 | .9981 |
| NJ | 36 | 1. | | 1 | .0364 | .9964 |
| NJ | 37 | 1. | | 1 | .9523 | .9998 |
| NJ | 38 | 1. | | 1 | .7515 | .9998 |
| NJ | 39 | 1. | | 1 | .3739 | 1.0000 |
| NJ | 40 | 1. | | 1 | .9293 | .9999 |
| NJ | 41 | 1. | | 1 | .6312 | .9998 |
| NJ | 42 | 1. | | 1 | .0095 | 1.0000 |
| NJ | 43 | 1. | | 1 | .4895 | .9783 |
| NJ | 44 | 1. | | 1 | .1016 | .9988 |
| NJ | 45 | 1. | | 1 | .8075 | .9996 |
| NJ | 46 | 1. | | 1 | .7392 | 1.0000 |
| NJ | 47 | 1. | | 1 | .2802 | .9966 |
| NJ | 48 | 1. | | 1 | .2684 | 1.0000 |
| NJ | 49 | 1. | | 1 | .6688 | .9880 |
| NJ | 50 | 1. | | 1 | .9003 | .9959 |
| NJ | 51 | 1. | | 1 | .3220 | 1.0000 |
| NJ | 52 | 1. | | 1 | .6284 | .9999 |
| NJ | 53 | 1. | | 1 | .4477 | .9507 |
| NJ | 54 | 1. | | 1 | .3892 | .9996 |
| HP | 55 | 2. | | 2 | .7584 | .7194 |
| HP | 56 | 2. | | 2 | .2447 | .6360 |
| HE | 57 | 2. | | 2 | .5793 | .8515 |
| HE | 58 | 2. | | 2 | .6683 | .6471 |
| HE | 59 | 2. | | 2 | .3091 | .9236 |
| HE | 60 | 2. | *** | 3 | .9947 | .7020 |
| HE | 61 | 2. | *** | 3 | .5959 | .5305 |
| HE | 62 | 2. | | 3 | .8611 | .6945 |
| HE | 63 | 2. | *** | 3 | .9543 | .7506 |
| HE | 64 | 2. | *** | 3 | .8118 | .6319 |
| HE | 65 | 2. | *** | 3 | .9357 | .7090 |
| HE | 66 | 2. | | 2 | .1894 | .9511 |
| HE | 67 | 2. | | 2 | .0732 | .9329 |
| HE | 68 | 2. | | 2 | .2644 | .9219 |
| HE | 69 | 2. | | 2 | .7567 | .7279 |
| HE | 70 | 2. | | 2 | .0955 | .7693 |
| HE | 71 | 2. | *** | 3 | .2570 | .7143 |
| HE | 72 | 2. | | 2 | .5199 | .8105 |
| HJ | 73 | 2. | *** | 3 | .5848 | .6889 |
| HJ | 74 | 2. | | 2 | .0055 | .9782 |
| HJ | 75 | 2. | | 2 | .1902 | .6774 |
| HJ | 76 | 2. | | 2 | .8654 | .7922 |
| HJ | 77 | 2. | *** | 3 | .9426 | .6317 |
| HJ | 78 | 2. | *** | 3 | .8798 | .6079 |
| HJ | 79 | 2. | | 2 | .5507 | .8853 |
| HJ | 80 | 2. | | 2 | .1384 | .9108 |
| HJ | 81 | 2. | *** | 3 | .8769 | .7353 |
| HJ | 82 | 2. | | 2 | .9332 | .7689 |
| HJ | 83 | 2. | | 2 | .9945 | .6613 |
| HJ | 84 | 2. | | 2 | .2365 | .9342 |
| HJ | 85 | 2. | | 2 | .1403 | .9134 |
| HJ | 86 | 2. | | 3 | .2854 | .6618 |
| HJ | 87 | 3. | | 3 | .9025 | .7761 |
| DP | 88 | 3. | | 3 | .1091 | .5936 |
| DP | 89 | 3. | | 3 | .5799 | .6239 |
| DE | 90 | 3. | | 3 | .4416 | .7146 |
| DJ | 91 | 3. | *** | 2 | .9201 | .6013 |
| DJ | 92 | 3. | | 3 | .3507 | .9210 |
| DJ | 93 | 3. | *** | 2 | .8638 | .7208 |
| DJ | 94 | 3. | | 3 | .5478 | .8006 |
| DJ | 95 | 3. | | 3 | .7375 | .7921 |
| DJ | 96 | | | | | |

Table 3.20: Affiliation Probabilities in $(N, H, D)$

| SUBCAT.& SAMPLE NO. | | ACTUAL GROUP | MISCLASS-IFIED | HIGHEST PROBABILITY GROUP | P(X/G) | P(G/X) | LEGEND |
|---|---|---|---|---|---|---|---|
| NP | 1 | 1. | | 1 | .1162 | 1.0000 | ACTUAL GROUP |
| NP | 2 | 1. | | 1 | .3755 | .9991 | |
| NP | 3 | 1. | | 1 | .2075 | .9868 | 1 = P |
| NP | 4 | 1. | | 1 | .3979 | .9997 | 2 = E |
| NP | 5 | 1. | *** | 3 | .5265 | .4812 | 3 = J |
| NP | 6 | 1. | | 1 | .4558 | .9996 | |
| NP | 7 | 1. | | 1 | .9147 | .9957 | MISCLASS. |
| NP | 8 | 1. | *** | 2 | .4970 | .4586 | *** |
| NP | 9 | 1. | | 1 | .5084 | .9935 | |
| NP | 10 | 1. | | 1 | .0090 | 1.0000 | |
| NP | 11 | 1. | | 1 | .0010 | .9999 | |
| NP | 12 | 1. | | 1 | .5019 | .9996 | |
| NE | 13 | 2. | *** | 3 | .2788 | .5439 | |
| NE | 14 | 2. | | 2 | .8522 | .5171 | |
| NE | 15 | 2. | *** | 3 | .8657 | .6006 | |
| NE | 16 | 2. | | 2 | .9759 | .5162 | |
| NE | 17 | 2. | *** | 3 | .2197 | .4521 | |
| NE | 18 | 2. | *** | 3 | .2370 | .6760 | |
| NE | 19 | 2. | *** | 3 | .0619 | .6160 | |
| NE | 20 | 2. | *** | 3 | .8975 | .5738 | |
| NE | 21 | 2. | | 2 | .7450 | .5224 | |
| NE | 22 | 2. | | 2 | .4903 | .6220 | |
| NE | 23 | 2. | | 2 | .0741 | .4480 | |
| NE | 24 | 2. | *** | 3 | .3760 | .5762 | |
| NE | 25 | 2. | | 2 | .3155 | .5743 | |
| NE | 26 | 2. | *** | 3 | .0263 | .6030 | |
| NE | 27 | 2. | | 2 | .9225 | .4978 | |
| NE | 28 | 2. | *** | 3 | .6154 | .4699 | |
| NJ | 29 | 3. | *** | 2 | .2530 | .5605 | |
| NJ | 30 | 3. | *** | 2 | .9450 | .5169 | |
| NJ | 31 | 3. | | 3 | .4904 | .4525 | |
| NJ | 32 | 3. | | 3 | .5338 | .5022 | |
| NJ | 33 | 3. | | 3 | .5404 | .5303 | |
| NJ | 34 | 3. | | 3 | .3325 | .5044 | |
| NJ | 35 | 3. | | 3 | .4640 | .6590 | |
| NJ | 36 | 3. | | 3 | .2804 | .6805 | |
| NJ | 37 | 3. | | 3 | .7505 | .5030 | |
| NJ | 38 | 3. | | 3 | .3641 | .6363 | |
| NJ | 39 | 3. | | 3 | .7136 | .5900 | |
| NJ | 40 | 3. | | 3 | .1343 | .7246 | |
| NJ | 41 | 3. | | 3 | .3017 | .6850 | |
| NJ | 42 | 3. | *** | 2 | .7090 | .5174 | |
| NJ | 43 | 3. | | 3 | .1533 | .6591 | |
| NJ | 44 | 3. | *** | 2 | .7872 | .5097 | |
| NJ | 45 | 3. | | 3 | .7130 | .5757 | |
| NJ | 46 | 3. | | 3 | .4535 | .6426 | |
| NJ | 47 | 3. | | 3 | .7065 | .5724 | |
| NJ | 48 | 3. | | 3 | .9891 | .5140 | |
| NJ | 49 | 3. | | 3 | .2137 | .6902 | |
| NJ | 50 | 3. | *** | 1 | .5770 | .8730 | |
| NJ | 51 | 3. | | 3 | .5104 | .5523 | |
| NJ | 52 | 3. | | 3 | .0230 | .6275 | |
| NJ | 53 | 3. | | 3 | .7623 | .5966 | |
| NJ | 54 | 3. | *** | 2 | .4335 | .5682 | |
| NJ | 55 | 3. | *** | 2 | .3813 | .5055 | |
| HP | 56 | 1. | | 1 | .1073 | .0797 | |
| HP | 57 | 1. | | 1 | .9179 | .9870 | |
| HE | 58 | 2. | | 2 | .6116 | .5824 | |
| HE | 59 | 2. | | 2 | .5471 | .5144 | |
| HE | 60 | 2. | | 2 | .1353 | .6896 | |
| HE | 61 | 2. | *** | 3 | .7327 | .5026 | |
| HE | 62 | 2. | | 2 | .1641 | .6034 | |
| HE | 63 | 2. | *** | 3 | .5176 | .6310 | |
| HE | 64 | 2. | | 2 | .8134 | .5882 | |
| HE | 65 | 2. | | 2 | .4059 | .6204 | |
| HE | 66 | 2. | *** | 1 | .2430 | .4420 | |
| HE | 67 | 2. | | 2 | .4009 | .6790 | |
| HE | 68 | 2. | | 2 | .9901 | .5282 | |
| HE | 69 | 2. | | 2 | .5532 | .5363 | |
| HE | 70 | 2. | | 2 | .1130 | .6758 | |
| HE | 71 | 2. | | 2 | .4505 | .5141 | |
| HE | 72 | 2. | *** | 1 | .3800 | .6400 | |
| HE | 73 | 2. | *** | 3 | .8601 | .5716 | |
| HJ | 74 | 3. | *** | 2 | .1781 | .5320 | |
| HJ | 75 | 3. | *** | 2 | .2181 | .7623 | |
| HJ | 76 | 3. | *** | 2 | .9112 | .5462 | |
| HJ | 77 | 3. | *** | 2 | .5700 | .5537 | |
| HJ | 78 | 3. | *** | 2 | .2791 | .6312 | |
| HJ | 79 | 3. | *** | 2 | .0717 | .5695 | |
| HJ | 80 | 3. | *** | 2 | .4802 | .4774 | |
| HJ | 81 | 3. | *** | 1 | .2159 | .5515 | |
| HJ | 82 | 3. | *** | 2 | .7508 | .5902 | |
| HJ | 83 | 3. | *** | 2 | .7203 | .5994 | |
| HJ | 84 | 3. | *** | 2 | .8300 | .5225 | |
| HJ | 85 | 3. | | 3 | .3433 | .4973 | |
| HJ | 86 | 3. | | 3 | .8749 | .4997 | |
| HJ | 87 | 3. | *** | 2 | .9857 | .5046 | |
| OP | 88 | 1. | | 1 | .3930 | .8039 | |
| OP | 89 | 1. | | 1 | .9703 | .9849 | |
| OP | 90 | 1. | | 1 | .5747 | .9994 | |
| OE | 91 | 2. | | 2 | .0780 | .6146 | |
| OJ | 92 | 3. | *** | 2 | .8931 | .5427 | |
| OJ | 93 | 3. | *** | 2 | .6749 | .5222 | |
| OJ | 94 | 3. | *** | 2 | .6680 | .5651 | |
| OJ | 95 | 3. | *** | 2 | .4008 | .5939 | |
| OJ | 96 | 3. | | 3 | .3907 | .5223 | |

Table 3.21: Affiliation Probabilities in (*P*, *E*, *J*)

| SUBCAT.& SAMPLE NO. | | ACTUAL GROUP | MISCLASS-FIED | HIGHEST PROBABILITY GROUP | P(X/G) | P(G/X) | LEGEND |
|---|---|---|---|---|---|---|---|
| NP | 1 | 1. | | 1 | .5855 | .9825 | **ACTUAL GROUP** |
| NP | 2 | 1. | | 1 | .5586 | .9992 | |
| NP | 3 | 1. | | 1 | .8815 | .6384 | |
| NP | 4 | 1. | | 2 | .3909 | .9121 | 1 = I |
| NP | 5 | 2. | | 2 | .3374 | .6367 | 2 = II |
| NP | 6 | 2. | *** | 3 | .7802 | .6390 | 3 = III |
| NP | 7 | 2. | | 2 | .6695 | .4021 | |
| NP | 8 | 2. | *** | 3 | .3842 | .5489 | |
| NP | 9 | 2. | *** | 3 | .8745 | .5265 | **MISCLASS.** |
| NP | 12 | 3. | *** | 2 | .7752 | .5944 | *** |
| NE | 13 | 2. | | 2 | .1550 | .9237 | |
| NE | 14 | 2. | | 2 | .8794 | .6825 | |
| NE | 15 | 2. | *** | 3 | .9402 | .7252 | |
| NE | 16 | 2. | | 2 | .1234 | .8997 | |
| NE | 17 | 2. | | 2 | .9147 | .5471 | |
| NE | 18 | 2. | *** | 1 | .5900 | .5177 | |
| NE | 19 | 2. | | 2 | .3171 | .7440 | |
| NE | 20 | 2. | | 2 | .7750 | .7768 | |
| NE | 21 | 3. | | 3 | .8350 | .5122 | |
| NE | 22 | 3. | | 3 | .2481 | .9394 | |
| NE | 23 | 3. | | 3 | .5373 | .5347 | |
| NE | 24 | 3. | *** | 2 | .7602 | .5795 | |
| NE | 25 | 3. | | 3 | .9436 | .7473 | |
| NE | 26 | 3. | *** | 2 | .9157 | .0522 | |
| NE | 27 | 3. | | 3 | .1058 | .8977 | |
| NE | 28 | 3. | | 3 | .5430 | .8543 | |
| NJ | 29 | 1. | | 1 | .7516 | .8294 | |
| NJ | 30 | 1. | | 1 | .7257 | .9105 | |
| NJ | 31 | 1. | *** | 3 | .0457 | .9388 | |
| NJ | 32 | 1. | | 1 | .3299 | .8163 | |
| NJ | 33 | 1. | | 1 | .8892 | .9965 | |
| NJ | 34 | 1. | | 1 | .2602 | .9845 | |
| NJ | 35 | 1. | | 1 | .4418 | .8449 | |
| NJ | 36 | 1. | | 1 | .5372 | .7965 | |
| NJ | 37 | 2. | | 2 | .9427 | .7798 | |
| NJ | 38 | 2. | | 2 | .7590 | .6217 | |
| NJ | 39 | 2. | | 2 | .4473 | .6673 | |
| NJ | 40 | 2. | | 2 | .6347 | .4685 | |
| NJ | 41 | 2. | *** | 3 | .4012 | .9120 | |
| NJ | 42 | 2. | | 2 | .4704 | .3985 | |
| NJ | 43 | 2. | | 2 | .5808 | .8305 | |
| NJ | 44 | 2. | | 2 | .8251 | .7655 | |
| NJ | 45 | 2. | | 2 | .1150 | .9311 | |
| NJ | 46 | 2. | *** | 3 | .5334 | .5999 | |
| NJ | 47 | 2. | | 2 | .1130 | .9336 | |
| NJ | 48 | 2. | *** | 3 | .7832 | .7620 | |
| NJ | 49 | 2. | | 2 | .8535 | .7383 | |
| NJ | 50 | 2. | *** | 3 | .5882 | .5803 | |
| NJ | 51 | 3. | | 3 | .0476 | .9729 | |
| NJ | 52 | 3. | | 3 | .2153 | .7953 | |
| NJ | 53 | 3. | | 3 | .1117 | .7974 | |
| NJ | 54 | 3. | | 3 | .2734 | .4665 | |
| HP | 55 | 3. | | 3 | .9197 | .5544 | |
| HP | 56 | 3. | | 2 | .7828 | .6490 | |
| HP | 57 | UNGRPD | | 3 | .9602 | .7594 | |
| HE | 58 | 2. | | 2 | .9900 | .0213 | |
| HE | 59 | 2. | | 2 | .9905 | .0409 | |
| HE | 60 | 2. | *** | 3 | 1.0000 | .6849 | |
| HE | 61 | 2. | *** | 3 | .1094 | .5221 | |
| HE | 62 | 2. | *** | 3 | .8620 | .8052 | |
| HE | 63 | 2. | *** | 1 | .8824 | .9469 | |
| HE | 64 | 3. | | 3 | .1807 | .9254 | |
| HE | 65 | 3. | *** | 1 | .5751 | .6243 | |
| HE | 66 | 3. | *** | 1 | .9580 | .8599 | |
| HE | 67 | 3. | *** | 2 | .9470 | .6289 | |
| HE | 68 | 3. | | 3 | .5706 | .8170 | |
| HE | 69 | 3. | | 3 | .9547 | .6147 | |
| HE | 70 | 3. | | 3 | .9622 | .7215 | |
| HE | 71 | 3. | | 3 | .5570 | .8756 | |
| HE | 72 | 3. | | 3 | .8750 | .7910 | |
| HE | 73 | 3. | | 3 | .9395 | .6344 | |
| HJ | 74 | 1. | | 1 | .1759 | .7125 | |
| HJ | 75 | 2. | | 2 | .9509 | .7194 | |
| HJ | 76 | 2. | | 2 | .7804 | .5853 | |
| HJ | 77 | 2. | | 2 | .7575 | .7946 | |
| HJ | 78 | 2. | | 2 | .9500 | .0951 | |
| HJ | 79 | 2. | *** | 3 | .7111 | .0702 | |
| HJ | 80 | 2. | | 2 | .5747 | .5746 | |
| HJ | 81 | 2. | | 2 | .7036 | .5477 | |
| HJ | 82 | 2. | | 2 | .6442 | .5804 | |
| HJ | 83 | 2. | | 2 | .7772 | .7400 | |
| HJ | 84 | 2. | *** | 3 | .4787 | .7074 | |
| HJ | 85 | 3. | | 3 | .9237 | .6380 | |
| HJ | 86 | 3. | *** | 2 | .5571 | .4984 | |
| HJ | 87 | 3. | *** | 2 | .6893 | .4024 | |
| DP | 88 | 1. | | 1 | .6550 | .9461 | |
| DP | 89 | 1. | *** | 3 | .6011 | .3987 | |
| DP | 90 | 3. | | 3 | .7368 | .5700 | |
| DE | 91 | UNGRPD | | 3 | .9315 | .6763 | |
| DJ | 92 | 1. | *** | 2 | .7042 | .4639 | |
| DJ | 93 | 1. | | 1 | .2385 | .9425 | |
| DJ | 94 | 2. | | 2 | .2393 | .5268 | |
| DJ | 95 | 2. | | 2 | .6748 | .5766 | |
| DJ | 96 | 3. | | 3 | .9272 | .5554 | |

Table 3.22: Affiliation Probabilities in (*I, II, III*)

Table 3.23: Grouping of Samples according to Affiliation Probabilities

| P(G/x) in (N, H, D) | | | P(G/x) in (P, E, J) | | | P(G/x) in (I, II, III) | | |
|---|---|---|---|---|---|---|---|---|
| Low | Medium | High | Low | Medium | High | Low | Medium | High |
| 32,33 (NJ) | 56 (HP) | 1-12 (NP) | 14 (NE) | 88 (DP) | 1-4 (NP) | 5 (II) | 3 (I) | 1,2 (I) |
| 57 (HP) | 58 (HE) | 13-28 (NE) | 16 (NE) | | 6-7 (NP) | 7 (II) | 19,20 (II) | 4 (I) |
| 59 (HE) | 71 (HE) | 29-31 (NJ) | 21-23 (NE) | | 9-12 (NP) | 14 (II) | 25 (II) | 13 (II) |
| 63 (HE) | 73 (HE) | 34-55 (NJ) | 25 (NE) | | 57 (HP) | 17 (II) | 28 (III) | 16 (II) |
| 70 (HE) | 77 (HJ) | 60 (HE) | 27 (NE) | | 89,90 (NP) | 21 (III) | 29 (I) | 22 (III) |
| 76 (HJ) | 80 (HJ) | 67-69 (HE) | 31-41 (NJ) | | | 23 (III) | 32 (I) | 27 (III) |
| 84 (HJ) | 83 (HJ) | 75 (HJ) | 43 (NJ) | | | 38 (II) | 35,36 (I) | 30 (I) |
| 87 (HJ) | 88 (DP) | 81 (HJ) | 45-49 (NJ) | | | 40 (II) | 37 (II) | 33,34 (I) |
| 89,90 (DP) | 96 (DJ) | 85,86 (HJ) | 51-53 (NJ) | | | 42 (II) | 39 (II) | 45 (II) |
| 91 (DE) | | 93 (DJ) | 56 (HP) | | | 49 (II) | 43 (II) | 47 (II) |
| | | | 58-60 (HE) | | | 54,55 (III) | 44 (II) | 51 (III) |
| | | | 62 (HE) | | | 56 (II) | 52,53 (III) | 64 (III) |
| | | | 64,65 (HE) | | | 58,59 (II) | 57* (III) | 88 (I) |
| | | | 68-71 (HE) | | | 69,70 (III) | 68 (III) | 93 (I) |
| | | | 85,86 (HJ) | | | 73 (III) | 71,72 (III) | |
| | | | 91 (DE) | | | 74 (I) | 77 (II) | |
| | | | 96 (DJ) | | | 75,76 (II) | 83 (II) | |
| | | | | | | 78,79 (II) | | |
| | | | | | | 81,82 (II) | | |
| | | | | | | 85 (III) | | |
| | | | | | | 90 (III) | | |
| | | | | | | 91* (II) | | |
| | | | | | | 94-96 (II) | | |

Total

| | Low | Medium | High |
|---|---|---|---|
| N: | 2 | — | 52 |
| H: | 7 | 7 | 8 |
| D: | 3 | 2 | 1 |

| | Low | Medium | High |
|---|---|---|---|
| P: | 1 | 1 | 13 |
| E: | 18 | — | — |
| J: | 23 | — | — |

| | Low | Medium | High |
|---|---|---|---|
| I: | 1 | 5 | 8 |
| II: | 21 | 9 | 4 |
| III: | 9 | 7 | 4 |

* Originally ungrouped, 57 was grouped into III and 91 into II.

Remark: The Table does not include misclassified samples.

Groupings confirm previous results: *N* stands apart from *H* and *D, P* from *E* and *J*, and, though to a lesser measure, *I* from *II* and *III*. On the other hand, most observations (samples) of *II* turn up as only vaguely related to *II* which, as a matter of fact, was already encountered when the rate of misclassification of *II* was found to be the highest (34 p.c., see Table 3.18).

Finally, the next Table 3.24 presents, for various analyses, the discriminating variables as they were incorporated, one after the other, in the Stepwise Discriminant Analysis, as well as their Varimax-rotated standardized Discriminant Function coefficients (those of the significant Discriminant Functions only are shown). (See Table 3.24, p. 121).

How the majority of the variables included in Table 3.24 "comport" themselves in each category can be gathered from Tables 3.2a and 3.2b. They list means and standard deviations of variables, found, by the U-statistic, as significantly discriminating between subcategories.

How the above findings may help the Bible scholar concerning the problem of the composition of the book will be left for him to ponder about. He should, however, be mindful of two particulars. For one thing, each of the above classifications uses a different set of discriminants. This phenomenon might be the outcome of significant differences in the composition of the group of linguistic criteria which create discrimination among subcategories, but may also be partially attributable, owing to the small number of observations, to sheer accident. It should therefore be treated with circumspection when subjected to Biblical and linguistic interpretation.

The other point which might prove to be meaningful is that only the subdivision of *N* into (*NP, NE, NJ*) resorts to employing DIS, a comprehensive criterion, as a discriminant variable. This is in full agreement with other observations, where *NP* included several samples, the language behavior of which, as manifested by DIS, was most deviant in comparison to others (see Section 3.3.2.).

**Resumé.** Discriminant Analysis aims at assessing the statistical significance of discrimination, into separate known source populations, of a group of items on the basis of their measured characteristics. In our enquiry, statistical evidence is sought for separating the 96 available samples into categories as defined by the Documentary, the Discourse and the Division hypotheses. Results yield high significance for discrimination between *N* and *H* + *D*, a milder one, though still high in terms of statistical significance, is noticed between *P* and *E* + *J* and between Divisions *I* and *II* + *III*. There is strong evidence that discrimination between Documents is much more pronounced in subcategories of *N*, i.e. *NP, NE, NJ*, than in the other two Sorts-of-Discourse, *H* and *D*.

Table 3.24: Varimax-Rotated Standardized Discriminant Function Coefficients

| Analysis | Discrim. Function | Variables and Coefficients | | | | |
|---|---|---|---|---|---|---|
| (N, H, D) | 1st | x19 1.096 | x11 .372 | x2 .695 | x27 −.497 | x53 −.023 |
| (P, E, J) | 1st | x3 −.796 | x1 .790 | x19 .032 | x25 .353 | x18 −.063 |
| (I, II, III) | 1st | x12 −.497 | x22 .507 | x29 .859 | x31 −.650 | x38 .010 |
|  | 2nd | −.088 | .007 | −.048 | −.187 | 1.013 |
| (NP, NE, NJ) | 1st | x3 .534 | DIS .793 | x21 −.411 | x51 −.162 | x5 .469 |
|  | 2nd | .072 | −.080 | .767 | −1.024 | .599 |
| (HP, HE, HJ) | 1st | x11 1.322 | x38 −.136 | x21 .005 | x35 1.209 | x22 −.875 |
|  | 2nd | −.086 | 1.047 | −.866 | −.300 | .360 |
| (NP, HP, DP) | 1st | x19 −11.841 | x29 11.389 | x25 9.569 | x53 5.201 | x52 −3.527 |
| (NE, HE, DE) | 1st | x19 1.012 | x11 .536 | x43 −.822 | x53 −.536 | x40 .029 |
| (NJ, HJ, DJ) | 1st | x19 .923 | x39 −.596 | x2 .602 | x17 −.114 | x34 −.047 |
|  | 2nd | .354 | .071 | .343 | .938 | .897 |

## 3.2.4.  PRELIMINARY CONCLUSIONS

We must pause here, before moving on to Phase II, and try to clarify what has emerged from the many analyses performed so far with regard to the much doubted homogeneity of Genesis.

First, the claim raised in Section 1.5.2. (end) that the set of linguistic criteria selected is adequate for describing the various fashions of language behavior in Genesis is indeed borne out by the fact that this set neatly and reasonably distinguishes between $N$ and $H + D$, even though this distinction was not the prime aim of this enquiry.

Second, although heterogeneity of sorts is traced in Genesis which is not attributable to the different Sorts-of-Discourse ($N, H, D$), it can hardly be explained by the Documentary Hypothesis, at least not in its simplistic traditional version. Rather, the Documentary Hypothesis, if not discarded *in toto* in view of the above results, should be examined anew and possibly reformulated according to the findings of Phase II of our investigation, i.e., the exploratory stage, which follows.

## 3.3.  **Phase II: An Exploratory Journey into Genesis**

## 3.3.1.  GENERAL

Phase I statistically evaluated current hypotheses concerning the composition of Genesis, with particular emphasis on the Documentary Hypothesis. The gist of what has emerged is that the hypothesis, as formulated by Wellhausen and his disciples, is in need of modification.

As outlined at the beginning of this Part — see Section 3.1.1. — we may now approach the next stage of our investigation, and set out on a fact-finding mission. Its object is to discover whether a better explanation than the one proposed by the hypotheses set in Section 3.2. may not present itself for the high heterogeneity of Genesis, revealed by the statistical analysis of Phase I. However, it must be clearly stated that no inferential statistical analysis is involved here. All that follows is descriptive in nature, our only goal being to detect groups of samples, which naturally tend to cluster together due to similarity in linguistic behavior, and to explore common features and explicable regularities in the data. It is our hope that, should any new hypothesis be conceived as a result of this inductive stage, later statistical analysis will ensue in proper and significant evidence, namely: that our findings are neither coincidental nor generated by sampling errors, but rather represent tangible characteristics of the source populations.

Six separate descriptive measures and methods are used:

(1)   Analysis of the distribution of the variable DIS (Section 3.3.2.);

(2)   Analysis of the distribution of the pattern vector of each sample, including location of outliers (Section 3.3.3.);

(3)  Cluster Analysis of samples (Section 3.3.4.);

(4)  *SSA1* (Smallest Space Analysis, Guttman's multidimensional scaling technique; Section 3.3.5.);

(5)  Reliability Analysis (Section 3.3.6.);

(6)  Factor Analysis (Q-mode; Section 3.3.7.).

All will be introduced, on intuitive grounds, in the descriptive paragraphs opening each section. Note 'that since no formal statistical analysis is performed here, outliers are included, and normality is not a precondition for the application of analyses (1) through (6).

## 3.3.2.  THE "DIS" DISTRIBUTION

The variable DIS, defined in Section 3.2.2.1., measures, as may be recalled, deviance from characteristic language behavior, represented by the means vector.  Thus, it may be employed to detect irregularities.

Values of DIS, rounded to integers, for each of the 96 samples may be read in Table 3.25.  (See Table 3.25, p. 124).

Table 3.25 shows that there are eight samples (nos. 1, 2, 3, 4, 9, 10, 11, 12) which are quite incongruous with the rest, having DIS values of at least 9, and another four (nos. 8, 67, 80, 81), which include outliers.  Exceptionally high values of DIS are those of nos. 4, 9, 10, 11. Table 3.26 details all these cases. (See Table 3.26, p. 124).

Inspecting Table 3.26, we realise that most of the samples belong to sub-category *NP*.  Moreover, not only is *NP* itself deviant in comparison with other subcategories, but it is also very heterogeneous within itself — viz. the comparatively wide range of variation of its DIS-values — and that to a much higher degree than could have been foreseen by the standard deviation of DIS for the entire sample set.

## 3.3.3.  ANALYSIS OF "PATTERN VECTOR" DISTRIBUTION

The "pattern vector" of a sample as presented in Matrix II is the roster of the 43 non-empty variables, all expressed in standard scores.  Since deviant samples can be identified by outlying values, studying the distribution of the "pattern vector" in each individual sample may well bring instructive information to light.  In other words: by resorting to the transposed matrix, where each sample is considered a separate "variable" (the values of the original 43 variables constituting now its "sample" of "observations") we may be able to locate samples of anomalous linguistic behavior.

Three features are examined in this quest:

(1)  The general shape of the distribution and outlying observations;

(2)  The dispersion, as measured by the standard deviation, of the "pattern vector" values for each sample.  Note, that since all values are

### Table 3.25: Rounded Values of DIS

|  | Sample no. | DIS |  | Sample no. | DIS |  | Sample no. | DIS |  | Sample no. | DIS |  | Sample no. | DIS |
|---|---|---|---|---|---|---|---|---|---|---|---|---|---|---|
| NP | 1 | 9 |  | 21 | 6 |  | 41 | 7 |  | 60 | 6 |  | 80* | 8 |
|  | 2 | 9 |  | 22 | 7 |  | 42 | 6 |  | 61 | 5 |  | 81* | 8 |
|  | 3 | 9 |  | 23 | 6 |  | 43 | 6 |  | 62 | 7 |  | 82 | 5 |
|  | 4* | 11 |  | 24 | 5 |  | 44 | 4 |  | 63 | 7 |  | 83 | 6 |
|  | 5 | 5 |  | 25 | 5 |  | 45 | 6 |  | 64 | 6 |  | 84 | 6 |
|  | 6 | 7 |  | 26 | 6 |  | 46 | 5 |  | 65 | 6 |  | 85 | 7 |
|  | 7 | 8 |  | 27 | 5 |  | 47 | 6 |  | 66 | 6 |  | 86 | 5 |
|  | 8* | 7 |  | 28 | 5 |  | 48 | 5 |  | 67* | 8 |  | 87 | 6 |
|  | 9 | 10 |  |  |  |  | 49 | 5 |  | 68 | 7 |  |  |  |
|  | 10* | 14 | NJ | 29 | 7 |  | 50 | 5 |  | 69 | 6 | DP | 88 | 7 |
|  | 11* | 12 |  | 30 | 6 |  | 51 | 6 |  | 70 | 5 |  | 89 | 6 |
|  | 12* | 9 |  | 31 | 7 |  | 52 | 5 |  | 71 | 6 |  | 90 | 6 |
|  |  |  |  | 32 | 6 |  | 53 | 5 |  | 72 | 5 |  |  |  |
| NE | 13 | 7 |  | 33 | 8 |  | 54 | 6 |  | 73 | 6 | DE | 91 | 6 |
|  | 14 | 7 |  | 34 | 7 |  | 55 | 5 |  |  |  |  |  |  |
|  | 15 | 4 |  | 35 | 6 |  |  |  | HJ | 74 | 5 | DJ | 92 | 6 |
|  | 16 | 8 |  | 36 | 6 | HP | 56 | 7 |  | 75 | 6 |  | 93 | 6 |
|  | 17 | 5 |  | 37 | 5 |  | 57 | 5 |  | 76 | 5 |  | 94 | 7 |
|  | 18 | 5 |  | 38 | 5 |  |  |  |  | 77 | 6 |  | 95 | 6 |
|  | 19 | 4 |  | 39 | 7 | HE | 58 | 8 |  | 78 | 5 |  | 96 | 6 |
|  | 20 | 5 |  | 40 | 6 |  | 59 | 5 |  | 79 | 5 |  |  |  |

Mean of Unrounded Values: 6.327; Standard Deviation: 1.618
* Includes outliers ($|z_i| \frac{2}{3} 3.5$ for any $z_i$)

### Table 3.26: Deviant Values of DIS

|  | Sample no. | DIS |  | Sample no. | DIS |  | Sample no. | DIS |  | Sample no. | DIS |
|---|---|---|---|---|---|---|---|---|---|---|---|
| 10 (NP, II) | | 14 | 9 (NP, II) | | 10 | 3 (NP, I) | | 9 | 80 (HJ, II) | | 8 |
| 11 (NP, III) | | 12 | 1 (NP, I) | | 9 | 12 (NP, III) | | 9 | 81 (HJ, II) | | 8 |
| 4 (NP, I) | | 11 | 2 (NP, I) | | 9 | 67 (HE, III) | | 8 | 8 (NP, II) | | 7 |

expressed in standard scores (for definition, see Section 3.1.4.4.), we expect random fluctuations from unity in "well-behaved" samples;

(3) The mean of the "pattern vector" values for each sample. Note, that for the same reason aforementioned, we expect random fluctuations from zero in "well-behaved" samples.

Starting with (1), Table 3.27 expounds, in broad terms, the distribution of "pattern vector" values in each sample. Included are outliers and frequency counts of variables, the rounded absolute values of which are 2, 3 or 4. In brackets, and adjacent to each count, those variables are specified that have values surpassing the numeral at the head of the column. (See Table 3.27, pp. 126-29).

To illustrate how this Table should be read, let us inspect the "pattern vector" of sample no. 9 ($NP$): there are ten variables, the rounded value of which is –2. Amongst them, five ($x14$, $x21$, $x27$, $x29$, $x40$) have values of less than –2. Likewise, there are two variables of the rounded value of +2, amongst which $x4$ is greater than +2.

Table 3.27 shows that in the $NP$ — subcategory, no. 5 (ch. 14!) is the only one in full conformity to the overall linguistic behavior of the entire Book of Genesis, and no. 6 (chs. 16-22) is almost as "normal". Very deviant values appear in nos. 4, 8(?), 10, 11 and 12. Other samples with such deviant values are nos. 67 ($HE$), 80-81 ($HJ$).

In contrast with $NP$, $HP$ and $DP$ display the highest degree of homogeneity among categories $H$ and $D$: all values are ±2.5, at the highest.

In $NJ$, a relatively high incidence of values exceeding ±2 is evidenced mainly in samples from Division $I$ — viz. nos. 29-36.

We turn now to the second feature under study (the dispersion of the "pattern vector" values). Table 3.28 shows standard deviations (as well as means, to be discussed later on) of the values in the "pattern vector" for each of the 96 samples. All 43 variables (see Section 3.1.4.3.), including those that had taken on a deviant value, participate in the calculation of these statistics. The data was taken from Matrix III (the transposed matrix). (See Table 3.28, p. 130).

The next table, Table 3.29, lists samples characterized by an exceptionally high standard deviation. (See Table 3.29, p. 131).

Taking a second look at Tables 3.26, 3.27 and 3.29 leads us to note two main peculiarities.

In Table 3.29, we find two deviant samples not included in Table 3.26, namely, nos. 33 and 58, whereas nos. 8 and 67 of Table 3.26 are missing, their standard deviations being .94 and 1.11, respectively. Also, three sets of samples in both tables are highly unlike the rest: $NP$(1-4, 7-12); $HJ$(80, 81); and $HE$(58, 67).

Now to the other peculiarity. Contrary to the aberrant nature of $NP$ which is characterized by outliers, nearly every remaining sample in Table 3.27 "conducts itself properly" — even those originating in the same chapters of Genesis, where deviant samples are drawn from. This rather bizarre picture emerges from Table 3.30. Here, each sample included either in

Table 3.27: Distribution of Deviant Variables in Individual Samples

| Sub-categ. | Samp. no. | −4 (I) | −3 (II) | −2⁻ (III) | +2⁺ (IV) | +3 (V) | +4 (VI) |
|---|---|---|---|---|---|---|---|
| | 1 | | 1 | 6(6, 8, 10) | 7(3, 14) | | |
| | 2 | | | 9(6, 9, 13, 22, 27) | 2(12) | 2(3, 14) | |
| | 3 | | 1(17) | 6(22, 51) | 3(3,16) | 1(50) | |
| | 4 | | 3(17, 18, 39) | 10(6, 8, 9, 13, 22, 27) | 3(4,5) | | |
| | 5 | | | | 2 | 1(34) | 1(14) |
| NP | 6 | | | 7(14, 26, 40) | 1 | | |
| | 7 | | | 3(14, 21, 29) | 4(11, 52) | 1(34) | |
| | 8 | 1(33) | | 4 | 1 | | |
| | 9 | | 1(12) | 10(14, 21, 27, 29, 40) | 2(4) | | |
| | 10 | 2(2, 29) | 4(12, 23, 41, 51) | 11(7, 8, 14, 20, 21, 25, 26, 27) | 3(4,5) | 2(16, 11) | 1(13) |
| | 11 | 1(12) | 4(2, 19, 25, 41) | 12(21, 22, 26, 27, 38, 39, 40) | 1(4) | 2(11, 53), 1(11) | |
| | 12 | | 1(51) | 5(14, 25, 26) | 2 | 1(50) | 1(16) |
| | 13 | | | 7(38) | 2(8) | | |
| | 14 | | 1(35) | 3(4) | 1 | 1(7) | |
| | 15 | | | 1 | | | |
| | 16 | | 1(43) | 6(10, 22, 38, 40) | 2(51) | | |
| | 17 | | | | 2 | | |
| | 18 | | | 3(22) | 2(8) | | |
| | 19 | | | | 1 | | |
| NE | 20 | | 1(35) | 1 | 5(33, 37) | | |
| | 21 | | | | | | |
| | 22 | | | 2(3, 19) | 2(20) | 1(22) | |
| | 23 | | | 3(5) | 2(4) | | |
| | 24 | | | 1 | 1 | | |
| | 25 | | 1(3) | 1 | | | |
| | 26 | | | 2 | 4 | 1(9) | |
| | 27 | | | 2 | | | |
| | 28 | | | 2 | | | |

Legend: Digits in cols. I–VI refer to the number of variables in a sample having the rounded value appearing at the top of the columns.

Table 3.27: Distribution of Deviant Variables in Individual Samples

*(Continued)*

| Sub-categ. | Samp. no. | $-4$ (I) | $-3$ (II) | $-2^-$ (III) | $+2^+$ (IV) | $+3$ (V) | $+4$ (VI) |
|---|---|---|---|---|---|---|---|
| | 29 | | 2 | | 3(6, 22) | 1(50) | |
| | 30 | 1(4) | 9 | | 2 | 1(16) | |
| | 31 | | 6(23, 38, 41) | | 1 | | |
| | 32 | | 1(27) | | 6(23, 25, 52) | 1(16) | |
| | 33 | | 1(40) | | 7(6, 25, 34, 38) | 2(16, 38) | |
| | 34 | | | | 1 | | |
| | 35 | | 3(10, 22) | | | | |
| | 36 | | 1(40) | | 3(18, 53) | | |
| | 37 | | 2 | | | | |
| | 38 | | 1 | | 2 | | |
| | 39 | | 1 | | 7(7, 19, 27, 28) | | |
| | 40 | | 2 | | 2 | | |
| | 41 | | 3(6, 40) | | 5(7, 18) | | |
| NJ | 42 | | 1(3) | | 3 | | |
| | 43 | | 1 | | 1 | 1(19) | |
| | 44 | | | | | | |
| | 45 | | 4(38) | | 2 | | |
| | 46 | | 3(40) | | | | |
| | 47 | | 3(22, 38) | | 2(7) | | |
| | 48 | | | | 1 | | |
| | 49 | | | | 2 | | |
| | 50 | | 3 | | 1(4) | | |
| | 51 | | 1 | | 3 | | |
| | 52 | | 2(23) | | | | |
| | 53 | | | | | | |
| | 54 | 1(35) | 2 | | | | |
| | 55 | | 1(14) | | 1 | | |
| HP | 56 | | 2(25) | | 4(37) | | |
| | 57 | | 1 | | 3 | | |

Table 3.27: Distribution of Deviant Variables in Individual Samples

*(Continued)*

| Sub-categ. | Samp. no. | −4 (I) | −3 (II) | −2⁻ (III) | +2⁺ (IV) | +3 (V) | +4 (VI) |
|---|---|---|---|---|---|---|---|
| | 58 | | 1(35) | 4(10, 22, 27) | 1(39) | | |
| | 59 | | 1(9) | 1 | 1 | | |
| | 60 | | | 3 | 2 | | |
| | 61 | | 1(51) | 1(10) | 4 | | |
| | 62 | | 1(11) | 1(18) | | | |
| | 63 | | | 3(22) | 4 | | |
| | 64 | | | 1 | 4(16, 23) | | |
| | 65 | | | 2(27) | 5(4, 20) | | |
| | 66 | | | 1(10) | 2(52) | | |
| HE | 67 | | | 1 | 2 | | 1(37) |
| | 68 | | | 1 | 5(29, 33) | 1(35) | |
| | 69 | | | 2 | 2(25) | 1(20) | |
| | 70 | | | | | | |
| | 71 | | | 1 | 2(16) | | |
| | 72 | | | | | | |
| | 73 | | | 1(4) | 2(33, 52) | | |
| | 74 | | | 2 | 3(5, 31) | | |
| | 75 | | | 1 | 2(27, 37) | | |
| | 76 | | | | 1 | | |
| | 77 | | | 1(9) | 2 | | |
| | 78 | | | | 1 | | |
| | 79 | | | | | | |
| | 80 | | | 2 | 3 | | |
| HJ | 81 | | | 1 | 4(25) | 1(37) | 1(52) |
| | 82 | | | 1 | 1 | 1(3) | 1(52) |
| | 83 | | | | 4(17, 41) | | |
| | 84 | | | 1 | 3(15, 29, 40) | | |
| | 85 | | | 1 | 6(52) | 1(37) | |
| | 86 | | | | 1 | | |
| | 87 | | | 1 | 2(20, 21) | | |

Table 3.27: Distribution of Deviant Variables in Individual Samples

| Sub-categ. | Samp. no. | $-4$ (I) | $-3$ (II) | $-2^-$ (III) | $+2^+$ (IV) | $+3$ (V) | $+4$ (VI) |
|---|---|---|---|---|---|---|---|
| DP | 88 | | | 1(51) | 5(20, 52) | | |
|  | 89 | | | 2(10) | 5 | | |
|  | 90 | | | 2(40) | 2(15, 52) | | |
| DE | 91 | | | 2(22) | 3(2) | | |
| DJ | 92 | | | 2(10) | 2(50) | | |
|  | 93 | | | | 2 | 2(23, 34) | |
|  | 94 | | | | 3(31) | 2(16, 34) | |
|  | 95 | | | 1 | 4(27) | | |
|  | 96 | | | 2(22) | 3 | | |

(Continued)

Table 3.28: Means and Standard Deviations of the Pattern Vector in
Individual Samples

| Sample no. | Sub-cat. | Mean | STD | Sample no. | Sub-cat. | Mean | STD | Sample no. | Sub-cat. | Mean | STD |
|---|---|---|---|---|---|---|---|---|---|---|---|
| 1 | NP | −.25 | 1.36 | 34 | | .27 | .99 | 67 | | .37 | 1.11 |
| 2 | | −.29 | 1.32 | 35 | | −.23 | .87 | 68 | | .18 | .98 |
| 3 | | −.32 | 1.35 | 36 | | −.11 | .84 | 69 | | .13 | .77 |
| 4 | | −.62 | 1.59 | 37 | | −.16 | .79 | 70 | | .16 | .72 |
| 5 | | −.01 | .81 | 38 | | −.13 | .85 | 71 | | .21 | .87 |
| 6 | | −.36 | 1.04 | 39 | | .09 | 1.14 | 72 | | .03 | .76 |
| 7 | | −.09 | 1.22 | 40 | | .06 | .90 | 73 | | .13 | .87 |
| 8 | | −.41 | .94 | 41 | | −.12 | 1.01 | | | | |
| 9 | | −.49 | 1.39 | 42 | | .19 | .90 | 74 | HJ | .26 | .76 |
| 10 | | −1.11 | 1.93 | 43 | | .05 | .91 | 75 | | .15 | .88 |
| 11 | | −.82 | 1.74 | 44 | | −.09 | .69 | 76 | | .27 | .78 |
| 12 | | −.25 | 1.38 | 45 | | −.02 | .95 | 77 | | .07 | .87 |
| | | | | 46 | | −.03 | .69 | 78 | | .09 | .72 |
| 13 | NE | −.30 | 1.00 | 47 | | −.24 | .90 | 79 | | .15 | .76 |
| 14 | | −.11 | 1.07 | 48 | | .04 | .74 | 80 | | .33 | 1.23 |
| 15 | | .00 | .68 | 49 | | −.03 | .82 | 81 | | .16 | 1.29 |
| 16 | | −.43 | 1.08 | 50 | | −.06 | .84 | 82 | | .11 | .80 |
| 17 | | .07 | .71 | 51 | | .07 | .91 | 83 | | .09 | .93 |
| 18 | | −.14 | .82 | 52 | | −.05 | .85 | 84 | | .31 | .81 |
| 19 | | .04 | .64 | 53 | | .08 | .78 | 85 | | .28 | 1.08 |
| 20 | | −.11 | .75 | 54 | | −.22 | .84 | 86 | | .11 | .75 |
| 21 | | .19 | .92 | 55 | | .08 | .79 | 87 | | .17 | .80 |
| 22 | | .03 | 1.06 | | | | | | | | |
| 23 | | −.17 | 1.01 | 56 | HP | −.18 | 1.01 | 88 | DP | .20 | .96 |
| 24 | | −.01 | .73 | 57 | | −.09 | .83 | 89 | | .18 | .89 |
| 25 | | .02 | .84 | | | | | 90 | | .06 | .88 |
| 26 | | .14 | .94 | 58 | HE | .00 | 1.28 | | | | |
| 27 | | −.06 | .78 | 59 | | .23 | .79 | 91 | DE | .06 | .91 |
| 28 | | −.22 | .75 | 60 | | −.05 | 1.02 | | | | |
| | | | | 61 | | .16 | .71 | 92 | DJ | .26 | .91 |
| 29 | NJ | .07 | 1.03 | 62 | | .13 | 1.01 | 93 | | .33 | .93 |
| 30 | | .07 | 1.00 | 63 | | .01 | 1.07 | 94 | | .39 | 1.02 |
| 31 | | −.29 | 1.00 | 64 | | .30 | .88 | 95 | | .26 | .92 |
| 32 | | −.07 | .89 | 65 | | .14 | .92 | 96 | | .07 | .90 |
| 33 | | .26 | 1.21 | 66 | | .14 | .88 | | | | |

Table 3.29: Samples Characterized by High Standard Deviation

| Sample no. | Subcate-gory | STD | Sample no. | Subcate-gory | STD | Sample no. | Subcate-gory | STD |
|---|---|---|---|---|---|---|---|---|
| 10 | NP | 1.93 | 1 | NP | 1.36 | 58 | HE | 1.28 |
| 11 | NP | 1.74 | 3 | NP | 1.35 | 80 | HJ | 1.23 |
| 4 | NP | 1.59 | 2 | NP | 1.32 | 7 | NP | 1.22 |
| 9 | NP | 1.39 | 81 | HJ | 1.29 | 33 | NJ | 1.21 |
| 12 | NP | 1.38 | | | | | | |

Table 3.30: Deviant Samples and Their Matches

| Sample no. | Sub-cat. | Matched Samples no. | Deviant Samples no. | Sample no. | Sub-cat. | Matched Samples no. | Deviant Samples no. |
|---|---|---|---|---|---|---|---|
| 1-4 | NP | 32-36 (NJ) 74 (HJ) 88, 89 (DP) 92, 93 (DJ) | 33 (NJ) | 67 | HE | 11 (NP) 24, 25 (NE) 53 (NJ) 86 (HJ) 90 (DP) 91 (DE) 96 (DJ) | 11 (NP) |
| 8-12 | NP | 14-28 (NE) 44-55 (NJ) 57 (HP) 59-73 (HE) 79-87 (HJ) 90 (DP) 91 (DE) 96 (DJ) | 67 (HE) 80, 81 (HJ) | 33 | NJ | 3 (NP) 74 (HJ) 88 (DP) 93 (DJ) | 3 (NP) |
| 58 | HE | 6 (NP) 13, 14 (NE) 41 (NJ) 56 (HP) 76 (HJ) 90 (DP) 91 (DE) 95 (DJ) | 6 (NP) | 80, 81 | HJ | 8 (NP) 14 (NE) 45-47 (NJ) 56 (HP) 59 (HE) 90 (DP) 91 (DE) 96 (DJ) | 8 (NP) |

Table 3.26 or in Table 3.29 is presented along with others taken from the same segment of Genesis. To illuminate this by sample no. 33($NJ$): its provenience is chs. 7 and 8, which also produced part of nos. 3($NP$), 74($HJ$), 88($DP$) and 93($DJ$). Of these, only the first reveals as deviant a language behavior as sample no. 33($NJ$). (See Table 30, p. 131).

The differences, manifested either in DIS-values (see Table 3.25) or in standard deviations (see Table 3.28), are striking, and reflect that the Documentary Hypothesis may indeed have some basis from the point of view of statistical linguistics; yet it requires a thorough rethinking and reformulation.

The implications of the fact that, when it comes to $N$, and unlike the cases of $H$ and $D$, samples attributed to $P$ differ so much from those attributed to $E$ and $J$, are discussed in Section 3.4.3.

Lastly, Table 3.28 relates to (3) above, and seems to suggest that the means of the samples form the following possible two clusters:

Sample nos. 1-55:   Nearly all means are either close to zero or strictly negative, with some values of $NP$-samples being extraordinarily negative. Exceptions (with their means) are:

21($NE$) : .19 | 33($NJ$) : .26 | 42($NJ$) : .19
26($NE$) : .14 | 34($NJ$) : .27

Samples nos. 56-96:   All means are strictly positive, except 56-57($HP$) and 60($HE$) which approach a near zero value.
Extraordinarily high values are found (in descending order of their means):

94($DJ$) : .39 | 80($HJ$) : .33 | 84($HJ$) : .31
67($HE$) : .37 | 93($DJ$) : .33 | 64($HE$) : .30

Note that samples nos. 67 and 80 were located as deviant in Table 3.26.

If a pattern lies concealed in these two groupings, apart from the obvious separation of $N$ from $H + D$, we were unable to spot it.

**Résumé.** A study of deviant values included in the "pattern vector" of samples shows that, excluding nos. 5,6 and 8, all other $NP$ samples are "malbehaved", while the linguistic behavior of $HP$ and $DP$ samples corresponds to that of the rest of Genesis. The deviant character of the majority of $NP$ samples manifests itself also in the wide dispersion of the "pattern vector" values as measured by standard deviations. Somewhat deviant samples are also found among those of subcategory $NJ$ in Division $I$.

## 3.3.4. CLUSTER ANALYSIS

3.3.4.1. **Description.** Cluster Analysis aims at creating homogeneous clusters of observations based on some proximity measure which reflects their similarity. The measure used here is the Euclidean distance. It is employed instead of the more commonly used Mahalanbolis-$D^2$ because of the relatively small correlations found between variables in our criteria set.

The Euclidean distance between samples $j$ and $k$ is defined by:

$$ d_{jk} = \sqrt{\sum_{i=1}^{43} (z_{ij} - z_{ik})^2} $$

where values of variables are expressed in standardized scores (for their definition, see Section 3.1.4.4.).

Cluster Analysis starts by calculating the Euclidean distance between each sample pair. It then tries to cluster samples progressively in such a manner that distances between samples within the same cluster are smaller than those between samples classified to different clusters.

Initially, each case is taken as a cluster of its own. Then, at each successive step, the two "nearest clusters" are combined (amalgamated), and treated from that step on as one new cluster. This process of amalgamation continues until all cases are fused into one comprehensive cluster.

The linkage principle by which two "nearest clusters" are combined is the average linkage rule. This rule is based on the arithmetic average of the Euclidean distances between all possible pairings of samples belonging to the two clusters. The resulting "amalgamation distance" between the two combined clusters is the Euclidean one, where the variables' values of each cluster, used to calculate the distance, are the sum of the values of all cases in the cluster.

The output of the program employed — see Section 3.1.4.1. — includes:

(a) A vertical tree diagram (dendogram) of clusters (e.g., Figure 3.11) where the numbers and the source subcategory of samples are printed at the top of the diagram. Each vertical column of "I"s denotes one single cluster, and the sign ($+$) the combination of two clusters. A horizontal line of ($-$) corresponds to a cluster formed in the amalgamation process. Samples belonging to one and the same cluster are located vertically above this line of ($-$). To the left of each line, the amalgamation distance is given between the two clusters combined.

(b) A histogram of distances between cases (not shown here).

(c) A shaded distance matrix after case clustering (e.g., Figure 3.12). Cases are here arranged in a vertical column, and to the right of each, the distances from all other cases located above it are listed. Thus, the distance between a case in the $j$-th line and another in the $i$-th line ($j > i$) can be traced in the $j$-th line at cell no. $i$ (from the left). Distances are marked by shades, the code of which is also printed next to the matrix: the darker the shade, the smaller the distance.

3.3.4.2. **Results.** The following analyses are carried out:

Cluster Analysis of the whole Book of Genesis (see Figures 3.11 and 3.12).

Cluster Analysis of $E + J$ (see Figures 3.13 and 3.14).

Cluster Analysis of $NE + NJ$ (see Figure 3.15).

These three analyses are run on the original data (Matrix I) prior to any transformation, outliers being included.

Figure 3.11 is the tree diagram and Figure 3.12 the shaded distance matrix resulting from Cluster Analysis of the whole Book of Genesis. (See Figures 3.11, 3.12, p. 135-36).

Both Figures tell the same, but in two different modes. Let us consider first Figure 3.11 and study the amalgamation process.

It is easy to see that, samples nos. 1, 2 and 4 disregarded, some clustering configuration is nested only in samples nos. 5($NP$) through 59($HE$), the numbers to be read in the uppermost line of Figure 3.11 from left to right. This is hereafter referred to as the main cluster. The remaining samples are added one at a time and fused separately and individually into the main cluster, which is an obvious indication for lack of any "local" homogeneity.

Figure 3.11 spotlights a number of conspicuous points.

Samples nos. 1, 2 and 4 are the most peculiar in the whole book of Genesis. While creating a cluster of their own which does not join the main cluster until a very late stage of the amalgamating process, they are also the most distant samples from the other $NP$-samples nos. 3, 7, 9-12. These, in turn, also exhibit exceptional linguistic behavior since they join the slowly amalgamating cluster as late as at the very end of the process (see for the location of these samples at the rightmost end of line 1 in Figure 3.11).

Thus, the above mentioned $NP$-samples seem to be of an out-of-the way character, on the one hand, and of non-uniform character, when perceived as one group, on the other. As if to add to this non-uniformity, note that sample no. 5($NP$) joins the main cluster at quite an early stage, not unlike nos. 6, 8($NP$), which amalgamate as one cluster much sooner than nos. 3, 7 and 9-12. Considering $NP$, then, as homogeneous, is not borne out in the light of these findings. So much for this subcategory.

Another conspicuous point presents itself with regard to category $J$, and that is that no $NJ$-sample of the group nos. 29-36 is part of the main cluster. It can hardly be a happy accident that all of these samples are from Division I, since almost all other samples which derive from that division, e.g., nos. 1-4 ($NP$), 74($HJ$), 88($DP$) and 93($DJ$) are also not included in the main cluster, no. 92($DJ$) being the only exception.

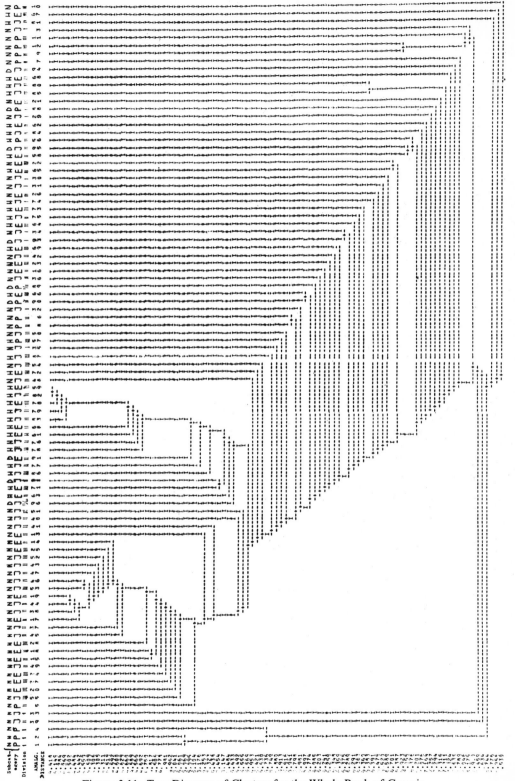

Figure 3.11: Tree Diagram of Clusters for the Whole Book of Genesis

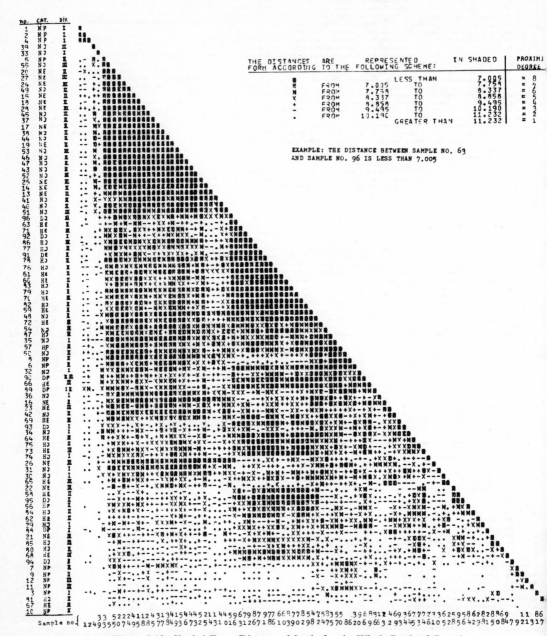

Figure 3.12: Shaded Form Distances Matrix for the Whole Book of Genesis

Returning to the main cluster, i.e., from no. 5(*NP*), onwards to no. 59(*HE*), in the same order as they appear in Figure 3.11, it may be instructive to list its constituents by subcategories, and to note their provenance in Genesis:

| | | | | |
|---|---|---|---|---|
| *NP* | : no. 5 | from chs. | | 11-16 |
| *NE* | : nos. 20, 27, 24, 15, 18, 28, 17, 19, 25, 14, 13 | ″ | ″ | 20-39, 41-50 |
| *NJ* | : nos. 55, 49, 45, 37, 38, 44, 53, 46, 47, 43, 52, 41, 40, 51 | ″ | ″ | 13-50 |
| *HP* | : none | | | |
| *HE* | : nos. 63, 71, 61, 60, 70, 59 | ″ | ″ | 21-39, 44-45 |
| *HJ* | : nos. 86, 77, 78, 76, 83, 79, 82 | ″ | ″ | 18-34, 38-47 |
| *DP* | : none | | | |
| *DE* | : no. 91 | ″ | ″ | 20-50 |
| *DJ* | : nos. 96, 92 | ″ | ″ | 3-6, 22-50 |

Chapters in the right hand column correspond in general to Division *II*, extending from somewhere around ch. 13 until approximately ch. 45.

Note, that apart from no. 5(*NP*), no other *P* sample is included in the above list. *P*, then, is not in keeping with the main body of Genesis, the Patriarchal Story.

Looking at it from yet another angle, let us inspect the last fifteen samples to combine with the main cluster (in order of their accession to it, as shown in Figure 3.11):

| | | | | | |
|---|---|---|---|---|---|
| 1. | no. | 68 (*HE,III*) | from chs. | | 42-43 |
| 2. | ″ | 94 (*DJ,II*) | ″ | ″ | 13-18 |
| 3. | ″ | 7 (*NP,II*) | ″ | ″ | 23-25 |
| 4. | ″ | 3 (*NP,I*) | ″ | ″ | 6-11 |
| 5. | ″ | 9 (*NP,II*) | ″ | ″ | 35-36 |
| 6. | ″ | 11 (*NP,III*) | ″ | ″ | 36-46 |
| 7. | ″ | 12 (*NP,III*) | ″ | ″ | 46-50 |
| 8. | ″ | 33 (*NJ,I*) | ″ | ″ | 7-8 |
| 9. | ″ | 39 (*NJ,II*) | ″ | ″ | 18-19 |
| 10. | ″ | 1 (*NP,I*) | ″ | ″ | 5 |
| 11. | ″ | 2 (*NP,I*) | ″ | ″ | 5-6 |
| 12. | ″ | 4 (*NP,I*) | ″ | ″ | 11 |
| 13. | ″ | 81 (*HJ,II*) | ″ | ″ | 27 |
| 14. | ″ | 67 (*HE,III*) | ″ | ″ | 42 |
| 15. | ″ | 10 (*NP,II*) | ″ | ″ | 36 |

Of these fifteen samples, seven are drawn from the first twenty chapters and six from the last fifteen, that is, from the two outer wings of Genesis. Two only, namely nos. 81(*HJ,II*) and 7(*NP,II*), derive from the innermost nucleus, which constitutes the majority of the main cluster's samples.

Reaching, finally, the central issue of this enquiry, the possible divergence of *E* from *J*, we cannot fail to see that there is no apparent distinction between the two.

We are turning now to Figure 3.12 (p. 139).  Five clusters have taken shape here:

(a)  Three gross (or basic) clusters, constituting the dark triangles at the utmost left, starting at sample no. 1(*NP*) and terminating at no. 59(*HE*);

(b)  Six small-sized groups of samples which, although not forming a cluster of their own, display a definite proximity to one, and only one, of the above basic clusters;

(c)  A group of samples relatively distant from the rest of the set;

(d)  A group of samples lying about equally near to two of the basic clusters;

(e)  A group of single samples showing *high* proximity to one, and one only, of the basic clusters.

The composition of (a) through (e) is specified below where the order of samples is prescribed by Figure 3.12.

(a)  Three basic clusters:

Cluster 1 (the uppermost triangle):
    nos. 1(*NP*), 2(*NP*), 4(*NP*)

Cluster 2 (the second triangle from the top):
    nos.  5(*NP*), 55(*NJ*), 20(*NE*), 27(*NE*), 24(*NE*), 49(*NJ*),
       ”    15(*NE*), 18(*NE*), 28(*NE*), 45(*NJ*), 37(*NJ*), 17(*NE*),
       ”    38(*NJ*), 44(*NJ*), 19(*NE*), 53(*NJ*), 46(*NJ*), 47(*NJ*),
       ”    43(*NJ*), 52(*NJ*), 25(*NE*), 14(*NE*), 13(*NE*), 41(*NJ*),
       ”    40(*NJ*), 51(*NJ*)

Cluster 3 (the third triangle from the top):
    nos. 96(*DJ*), 63(*HE*), 71(*HE*), 92(*DJ*), 86(*HJ*), 77(*HJ*),
       ”    91(*DE*), 78(*HJ*), 76(*HJ*), 61(*HE*), 60(*HE*), 83(*HJ*),
       ”    79(*HJ*), 70(*HE*), 82(*HJ*), 59(*HE*)

(b)  Subclusters of the basic clusters:

Cluster A (subcluster of Cluster 3):  nos. 32(*NJ*), 90(*DP*), 66(*HE*), 89(*DP*)
Cluster B (subcluster of Cluster 2):  ”  36(*NJ*), 16(*NE*), 23(*NE*), 42(*NJ*),
                                                69(*HE*)
Cluster C (subcluster of Cluster 3):  ”  93(*DJ*), 64(*HE*), 75(*HJ*), 73(*HE*),
                                                74(*HJ*)
Cluster D (subcluster of Cluster 2):  ”  26(*NE*), 31(*NJ*), 30(*NJ*)
Cluster E (subcluster of Cluster 3):  ”  58(*HE*), 95(*DJ*), 56(*HP*), 84(*HJ*),
                                              62(*HE*)
Cluster F (subcluster of Cluster 3):  ”  68(*HE*), 94(*DJ*)

(c) Outcast samples: a number of samples are lying relatively remote, compared with any other sample or group of samples in the set. They are listed below, and the nearest samples are detailed for each one. Proximity degrees (P.D.) are added in the right margin in accordance with the code of shades in Figure 3.12. The higher the P.D., the nearer to the samples enumerated after the colon lies the sample which is heading the line; source chapters of this sample are given in brackets:

| | | |
|---|---|---|
| 39(*NJ*) (chs. 18-19) | : 5(*NP*), 45(*NJ*), 44(*NJ*), 19(*NE*), 43(*NJ*) | P.D. = 7 |
| 33(*NJ*) (chs. 7-8) | : 34(*NJ*) | P.D. = 7 |
| | 54(*NJ*), 32(*NJ*), 90(*DP*), 66(*HE*), 88(*DP*) | P.D. = 6 |
| 29(*NJ*) (chs. 2) | : 54(*NJ*), 22(*NE*) | P.D. = 7 |
| 88(*DP*) (chs. 6-9) | : 66(*HE*), 90(*DP*) | P.D. = 8 |
| | 65(*HE*), 89(*DP*), 50(*NJ*), 61(*HE*) | P.D. = 7 |
| 34(*NJ*) (chs. 8) | : 93(*DJ*) | P.D. = 8 |
| | 89(*DP*), 54(*NJ*), 40(*NJ*), 19(*NE*), 17(*NE*), 33(*NJ*), 64(*HE*), 30(*NJ*) | P.D. = 7 |
| 65(*HE*) (chs. 41) | : 89(*DP*), 69(*HE*) | P.D. = 8 |
| | 70(*HE*), 61(*HE*), 78(*HJ*), 27(*NE*) | P.D. = 7 |
| 22(*NE*) (chs. 40-41) | : 55(*NJ*), 65(*HE*) | P.D. = 8 |
| | 96(*DJ*), 42(*NJ*), 23(*NE*), 25(*NE*), 44(*NJ*), 27(*NE*), 29(*NJ*) | P.D. = 7 |
| 21(*NE*) (chs. 39-40) | : 55(*NJ*) | P.D. = 8 |
| | 69(*HE*), 42(*NJ*), 25(*NE*), 17(*NE*) | P.D. = 7 |
| 85(*HJ*) (chs. 37-38) | : 80(*HJ*) | P.D. = 8 |
| | 73(*HE*), 81(*HJ*) | P.D. = 7 |
| 7(*NP*) (chs. 23-25) | : 8(*NP*), 55(*NJ*) | P.D. = 7 |
| | 6(*NP*), 50(*NJ*), 57(*HP*), 44(*NJ*), 17(*NE*), 37(*NJ*), 28(*NE*), 20(*NE*) | P.D. = 6 |
| 9(*NP*) (chs. 35-36) | : 12(*NP*) | P.D. = 8 |
| | 36(*NJ*) | P.D. = 7 |
| | 8(*NP*) | P.D. = 6 |
| 12(*NP*) (chs. 46-50) | : 9(*NP*) | P.D. = 8 |
| | 36(*NJ*), 3(*NP*) | P.D. = 6 |
| 11(*NP*) (chs. 36-46) | : 12(*NP*) | P.D. = 5 |
| | 8(*NP*) | P.D. = 4 |
| 3(*NP*) *(chs. 6-11)* | : 57(*HP*) | P.D. = 8 |
| | 12(*NP*), 6(*NP*), 8(*NP*), 50(*NJ*), 20(*NE*) | P.D. = 6 |
| 81(*HJ*) (chs. 27) | : 80(*HJ*) | P.D. = 7 |
| | 87(*HJ*) | P.D. = 6 |
| 67(*HE*) (chs. 42) | : all samples | only P.D. ≤ 5 |
| 10(*NP*) (chs. 36) | : 9(*NP*) | P.D. = 7 |
| 80(*HJ*) (chs. 26-27) | : 85(*HJ*) | P.D. = 8 |
| | 73(*HE*), 81(*HJ*) | P.D. = 7 |

Trivial as this list of eighteen items looks, it has a few surprises in store. Let us first rearrange the samples by subcategories:

*NP*(3,7,9,10,11,12);  *NE*(21,22);  *NJ*(29,33,34,39);  *HE*(65,67);  *HJ*(80,81,85); *DP*(88).

One cannot overlook that nearly consecutive text blocks are represented here, including almost all samples of *NP* which are not part of the very far basic Cluster 1, uppermost in Figure 3.12 (nos. 1, 2 and 4).

When the source chapters of these blocks are traced, we realize that while the origin of both the *NE* and *HE* samples is chs. 39-42 (Division *III*), the great majority of the *NJ* samples are formed by Division *I*, a fact already referred to above.  Outcast samples of *NP* have source chapters which are spread throughout the whole book.

(d)   Samples of high proximity to both basic Clusters 2 and 3:

48(*NJ*), 72(*HE*), 54(*NJ*), 35(*NJ*), 57(*HP*), 50(*NJ*).

All these, except no. 35(*NJ*), come from chs. 34-50, that is, mainly, Division *III*.

(e)   Single samples of high proximity to one basic Cluster only:

8(*NP*), 6(*NP*) — both close to Cluster 2.

Since what is at stake in the first place is the relationship between *E* and *J*, let us now carry out the Cluster Analysis somewhat further, and focus it on these Documents only.  The relevant graphic displays are Figure 3.13, the tree diagram, and Figure 3.14, the shaded matrix.  (See Figures 3.13, 3.14, pp. 142-43).

Among the 36 samples which make up the main cluster in Figure 3.13, and which produce the only clustering configuration, there is none from Division *I*.  A demarcation in the composition of the main cluster is recognizable between *N* and *H* + *D*.  Nothing of this sort may be noticed among the rest of the samples as they are added to the main cluster one at a time.

The last samples to accrue to the main cluster are the fifteen following, numbered here in order of their amalgamation:

|  |  |  |
|---|---|---|
| 1. no. 95(*DJ*) | 6. no. 21(*NE*) | 11. no. 29(*NJ*) |
| 2. no. 58(*HE*) | 7. no. 62(*HE*) | 12. no. 39(*NJ*) |
| 3. no. 85(*HJ*) | 8. no. 68(*HE*) | 13. no. 67(*HE*) |
| 4. no. 80(*HJ*) | 9. no. 94(*DJ*) | 14. no. 33(*NJ*) |
| 5. no. 84(*HJ*) | 10. no. 22(*NE*) | 15. no. 81(*HJ*) |

By and large, their source is again either the first twenty or the last fifteen chapters of the book.

Inspecting now Figure 3.14, we note that a rather homogeneous group is created by samples nos. 37-55($NJ$) drawn from Divisions $II$ and $III$, with only nos. 39, 40, 42, 50, 51 and 54 lying somewhat distant from the main cluster.

Concerning the outcast samples of $NE$, the majority, i.e., nos. 26, 23, 21, 22 in Figure 3.14, originate in Division $III$. Nearly the same applies to the outcast $HE$ samples (nos. 71, 64, 69, 73, 66, 63, 65, 58, 62, 68, 67), to the exclusion of nos. 58 and 62.

Finally, Figure 3.15 the clustering map of $NE + NJ$: it is again apparent that relatively isolated samples belong to $NE(III)$ and to $NJ(I)$. (See Figure 3.15, p. 144).

**Résumé.** Cluster Analysis of the entire book, carried out on the original data, results in three basic clusters: (a) the three $NP$ samples nos. 1, 2, 4; (b) the great majority of $N$ samples, originating in $E$ and $J$; (c) $H$ and $D$ samples not originating in $P$. Relatively isolated are a few $NE$ samples from Division $III$, a few $NJ$ samples from Division $I$, and a number of $P$ samples from all three Sorts-of-Discourse.

Cluster Analysis of $E + J$ creates one main cluster where a clear distinction between $N$ and $H + D$ only is discernable, and where Division $I$ is not represented at all. Most $NE$ and $HE$ outcasts are from Division $III$.

The most remote samples stem either from the first twenty or from the last fifteen chapters.

## 3.3.5. SMALLEST SPACE ANALYSIS ($SSA1$)

3.3.5.1. **Description.** Smallest Space Analysis (hereafter denoted ($SSA1$) after its programmed version as used here) is a multidimensional scaling technique which attempts to reduce the dimensionality of the "pattern vector" while preserving monotonicity among points in the original space. Yet, before we introduce $SSA1$, a few words are in place on how other techniques function in this regard.

Distance relations may be studied by various approaches, such as Factor Analysis, Discriminant Analysis and others. All share a common characteristic, namely, the desire to represent patterns as points in a coordinate space in such a manner that will meet two requirements:

(a) The Monotonicity Requirement: Let $d_{ij}$ be the Euclidean distance between the representative points of two patterns $M_i$ and $M_j$ in some space. Then, the dimensionality $m$ of this space is sought which will satisfactorily fulfill the Monotonicity Requirement, that is, that $d_{ij}$ be smaller than $d_{kl}$, whenever the observed data indicates that $M_i$ is closer to $M_j$ than $M_k$ is to $M_l$ — whatever the term "closer" may mean here.

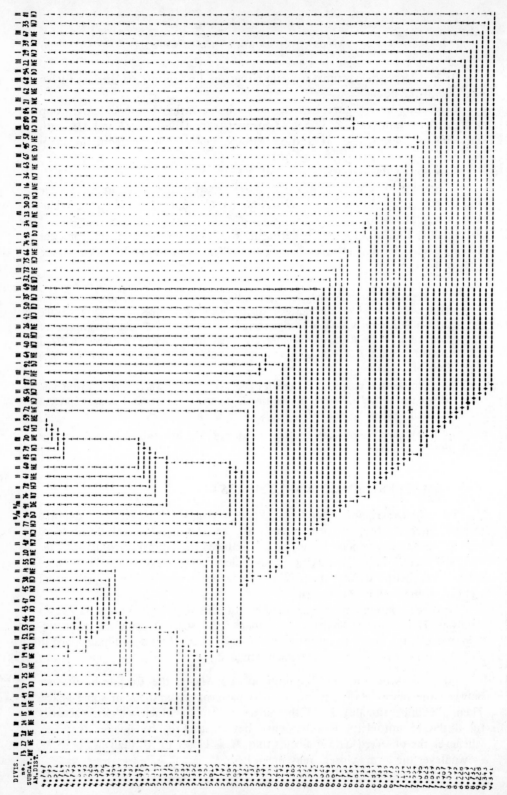

Figure 3.13: Tree Diagram of Clusters for $E$ and $J$

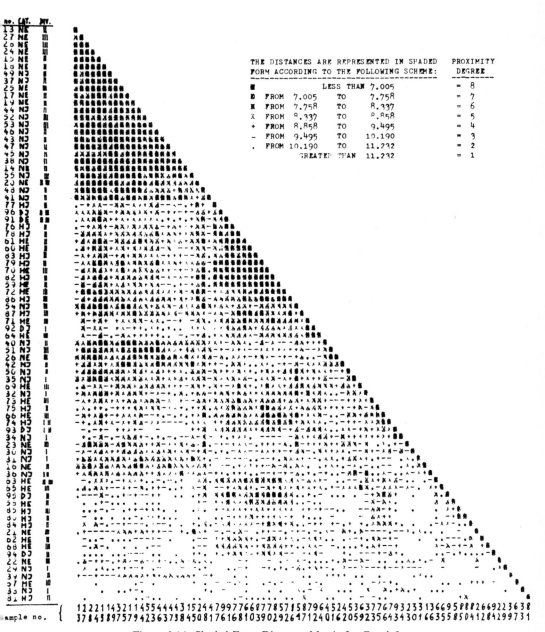

THE DISTANCES ARE REPRESENTED IN SHADED          PROXIMITY
FORM ACCORDING TO THE FOLLOWING SCHEME:          DEGREE

| | | | | |
|---|---|---|---|---|
| ▇ | | LESS THAN 7.005 | | = 8 |
| ▣ | FROM 7.005 | TO | 7.758 | = 7 |
| ✕ | FROM 7.758 | TO | 8.337 | = 6 |
| X | FROM 8.337 | TO | 8.858 | = 5 |
| + | FROM 8.858 | TO | 9.495 | = 4 |
| − | FROM 9.495 | TO | 10.190 | = 3 |
| . | FROM 10.190 | TO | 11.232 | = 2 |
| | | GREATER THAN | 11.232 | = 1 |

Figure 3.14: Shaded Form Distances Matrix for *E* and *J*

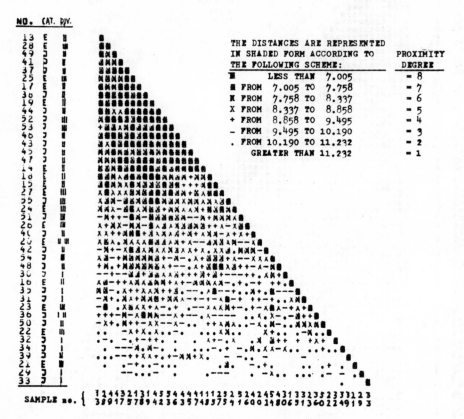

THE DISTANCES ARE REPRESENTED
IN SHADED FORM ACCORDING TO    PROXIMITY
THE FOLLOWING SCHEME:       DEGREE

| | | | | |
|---|---|---|---|---|
| ▓ | LESS THAN | | 7.005 | = 8 |
| ▩ FROM | 7.005 | TO | 7.758 | = 7 |
| X FROM | 7.758 | TO | 8.337 | = 6 |
| X FROM | 8.337 | TO | 8.858 | = 5 |
| + FROM | 8.858 | TO | 9.495 | = 4 |
| - FROM | 9.495 | TO | 10.190 | = 3 |
| . FROM | 10.190 | TO | 11.232 | = 2 |
| | GREATER THAN | | 11.232 | = 1 |

Figure 3.15: Shaded Form Distances Matrix for *NE* and *NJ*

(b) The Smallest Space Requirement: Monotonicity should be satisfied by as few dimensions as possible.

In common with these two requirements, a third must be met in metric approaches (such as some of the aforementioned analyses): that the distance $d_{ij}$ between the representative points in the desired space be related to the original distance (the "proximity" index) $D_{ij}$ by some specified metric formula.

*SSA1*, not being a metric approach, need not satisfy this third condition and centers solely on the Monotonicity and the Smallest Space Requirements, thus allowing its input data to be measured in a scale as low as the ordinal one. Since *SSA1* does not specify any explicit mathematical relationship between $d_{ij}$ and $D_{ij}$, fewer constraints are imposed, and a representative space may be derived which has a much lower dimensionality than the one possibly derived from corresponding metric approaches.

Consequently, *SSA1* is a by far more powerful method for describing mutual relationships between patterns (or variables, as is frequently the case). The reader may ask here why not be contented with the Cluster Analysis of Section 3.3.4. Admittedly, in Pattern Recognition practice it is often sensed that resorting to both methods for discovering homogeneous clusters and their relationships is redundant. Kruskal and Wish, however, refute this objection, holding as we do that the conclusion derived from both Cluster Analysis and *MDS* are complementary [12].

In this context, we would like to remark upon one more feature which renders the two methods, i.e., Cluster Analysis and *SSA1*, as standing each on its own. Whereas the former uses Euclidean distances, the latter is based, in our study, on correlational analysis. The two, it is true, are not completely independent, yet each is of a unique discriminating power.

A last detail worth drawing attention to is the fashion in which *SSA1* was adapted to our present needs. Whilst *SSA1* originally tries to locate variables in the smallest space possible, it is our objective here to do so with patterns (samples) rather than with variables. What we did, and reported upon, in Section 3.3.3., in order to apply analysis of "pattern vector" distributions, is therefore relevant here, too, and the transposed Matrix III is put to use.

Prior to detailing the analysis and its results, a few of the statistics in the exhibited output are defined.

The first and most indicative statistic measuring to what extent the Monotonicity Requirement was fulfilled is the coefficient of alienation $k$, $k = \sqrt{1-\lambda^2}$, where $\lambda$, the second statistic, is a proportionality measure. It assumes its maximum value of 1 if, and only if, the Monotonicity Requirement

---

[12] J. B. Kruskal and M. Wish, *Multidimensional Scaling* (Beverley Hills: Sage Publications, 1978).

is fully kept, namely, $d_{ij} = \alpha D_{ij}$ (for all $i \neq j$, where $\alpha$ is a proportionality coefficient). The minimum value of $\lambda$ is zero, which then signifies a complete lack of association between $d_{ij}$ and $D_{ij}$. It is the aim of *SSA1* to find coordinates in the smallest space that maximize $\lambda$.

The coefficient of alienation $(k)$ varies in the range $(0,1)$, but $k$ of about .15 or less is conventionally and usually considered satisfactory for fulfilling the Monotonicity Requirement.

A third statistic, not independent of $k$, is the normalized $\psi$: $\psi^2 = 1 - (1 - k)^2$.

The analyses run are:

(1)  *SSA1* for the entire Book of Genesis.  Only a limited group of 32 samples is included because of program limitations, but all 43 variables are used.

(2)  *SSA1* for each of the categories defined by the Discourse and the Division hypotheses.

(3)  *SSA1* for $NE + NJ$.

Only two-dimensional solutions are pursued in these runs.  A three- or more-dimensional one may have improved the fit, but it is not being sought here because any gain in accuracy might be offset by difficulties in visualizing and interpreting the inter-relationship between the samples.

3.3.5.2.  **Results.**  Graphic presentation of the multidimensional scaling in the various analyses is shown in the following Figures:

| | | |
|---|---|---|
| The whole book | (32 samples): | Figure 3.16 |
| Category *N* | (37 samples): | Figure 3.17 |
| Category *H* | (21 samples): | Figure 3.18 |
| Category *D* | ( 9 samples): | Figure 3.19 |
| Division *I* | (16 samples): | Figure 3.20 |
| Division *II* | (48 samples): | Figure 3.21 |
| Division *III* | (30 samples): | Figure 3.22 |
| Subcat. *NE + NJ* | (43 samples): | Figure 3.23 |

(See Figures 3.16-3.23, pp. 147-54).

These eight Figures are the visual part only of the computer output of *SSA1*.  The rest (the distance of each point from the centroid and the coordinates of the points and centroids in the space diagrams as well as, for each diagram, the normalized $\psi$, the number of iterations needed to achieve a solution and the alienation coefficient) are deferred to Appendix 3.B, and the discussion of some of the individual deviant samples to Section 3.4.

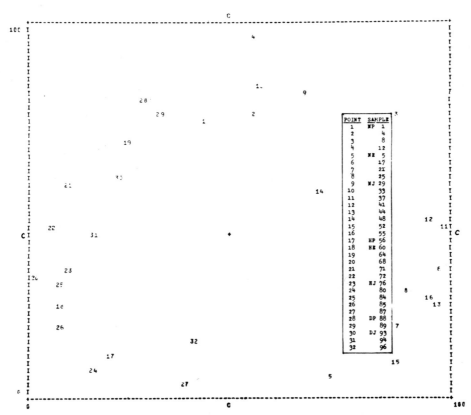

Figure 3.16: Scatter Diagram of Samples in the Reduced Space
for the Whole Book of Genesis

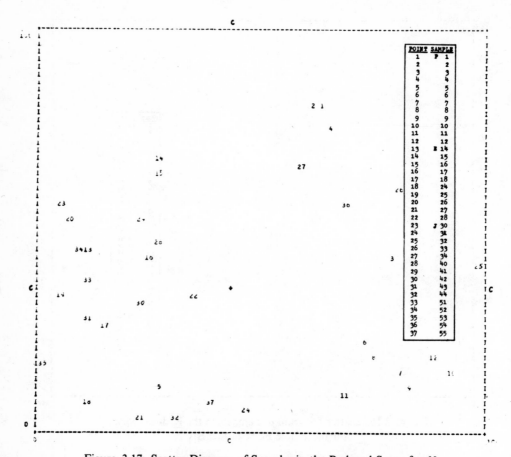

Figure 3.17: Scatter Diagram of Samples in the Reduced Space for *N*

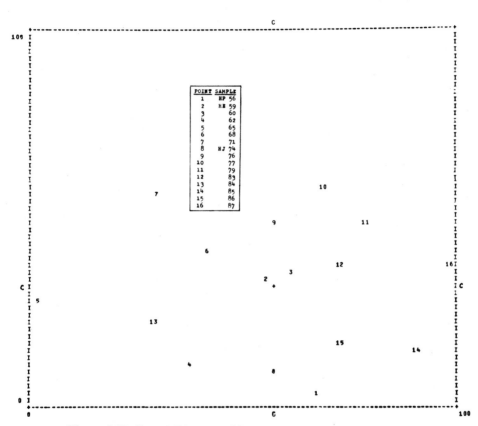

Figure 3.18: Scatter Diagram of Samples in the Reduced Space for *H*

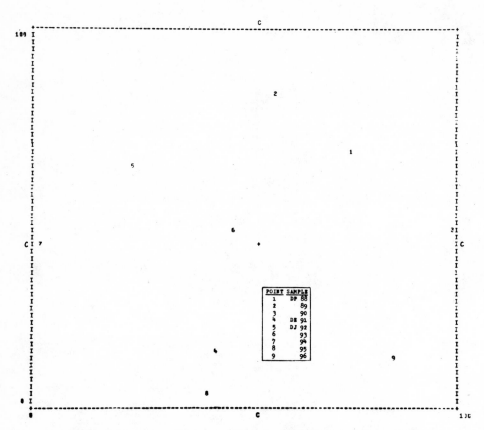

Figure 3.19: Scatter Diagram of Samples in the Reduced Space for *D*

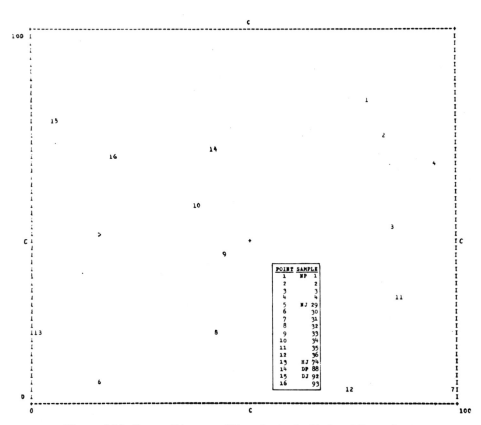

Figure 3.20: Scatter Diagram of Samples in the Reduced Space for *I*

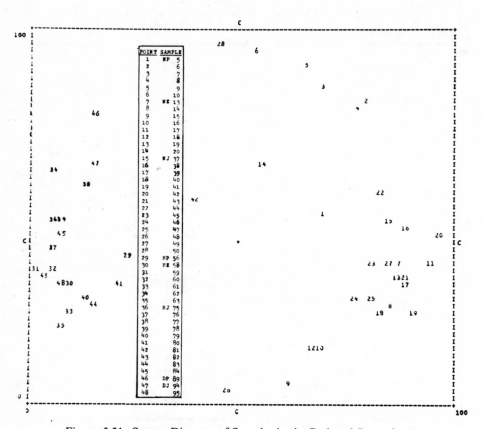

Figure 3.21: Scatter Diagram of Samples in the Reduced Space for *II*

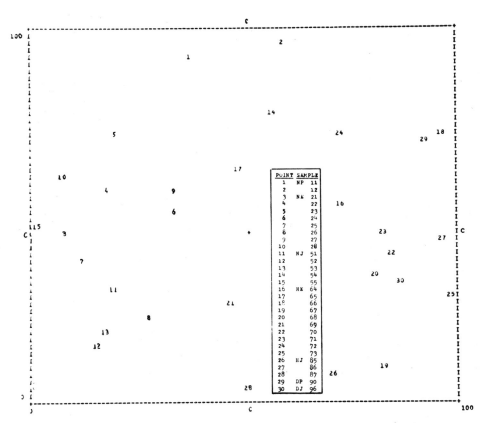

Figure 3.22: Scatter Diagram of Samples in the Reduced Space for *III*

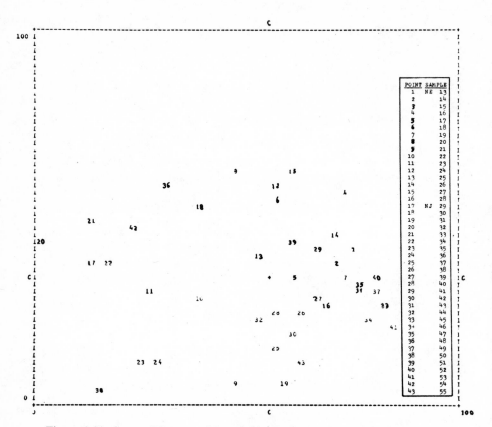

Figure 3.23: Scatter Diagram of Samples in the Reduced Space for *NE* and *NJ*

3.3.5.2.1. *Analysis of the Whole Book* (Figure 3.16). Three clusters are in full view:

— Cluster 1: nos. 1(*NP*), 4(*NP*), 8(*NP*), 12(*NP*), 29(*NJ*), 33(*NJ*) — with 8(*NP*) somewhat remote;

— Cluster 2: nos. 5(*NP*), 17(*NE*), 21(*NE*), 25(*NE*), 37(*NJ*), 41(*NJ*), 44(*NJ*), 48(*NJ*), 52(*NJ*), 55(*NJ*) — with 5(*NP*) and 48(*NJ*) somewhat remote;

— Cluster 3: the rest, consisting solely of *H* and *D* samples.

Three points immediately strike the eye:

(a) the unblurred line dividing *N* and *H* + *D*, (b) Cluster 1 being on the whole made up of *NP* and of *NJ* samples from Division *I*, and (c) Cluster 2 consisting principally of *NE* samples and of *NJ* samples not belonging to Division *I*.

3.3.5.2.2. *Analyses of N, H and D* (Figures 3.17-19). The total number of *N* samples is 55, of which only 37, semi-arbitrarily chosen to participate in this analysis (deliberately including all *NP* samples) appear in Figure 3.17. Four clusters are visible:

— Cluster 1: nos. 1(*NP*), 2(*NP*), 3(*NP*), 4(*NP*), 32-34(*NJ*), 54(*NJ*), with nos. 3(*NP*) and 32(*NJ*) slightly on the side;

— Cluster 2: nos. 6-12(*NP*);

— Cluster 3: nos. 5(*NP*), 24(*NE*), 27(*NE*), 31(*NJ*), 44(*NJ*), 53(*NJ*), 55(*NJ*), with no. 53(*NJ*) fairly remote;

— Cluster 4: nos. 15-18(*NE*), 25-26(*NE*), 28(*NE*), 30(*NJ*), 40-43(*NJ*), 51-52(*NJ*).

Cluster 1 stands plainly for Division *I* with no. 54(*NJ*) as a strange adjunct. Cluster 2 represents the highly homogeneous *NP* samples that do not belong to Division *I*, although, as might already be anticipated, no. 5 (*NP*) is absent. Cluster 3 is composed foremostly of *NE* samples and *NJ* samples from Division *III* — witness nos. 24, 27, 53, 55.

No distinct configuration is detectable within either *H* or *D*. All the same, some samples in the *H*-analysis lie exceedingly isolated from the centroid. They are (note that the distance unit is arbitrary because only comparison between distances is meaningful):

no. 65(*HE*) from chs. 41  :  distance from the centroid is 58
no. 87(*HJ*)   ”    ”  47-50:    ”     ”     ”     ”    ” 43
no. 71(*HE*)   ”    ”  44-45:    ”     ”     ”     ”    ” 39
no. 85(*HJ*)   ”    ”  37-38:    ”     ”     ”     ”    ” 39

The entire group thus consists of samples from Division *III*.

3.3.5.2.3.  *Analyses of I, II and III* (Figures 3.20-32).  All pertinent samples are included here.  Observing the configuration pattern of sample points in the reduced space, reveals major differences between the three Divisions and, therefore, confirms once more that the latter play a major role in the changeful language behavior of Genesis.

When one reviews, first, the *SSA1* analysis of Division *I*, definite clusters hardly meet the eye.  Still, the three samples of *NP,* by now familiar as typical, are grouped together again (nos. 1, 2 and 4), and so are those of *D* (nos. 88, 92, 93).  *NJ* and *HJ* samples, on the other hand, are scattered in all directions, thus demonstrating little homogeneity.  Strangely enough, *N* and *H+D* are for once not separated from each other.

In Division *II*, three distinct clusters appear:

— Cluster 1: nos. 6-10(*NP*), 50(*NJ*)

— Cluster 2: nos. 5(*NP*), 13-20(*NE*), 37-49(*NJ*), with nos. 5(*NP*), 15(*NE*), 16(*NE*), 18(*NE*), 20(*NE*), 48(*NJ*) somewhat remote.

— Cluster 3: nos. 56(*HP*), 58-63(*HE*), 75-84(*HJ*), 89(*DP*), 94-95(*DJ*), with nos. 81(*HJ*) and 89(*DP*) farther away.

This clustering suggests a strong distinction between the three groups *NP, NE + NJ* and *H + D,* yet none whatsoever between *E* and *J,* either in *N* or in *H + D.*  As so often before, *P* is different, but only within *N.*

Three cases are rather exceptional: nos. 50(*NJ*), since it is attached to the *NP* cluster; 5(*NP*), since it joins the *NE + NJ* group; and 20(*NE*), lying almost midway between the two groups *NP* and *NE + NJ.*  We recall, however, that samples adjacent to no. 20, namely, nos. 21 and 22, are among the last to amalgamate with the main cluster as discussed in Section 3.3.4.2., and that no. 5 was already located as deviant within its assumed subcategory.

Finally, Division *III.*  It is true that consecutive samples occupy common areas in the space diagram, Figure 3.22.  Yet a strong imagination is needed in order to notice any clustering configuration.  One which might be suggested by the scatter of points is:

— Cluster 1: nos. 21-28(*NE*), 51-53(*NJ*), 55(*NJ*)

— Cluster 2: nos. 54(*NJ*), 64-73(*HE*), 85-87(*HJ*), 90(*DP*), 96(*DJ*) with the following six at a distance: nos. 54(*NJ*), 65(*HE*), 67(*HE*), 69(*HE*), 85(*HJ*) and 87(*HJ*)

— Cluster 3: nos. 11-12(*NP*)

Thus, the very same discrimination as realized in the analysis of Division *II* is repeated in Division *III*, although the clustering effect is much less manifested here, as shown also by the alienation coefficients:

For Division *I* (16 samples):    .2276 (no. of iterations to reach
                                                     a solution — 11)

For Division *II* (48 samples):   .2397 (no. of iterations to reach
                                                     a solution — 6)

For Division *III* (30 samples):  .2861 (no. of iterations to reach
                                                     a solution — 6)

Recall that the smaller the coefficient, the better the Monotonicity Requirement is met.

3.3.5.2.4. *Analysis of NE + NJ* (Figure 3.23). With all respective samples included, *SSA1* yields two groups: one is a highly concentrated cluster, the samples of the other are in random disarray. The two groups are composed as follows:

Group 1:   no. 13(*NE*) from chs. 20-21
                no. 14(*NE*) from chs. 21-28
                no. 17(*NE*) from chs. 30
                no. 19(*NE*) from chs. 31-35
                nos. 25-26(*NE*) from chs. 42-45
                no. 28(*NE*) from chs. 48-50
                no. 31 (*NJ*) from chs. 3-4
                nos. 37-47(*NJ*) from chs. 13-32
                no. 49(*NJ*) from chs. 33-34
                nos. 51-53(*NJ*) from chs. 37-47
                no. 55(*NJ*) from chs. 47-50.

Group 2:   no. 15-16(*NE*) from chs. 28-30
                no. 18(*NE*) from chs. 30-31
                no. 20-24(*NE*) from chs. 35-42
                no. 27(*NE*) from chs. 45-48
                no. 29-30(*NJ*) from chs. 2-3
                no. 32-36(*NJ*) from chs. 4-13
                no. 48(*NJ*) from chs. 32-33
                no. 50(*NJ*) from chs. 34-37
                no. 54(*NJ*) from chs. 47.

A conclusion arrived at earlier (in Section 3.3.4.) is echoed here: while samples of subcategories *NE* and *NJ* form a single homogeneous cluster within Division *II*, the main body of Genesis (chs. 12-36), the greater part of "almost consecutive" outliers of subcategory *NJ* belong to Division *I*, and most "almost consecutive" ones of subcategory *NE* to Division *III*. Furthermore, whereas Group 1 comprises 80% of the samples belonging to

Division *II* (which constitute 67% of all samples of Group 1), Group 2 contains 65% of the samples belonging to either Division *I* or *III* (which constitute about 80% of all samples of Group 2).  Thus, the greater part of samples belonging to the heterogeneous Group 2 derive from Division *I* or *III*, while the greater part of samples belonging to Division *II* affiliate to the homogeneous Group 1, irrespective of their source documents.

It follows that the assumption that *E* is homogeneous and separate from *J* is rather dubious.  The high alienation coefficient achieved in this analysis (.3076) is another sign of the separation of *NE* from *NJ* being most unlikely.

**Resumé.** *SSA1* indicates that *N*-samples and *H* + *D* samples are dissimilar on the whole.  Also dissimilar are *NP,* on the one hand, and *NE* + *NJ,* on the other.  Clustering pattern varies from one Division to the other.  As far as these are concerned, compact clustering is evidenced in Division *II* where *NP, NE* + *NJ* and *H* + *D* are distinct.  No support can be found for separating *E* from *J*, either in their entirety or when subcategorized into *N, H* and *D*.  Several samples belonging to one Document seem rather related to another, and their original attributions should therefore be reconsidered.

## 3.3.6.  RELIABILITY ANALYSIS

3.3.6.1.  **Description.** The term "reliability" bears different meanings in different branches of science and technology.  Here we use it in the same sense as in the social sciences, where it refers to one of the basic requirements and a precondition for the application of any measurement device, be it a personality test, an attitude questionnaire or else.

To get an intuitive grasp of what reliability means in the social sciences, suppose that a test is being administered to a group of people, the purpose of which is to measure a certain personality trait, for instance, dogmatism. Were the test free of any measurement error, we would expect the score received by a testee to reflect the trait as revealed in his personality, and the variance of the actual scores to reflect the variance of the "true level" of dogmatism, as it prevails in the population.  If this expectation is fulfilled, the test may be called good because it produces scores representative of the "true" variation in dogmatism existing in the population.  Unfortunately, every test, like any measurement tool, incorporates an error component, so that the variance of the observed scores will be higher than the variance of the "true scores".

Put in algebraic terms, any measured score can be presented as a sum of two components, namely,

$$x_i = t_i + e_i$$

where

$x_i$ = the score actually obtained for testee $i$
$t_i$ = the "true score" of testee $i$
$e_i$ = the error deviation from the "true score" for testee $i$.

Assuming reasonably that the two components, $t_i$ and $e_i$, are statistically independent, it follows from a well-known theorem in statistics that the variance of $x$ will be

$$\sigma_x^2 = \sigma_t^2 + \sigma_e^2$$

where

$\sigma_x^2$ = the variance of the observed scores
$\sigma_t^2$ = the variance of the "true scores"
$\sigma_e^2$ = the variance of the errors.

Since a test may be termed good if it produces a small error variance, the natural index of the quality of a test is the ratio between the "true score" variance and the observed score variance,

$$\frac{\sigma_t^2}{\sigma_x^2} = \frac{\sigma_x^2 - \sigma_e^2}{\sigma_x^2}.$$

This ratio is defined as the reliability of a test and assumes its maximum value of 1.0 when no error component is present. The minimum value is of course zero.

How reliability should be assessed is another question. Since the "true scores" are never known, the exact value of the variances of $t$ and $e$, and hence of the reliability itself, can only be estimated. Various ways of doing so have been developed, the most common of which is Cronbach's index of reliability, known as Cronbach's Alpha.

Let a test be composed of $k$ measures (such as items, jugdments, opinions of experts and the like). Then, Cronbach's index of reliability is calculated according to the formula

$$\alpha = \frac{k}{k-1}\left[1 - \frac{\sum_{(i)} S_i^{\,2}}{S_T^2}\right] \quad \text{(Cronbach's Alpha)}$$

where

$$S_i^2 = \text{the observed variance of measure } i$$
$$S_T^2 = \text{the variance of the sum over the } k \text{ measures.}$$

Cronbach's Alpha is a standardized Alpha, $\alpha_s$, where the input of an item is expressed in terms of its standard deviation. Actually, this statistic utilizes the average correlation between items and is calculated by the formula

$$\alpha_S = \frac{k\,\bar{r}}{1 + (k-1)\,\bar{r}}$$

where

$$\bar{r} = \text{mean interitem correlation}$$

An alternative way to measure reliability is associated with a specific experimental procedure which results in the "test-retest reliability". According to this approach, the test is administered twice to the same group of people, with a time interval between the test and the retest. Fluctuations of scores are considered to constitute the error component of the measurement. It can be shown that the correlation between the scores of the first and those of the second administrations is in effect an estimate of reliability as defined above.

A third approach which avoids some of the imperfections inherent in the test-retest procedure produces still another kind of estimate — the Split-Half reliability. Here, the group of items comprised in the test is split into two halves, and a score is obtained for each. The correlation between scores of the two halves may then serve as a measure of reliability. Since reliability increases with the length of the test, and since the correlation is calculated with a number of pairs which is half the number of all test items, a correction is needed. This correction is accomplished with the "Spearman-Brown's Prophecy Formula".

$$\text{Spearman-Brown Reliability} = \frac{2r_{xy}}{1 + r_{xy}}$$

where $r_{xy}$, the "correlation between forms", is the correlation between the total score of items in the first half and that of the second half (henceforth denoted Part I and Part II, respectively).

Another, fourth, index which measures Split-Half reliability is "Guttman's Split-Half". Unlike the aforementioned one, this measure does not necessarily presume equal reliabilities or equal variances for the two halves.

All four measures appear in the output of the computer program used for Reliability Analysis and will be referred to when results are discussed.

Still, the connection between reliability as defined above and the problem which lies at the center of our research has not yet been clarified, and the reader is bound to wonder how Reliability Analysis can be employed in the present exploratory stage.

To gain a better understanding of how this is done here, let us take a closer look at what reliability of a test means. We recall that reliability actually measures the extent to which the "true score" is obtained by a test. Since a test comprises many items, each presumably measuring the same trait, we call it reliable if inter-item correlations are high. Put differently, consistency among items in the way they measure a trait gives an indication of the test's reliability. Now, measuring consistency of language behavior is precisely the task we are facing here. Asking whether two samples originated in the same population amounts, in the last analysis, to asking whether the language behavior of the two, as demonstrated in the pattern vector, is consistent.

The analogy with determining a test's reliability now becomes plain. In assessing the latter in psychology, a group of measures, i.e., the test items, is applied to a group of people, and consistency among measures is established through the reliability index. In our case, we are confronted with an analogous situation. A group, not of people, but of 43 variables, is measured by "items", that is, here, by 96 samples, and consistency, in other words, homogeneity, among samples is searched for. And just as low reliability of a psychological test is evidential of that not all items measure the same trait, so will here low reliability point to the fact that the source population of the samples is not homogeneous.

In accordance with this approach, where our samples turn into items, or "variables", of a test, and where our original variables turn into "cases" to which a test is administered, the transposed matrix — see Section 3.1.4.5. — is called for and Reliability Analysis applied to it. The output of this analysis includes not only overall reliability measures, but other statistics, helpful in detecting unreliable "items" (in our case, deviant samples), as well. Definitions of these statistics and of other terms appearing in the results (Section 3.3.6.2.) are:

— Scale: the group of "items" (samples) to be analysed;
— Statistics for Part I: statistics calculated separately for "items" (samples) included in the first half of the scale (the Split-Half procedure);
— Inter-item correlations: correlations between "items" (samples) calculated over all "cases" (variables) included in the analysis;
— Item-total correlation: the correlation between an "item" (sample) and the sum of all other "items" (samples);
— Correlation between forms: the correlation between the sum of the "items" (samples) in Part I and the sum of those in Part II (the Split-Half procedure).

Prior to discussing reliability statistics referring to entire scales, a detailed analysis of mutual correlational relationships between samples will be performed. Detection of either exceptionally high negative correlations, or of samples non-positively correlated with the majority of the remaining samples in the scale, may sort out deviants.

Thirteen scales are defined for this purpose and for the rest of the analyses, in accordance with the central, i.e. the Documentary, hypothesis, and with the Sort-of-Discourse hypothesis:

| Scale | $N$ | $H$ | $D$ | $P$ | $E$ | $J$ | $NP$ | $NE$ | $NJ$ | $HE$ | $HJ$ | $DP$ | $DJ$ |
|-------|-----|-----|-----|-----|-----|-----|------|------|------|------|------|------|------|
| no. of items (samples) | 55 | 32 | 9 | 17 | 33 | 46 | 12 | 16 | 27 | 16 | 14 | 3 | 5 |

where $HP$ and $DE$, because of an insufficient number of "items" (samples), are excluded. Deviant samples are included owing to the explorative nature of the present stage of the investigation.

3.3.6.2. **Results.**

3.3.6.2.1. *Analysis of Inter-Sample Correlations.* Summary statistics of the distribution of inter-sample correlations are featured in Table 3.31. (See Table 3.31, p. 163).

Mostly non-positively correlated samples, that is, those sharing strictly non-positive correlations with other samples, and for which the number of non-positive correlations is no less than that of the positive ones, are listed in Table 3.32. (See Table 3.32, p. 164).

What can be learned from the last two Tables is summarized as follows under (a), (b) and (c):

(a) $H$ and $D$ are more homogeneous than $N$, both in terms of the mean and of the dispersion of the inter-sample correlation. When, however, subcategories within $N$, $H$ and $D$ are examined separately, a more detailed picture obtains: the dispersion of the inter-sample correlation in $NJ$ and $NP$ is very high, while that in $NE$ resembles in magnitude the one in subcategories within $H$ and $D$. Thus, whereas $H$ and $D$ as well as $NE$ are of a comparatively similar degree of homogeneity, both $NJ$ and $NP$ show, as far as inter-sample correlation is concerned, a high measure of variation in intensity. The homogeneity of $NE$, here unexpectedly higher than that of $NJ$ and $NP$, may well be caused by $E$ being the only Document not represented in all three Divisions. Existence of separate clusters within $NJ$ and $NP$ is thus perhaps intimated. That such clusters are indeed there, is proved by Table 3.33 (See Table 3.33, p. 165).

Table 3.31: Means, Extreme Values and Variances of Inter-Sample Correlations

| Categ. or Subcateg. | No. of Samples | Mean Correlation | Minimum Correlation | Between nos. | Maximum Correlation | Between nos. | Variance |
|---|---|---|---|---|---|---|---|
| N | 55 | .0794 | -.5316 | (33,53) | .7831 | (1,4) | .046 |
| H | 32 | .1806 | -.3378 | (58,69) | .7194 | (59,70) | .037 |
| D | 9 | .1498 | -.2130 | (94,96) | .6140 | (91,95) | .038 |
| P | 17 | .1304 | -.5574 | (3,56) | .7831 | (1,4) | .064 |
| E | 33 | .0122 | -.6115 | (13,64) | .7194 | (59,70) | .059 |
| J | 46 | .0088 | -.5869 | (31,96) | .6793 | (79,83) | .056 |
| NP | 12 | .1989 | -.2612 | (2,9) | .7831 | (1,4) | .069 |
| NE | 16 | .1641 | -.3767 | (15,21) | .4958 | (14,25) | .033 |
| NJ | 27 | .1043 | -.5316 | (33,53) | .6739 | (43,49) | .060 |
| HP | 2 | -.2284 | — | — | — | — | — |
| HE | 16 | .1894 | -.3378 | (58,69) | .7194 | (59,70) | .036 |
| HJ | 14 | .2429 | -.0628 | (84,85) | .6793 | (79,83) | .028 |
| DP | 3 | .3562 | .1136 | (89,90) | .5271 | (88,90) | .037 |
| DE | 1 | — | — | — | — | — | — |
| DJ | 5 | .1360 | -.2130 | (94,96) | .3946 | (92,94) | .036 |

Remark: Pairs of samples between which the extreme correlation occurs are given in brackets.

Table 3.32: "Foreign" Samples, Mostly Non-Positively Correlated (n.p.c.)
with Other Samples of the Same Subcategory

| Sub-category | No. of Samples | P.c. of n.p.c. Samples | n.p.c. Samples |
|---|---|---|---|
| NP | 12 | 33 | 1(8), 2(8), 4(6), 5(10) |
| NE | 16 | 12 | 20(11), 21(10) |
| NJ | 27 | 33 | 29(20), 32(20), 33(17), 34(16), 35(18), 36(14), 48(18), 50(17), 54(15) |
| HE | 16 | 25 | 65(9), 67(9), 69(9), 72(8) |
| HJ | 14 | 0 | none |
| DP | 3 | 0 | none |
| DJ | 5 | 0 | none |

Remarks: (1) Digits in brackets are the count of samples with which the sample whose no. appears in front of the brackets, is non-positively correlated.

(2) Although not "mostly non-positively correlated", two *NJ*-samples still retain an exceptionally high rate of non-positive correlations with other samples in their subcategory: no. 30(10) and no. 31(7).

Table 3.33: Extremely Correlated Samples for Individual Scales

| Category or Subcat. | No. of Samples | Percentage of I.-S.N.C. | Samples Extremely Correlated with Total | |
|---|---|---|---|---|
| | | | Low ($r \leq .0$) | High ($r \geq .50$) |
| N | 55 | 37.4 | 1, 2, 4, 10, 20, 29, 30, 32-34, 48, 50, 53 | 28, 43 |
| H | 32 | 16.9 | 57, 69 | 58-61, 68, 70, 75, 76, 78, 82, 83 |
| D | 9 | 25.0 | — | — |
| P | 17 | 35.3 | 5, 56 | 3, 10-12 |
| E | 33 | 50.0 | 13-17, 19-23, 26, 28, 62, 64-67, 69, 73 | — |
| J | 46 | 49.6 | 29, 32-38, 41, 48, 50, 54, 55, 74, 77, 78, 80-82, 84-86, 92-96 | — |
| NP | 12 | 33.3 | 5 | 3, 10-12 |
| NE | 16 | 16.2 | 20 | 14, 25, 28 |
| NJ | 27 | 33.3 | 29, 32, 33, 35, 48, 50, 54 | 38, 39, 43 |
| HP | 2 | — | — | — |
| HE | 16 | 9.5 | — | 59-61, 68, 70 |
| HJ | 14 | 3.8 | — | 76, 79, 80, 82, 83 |
| DP | 3 | — | — | 88 |
| DE | 1 | — | — | — |
| DJ | 5 | 33.3 | 96 | — |

* I.-S.N.C. = Inter-Sample Negative Correlations.

The percentages of negative ones among the $n(n-1)/2$ correlations which may be calculated between $n$ items are given in the third column of this Table. When these percentages are arranged, per categories and subcategories, in increasing order, we obtain the following list:

| HJ | HE | NE | H | D | DJ | NP | NJ | P | N | J | E |
|----|----|----|----|----|----|----|----|----|----|----|----|
| 3.8 | 9.5 | 16.2 | 16.9 | 25.0 | 33.3 | 33.3 | 33.3 | 35.3 | 37.4 | 49.6 | 50.0 |

*NE* turns out here too as homogeneous as any other of the samples of *H* or *D*, which only reflects what has been said above.

(b)  In a comparison between *P, E* and *J, P*'s homogeneity is the highest: its mean inter-sample correlation is .13, while that of *E* and *J* only about .01. (Whether the difference is statistically significant is not dealt with here.)  The exclusion of *P*'s non-*N* samples would not meaningfully alter the rate of negative correlations.

(c)  The composition of samples mostly non-positively correlated with others in their subcategory — see Table 3.32 — defines as outcasts

in *NP*: the cluster of nos. 1, 2, 4 in addition to no. 5;
in *NE* and *HE*: mainly samples from chs. 35-44, most of which were already elsewhere detected as outliers;
in *NJ*: mostly samples from Division *I* (nos. 29, 32-26).

3.3.6.2.2.  *Analysis of Item-Total Correlations.*  The total of a scale is here defined as the sum of all "items" (samples) in a scale, and the total of an "item" is the sum of all 43 non-empty variables which comprises the pattern vector of the specific "item" (sample).  We specified in the two right-hand columns of Table 3.33 every sample whose correlation with the total of the scale is either very high (at least .50) or low (non-positive).  This total does not include the sample with which it is being correlated.

What information may be culled from this Table?

(a)  The most heterogeneous clusters are *E* and *J*.  They cannot possibly be considered homogeneous since nearly half the samples included in each are non-positively correlated with the total.

(b)  Regarding the proportion of samples positively correlated with the total, *H* is very homogeneous.  *D,* in contrast, enjoys neither extremely positive nor any non-positive correlations.  Of the three Sorts-of-Discourse, *N* is the least homogeneous.

(c)  The list of samples non-positively correlated with the total in each scale strengthens several of former observations.

For once, in *N,* the "alien" samples belong mainly to Division *I* (nos. 1, 2, 4, 29, 30, 32-34) or to Division *III* (nos. 10, 20, 50, 53).  The sole exception is no. 48(*NJ*).

Another instance is $E$, where the number of samples negatively correlated with the total is rather high. The only specious explanation of this fact is the existence of different Sorts-of-Discourse in this category. This interpretation gains support from the exceedingly small number of non-positively correlated samples found when $E$ is divided into its constituents $NE$ and $HE$.

A third observation confirmed here is $J$ being conspicuous by the absence, in the group of non-positively correlated samples, of nos. 39-40 and 42-47. These eight samples form a large portion of Division $II$, especially chs. 18-32. Dividing Genesis into the three Divisions as done at the outset of this study (Section 1.4.1.) is hereby vindicated again. It becomes even more borne out by examining the extremely correlated samples of subcategory $NJ$: only two (nos. 48, 50) of those non-positively correlated are from Division $II$, although this Division accounts for more than half of all $NJ$-samples. On the other hand, all samples very highly positively correlated with the total, either in $NJ$ or in $HJ$, are drawn from the same Division $II$.

Finally, the notorious sample no. 5($NP$): it is negatively correlated with all other $NP$-samples — correlations are not given in the Table — the only exception being no. 7($NP$), which no. 5 is slightly positively correlated with. How to solve this apparent riddle is discussed in Section 3.4.

3.3.6.2.3. *Reliability Measures.* In Table 3.34, reliability measures and various statistics are given which indicate homogeneity within subcategories. (See Table 3.34, p. 168).

Table 3.34 leads to a number of conclusions, some of which merely reiterate, and thus confirm, previous ones:

(a) $E$ and $J$ are highly heterogeneous, the very negative correlations between forms being probably the result of that Part I mostly consists of $N$-samples and Part II mostly of $H$- and $D$-samples. (The order of samples within each category follows Table 1.3.) This interpretation is sustained by the high $\alpha$ achieved within Parts I and II. The same picture emerges from observing the overall standard $\alpha$. On the other hand, the high value of the reliability statistics in $P$ is exceptional since it is so despite $P$ comprising here both $N$ and $H + D$. This finding, however, repeats results presented in Table 3.15 (Section 3.2.3.3.2.).

(b) Judged either by reliability measures or by the correlations between forms, $DJ$ is notably more heterogeneous than any other subcategory.

**Résumé.** $H$ is highly more homogeneous than $D$ and both are much more so than $N$. When, however, $N$ is subdivided per Documents, $NE$ is found more homogeneous than $NJ$ and $NP$. This is not featured either in $H$ or in $D$. Comparison of Documents shows that $P$'s homogeneity is higher than both $E$'s and $J$'s. Deletion of non-$N$ from $P$ does not substantially alter this. $E$ and $J$ are even more heterogeneous than $N$, $H$, or $D$. The effect of Divisions as proposed manifests itself in groups of outlying samples, with each group originating in only one Division. Sample no. 5($NP$) is alien within the $NP$-subcategory.

Table 3.34: Reliability Statistics

| Category or Subcateg. | No. of Samples | Overall Standardized α | Correlation betw. Forms | Split-Half Statistics | | | | Reliability | |
|---|---|---|---|---|---|---|---|---|---|
| | | | | Part I | | Part II | | Spearman-Brown's | Guttman's |
| | | | | α | No. of Items | α | No. of Items | | |
| N | 55 | .8259 | .4404 | .6757 | 28 | .7530 | 27 | .6115 | .6089 |
| H | 32 | .8758 | .6765 | .7646 | 16 | .8064 | 16 | .8070 | .8068 |
| D | 9 | .6132 | .3585 | .5550 | 5 | .3908 | 4 | .5299 | .5205 |
| P | 17 | .7182 | .4916 | .6611 | 9 | .5608 | 8 | .6598 | .6554 |
| E | 33 | .2906 | -.5924 | .6609 | 17 | .7864 | 16 | negative | negative |
| J | 46 | .2892 | -.5953 | .7226 | 23 | .7268 | 23 | negative | negative |
| NP | 12 | .7487 | .1849 | .7057 | 6 | .8084 | 6 | .3120 | .3031 |
| NE | 16 | .7585 | .3348 | .7020 | 8 | .6955 | 8 | .5017 | .5016 |
| NJ | 27 | .7588 | .4143 | .6248 | 14 | .7046 | 13 | .5861 | .5838 |
| HP | 2 | — | — | — | — | — | — | — | — |
| HE | 16 | .7890 | .6754 | .6853 | 8 | .5646 | 8 | .8062 | .7941 |
| HJ | 14 | .8179 | .6846 | .7204 | 7 | .6283 | 7 | .8127 | .8127 |
| DP | 3 | .6241 | .3887 | .5982 | 2 | — | 1 | .5800 | .4984 |
| DE | 1 | — | — | — | — | — | — | — | — |
| DJ | 5 | .4403 | .0769 | .5727 | 3 | .2936 | 2 | .1455 | .1322 |

## 3.3.7. FACTOR ANALYSIS (Q-TECHNIQUE)

3.3.7.1. **Description.** The method of Factor Analysis has already been described in Section 3.2.3.2.1. so that a certain familiarity with it may be presupposed here. Yet its objective at this juncture is not the same. While in the foregoing application basic factors, governing the behavior of linguistic variables, were searched for, we pursue now an explorative goal, namely: to create homogeneous clusters of samples. For this, we summon Factor Analysis to our aid in what is known as the *Q*-mode. Based on correlational analysis, it tries to cluster together samples that are highly positively correlated. Factors, this time, are therefore interpreted as indicatory of existence of sample clusters. Consequently, outstanding loads, shared in a single factor by a group of "variables" (samples), are investigated for any meaning that may possibly be attached to the emergent cluster. With that end in our mind, we again make use of the transposed matrix, where samples are turned into "variables", and *vice versa*.

Six separate analyses are performed on *N, H, D, P, E,* and *J.* Each is run twice: once with orthogonal rotation, utilizing Varimax technique, and another time with oblique (non-orthogonal) rotation. Since descriptive characteristics only are sought here, the deviant samples — see Section 3.1.4.3. for their definition — were included. Only the first two factors derived in the analysis will be considered.

3.3.7.2. **Results.** Table 3.35 presents exceptional "variables" (samples), the loads of which are either zero or strictly negative (for the meaning of the term "load" see Section 3.2.3.2.2.). Table 3.36 presents exceptional "variables" (samples) in the oblique rotation, the correlations of which with the factor are either zero or strictly negative. (See Tables 3.35, 3.36, pp. 170-71).

Observing both Tables, the cluster pattern revealed is quite similar to that in Section 3.3.5., which is little wonder as both techniques are based on correlational analysis. What the various factors stand for will be discussed below, separately for *N, H, D,* and *P, E, J.*

Scatter diagrams of the samples in the factor space (derived from Varimax rotation), for each of the analyses, are shown in Figures 3.24 through 3.29. (See Figures 3.24-3.29, pp. 172-77).

3.3.7.2.1. *Analyses of N, H, D.* (Figures 3.24-3.26). The first factor in *N* (Table 3.35), in both modes of rotation, essentially excludes most *NP*-samples as well as those *NJ*-samples that stem from Division *I,* since they have zero or negative loads here. It therefore stands for *NE + NJ* in Divisions *II* and *III.* A noteworthy detail is that sample no. 5 (*NP*), which has already so many times before proved to stand out of *P,* also loads high on this factor.

The meaning of the second factor is difficult to interpret from the reject samples, i.e., those of low loads. However, examining the highest positive loads (not given here) leaves no doubt that this factor stands for samples nos. 6-12, the entire *NP*-subcategory in Divisions *II* and *III.* Interestingly

Table 3.35: Samples with Non-Positive Loads Derived from Factor Analysis
with Orthogonal (Varimax) and Oblique Rotations

| Categ-ory | Factor | P.c. of Explained Variation | Method of Rotation | |
|---|---|---|---|---|
| | | | Orthogonal (Varimax) | Oblique |
| N | 1st | 17.5 | nos. 1-4, 7-12, 20, 29, 32-36, 50, 54 | nos. 1-4, 7-12, 20, 29, 32-36, 50, 54 |
| | 2nd | 9.7 | » 1, 2, 4, 5, 14-19, 24-27, 29, 30, 34, 39-43, 45-49, 51-54 | » 1, 2, 4, 5, 14-19, 24-27, 29, 30, 33, 34, 39-43, 45-49, 51-54 |
| H | 1st | 24.8 | » 57, 64, 65, 69, 77, 78, 81 | » 51, 64, 65, 69, 77, 78, 87 |
| | 2nd | 8.7 | » 57, 62, 64-66, 71-73, 84 | » 56, 58, 63, 66, 72, 74, 79, 83, 87 |
| D | 1st | 26.0 | » 96, 96 | » 91, 94-96 |
| | 2nd | 20.0 | » 88, 89, 92 | » 88-91, 93, 95, 96 |
| P | 1st | 25.2 | » 1, 2, 4, 5, 56, 88-90 | » 1, 2, 5, 56, 88-90 |
| | 2nd | 19.9 | » 5-9, 11, 12, 56, 57 | » 6-9, 11, 12, 56, 57 |
| E | 1st | 21.4 | » 13, 14, 16-28, 67, 69 | » 13, 14, 16-28, 67, 69 |
| | 2nd | 10.5 | » 20-22, 27, 58-73, 91 | » 14-18, 21-28, 59-61, 64, 65, 68-72 |
| J | 1st | 18.3 | » 29, 30, 32-37, 48, 50, 54, 74-87, 92-96 | » 29, 30, 32-36, 48, 50, 54, 74-87, 92-96 |
| | 2nd | 12.4 | » 29-51, 53-55, 77, 92-94 | » 29-51, 53-55, 77, 92-94 |

Table 3.36: Non-Positive Correlations between Factors Derived by Factor Analysis and Individual Samples (by Oblique Rotation)

| Category | Factor | Correlations |
|---|---|---|
| N | 1st | nos. 1-4, 7-12, 20, 29, 32-36, 50, 54 |
|   | 2nd | » 1, 2, 4, 5, 14-19, 24-27, 30, 34, 39-43, 45-49, 51-54 |
| H | 1st | » 69 |
|   | 2nd | — |
| D | 1st | » 95, 96 |
|   | 2nd | » 88, 90, 96 |
| P | 1st | » 1, 2, 4, 5, 56, 88-90 |
|   | 2nd | » 5-9, 11, 12, 56, 57 (and 10, positive, but very low) |
| E | 1st | » 13, 14, 16-28, 67, 69 |
|   | 2nd | » 14-18, 21-28, 59-61, 64, 65, 68-72 |
| J | 1st | » 29, 30, 32-36, 48, 50, 54, 74-87, 92-96 |
|   | 2nd | » 29-51, 53-55, 77, 92-94 |

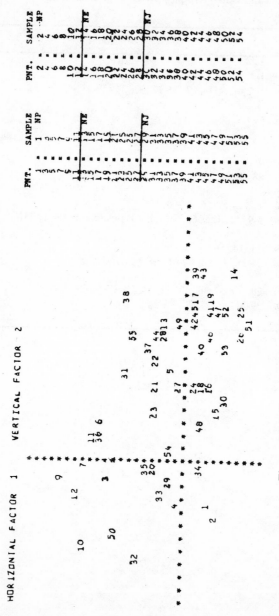

Figure 3.24: Scatter Diagram of *N*-Samples in the Factor Space

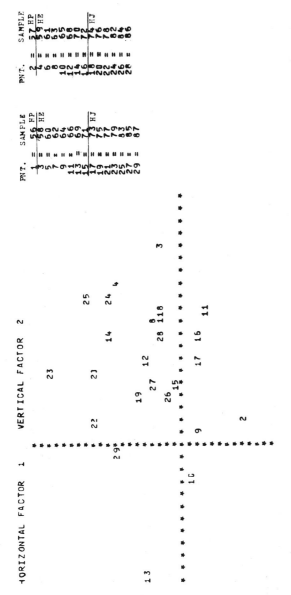

Figure 3.25: Scatter Diagram of *H*-Samples in the Factor Space

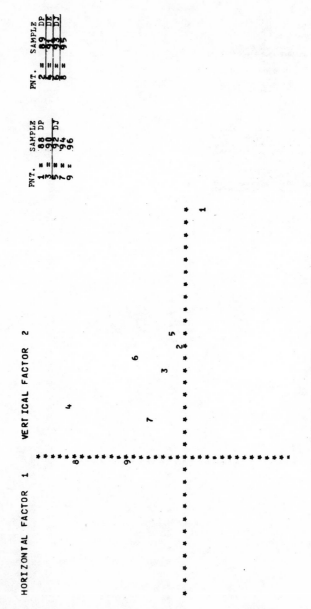

Figure 3.26: Scatter Diagram of *D*-Samples in the Factor Space

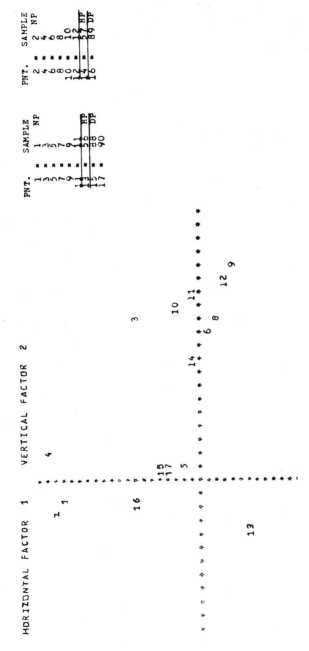

Figure 3.27: Scatter Diagram of *P*-Samples in the Factor Space

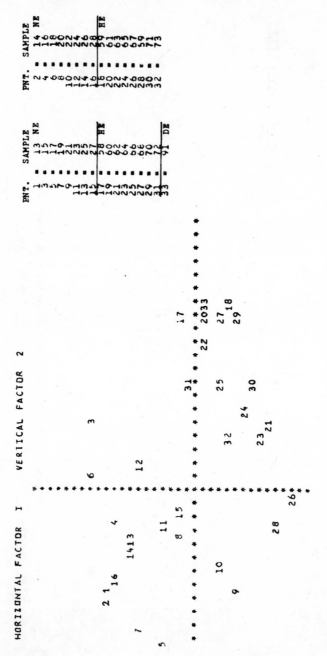

Figure 3.28: Scatter Diagram of *E*-Samples in the Factor Space

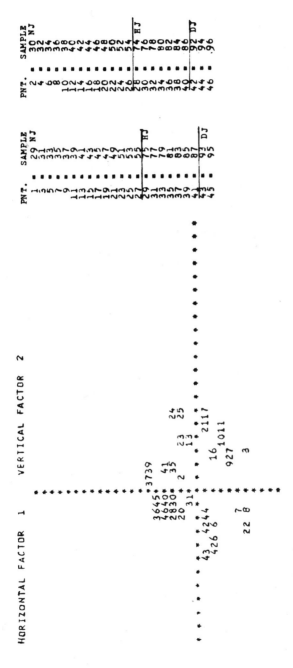

Figure 3.29: Scatter Diagram of *J*-Samples in the Factor Space

enough, sample no. 3 (*NP, I*) also loads high on this factor, thus indicating its affiliation to nos. 6-12. This fact connects nicely with a previous experience of ours: it is no. 3 (*NP*) which is missing in the cluster formed by nos. 1, 2, 4 (all *NP*) in Figure 3.11.

Regarding *H* (Figure 3.25), the first factor excludes samples nos. 57(*HP*) 64-65(*HE*), 69(*HE*), 77-78(*HJ*) and 87(*HJ*). The second excludes the only two *HP*-samples (nos. 56, 57), nine of the sixteen *HE*-samples (nos. 58, 62-66, 71-73) and four of the fourteen *HJ*-samples (nos. 74, 79, 83, 84). No plausible interpretation, in terms of our three hypotheses, can be offered for this list.

In *D* (Figure 3.26), the first factor does not include *DE*- and *DJ*-samples from Divisions *II* and *III*, and the second essentially excludes all *D*-samples except nos. 92(*DJ*) and 94(*DJ*). What this means we again feel unable to fathom. Note that Table 3.35 and the respective Figures are complementary in the preceding and following interpretations.

3.3.7.2.2. *Analyses of P, E, J* (Figures 3.27 – 3.29). Taking *E* first (Figure 3.28), its first factor essentially excludes *NE*-samples, and thus stands for *H + D*. The other excludes, in the Varimax rotation, all non-*NE*-samples, with nos. 20-22 and 27 as exceptions. Hence, it stands for *NE*. But when coefficients of the initial Factor Matrix, derived by the method of "principal axis factoring with iterations" prior to any rotation, are studied, the highest loads to appear for the second factor, are those of samples nos. 13-20 (except 17), 58, 63, 73 and 91. Evidently, this factor stands for *NE* in Division *II* alone, and it is only after employing Varimax rotation that the rest of *NE*-samples, namely those of Division *III*, are here included. This observation is no more than a repetition of an earlier one where the distinction between *NE + NJ* and *H + D* came out sharper in Division *II* than in Division *III* (see the *SSA1* analysis of Division *II* as compared with Division *III* in section 3.3.5.2.3.).

In the oblique rotation, the second factor loads high only on samples nos. 13, 20, 58, 62, 63, 67, 73, which is once more hard to understand. Note, however, that both samples nos. 13 and 58 derive from chs. 20-21, and that the three samples nos. 20, 62, 63 from chs. 31-39.

The first factor in *J* (Figure 3.29) essentially excludes *NJ*-samples of Division *I* and all *H + D*-samples. By way of elimination, it therefore stands for *NJ*-samples not deriving from Division *I*.

*J*'s second factor excludes all *NJ*-samples except no. 52, and *DJ*-samples from Division *I* and *II* up to ch. 18, so that it represents *H + D*-samples to the exclusion of the first three *DJ*-samples (nos. 92-94). We are impressed, incidentally, by one circumstance: whereas there is no distinction in *H* between Division *I* and *II*, there is a break around ch. 18 that divorces nos. 92-94 (*DJ*) from nos. 95-96 (*DJ*).

Focusing now on *P* (Figure 3.27), we find its first factor to exclude non-*NP*-samples, with no. 57(*HP*) as an exception, and *NP*-samples from Division *I*, except, again, no. 3(*NP*). It stands, then, for *NP*-samples from Division *II* and *III*.

The second factor of *P* excludes all *HP*-samples, and *NP*-samples not derived from Division *I*. It therefore stands for *NP*-samples from this Division and for *DP*-samples. Admittedly, the combination of *NP*-samples from Division *I* and *DP*-samples in one factor is puzzling and needs some clarification. A possible one will be proposed in Section 3.4. Note that a similar phenomenon occurred in *J*: there, *DJ*-samples from Division *I* were excluded from the second factor together with *NJ*-samples.

In conclusion, it is important to take notice of one eventuality: the percentage of explained variation, yielded by the first two derived factors, is by one half higher in *P* (45.1 p.c.) than in *E* (31.9 p.c.) and *J* (30.7 p.c.). With mounting frequency, we encounter *P* as a *corpus* apparently apart and of its own unique language behavior.

**Résumé.** Interpretation of the derived factors reveals the influence of the Divisions' character in every analysis. Within *N*, *NP* is separated from NE + NJ in Division *II* and *III*, but not in Division *I*, Factors derived in the *H*- and *D* analyses are not interpretable. In *E*, the separation between *N* and *H* + *D* is prominent, whereas it is much weaker between *NE*-samples from Division *II* and *III* remaining *E*-samples. Analysis of *J* results in a distinction between *N* from Divisions *II* and *III* and *H* + *D*. Thus, *NJ*-samples drawn from Division *I* differ from all other *NJ*-samples. As to *P*, *NP* in Divisions *II* + *III* is dissimilar to *NP* in Division *I* and to *DP*-samples.

## 3.4. Conclusions

With all our statistical analyses and their results put forward, it remains for us to sum up. Yet before doing so, we wish to anticipate one point of criticism which may be voiced by statisticians and reply to it.

## 3.4.1. A POSSIBLE OBJECTION

The main objection, we can foresee, will be directed against the relatively low ratio of the number of samples ("observations") to the number of variables used in the multivariate analyses, especially in the Discriminant Analysis.

The issue of determining the requisite number of observations, given maximum tolerated error probabilities (misclassification error probability or type II error probability) is a source of much confusion in applied statistics. As realized in Discriminant Analysis in particular, the crux of the problem lies in the following dilemma: given fixed training data size, there ensues a trade-off between the information added by one more dimension and the loss in accuracy of the estimates of the joint conditional densities due to the added number of "parameters" that have to be estimated.[13] Put in different terms:

---

[13] See J. W. Van Ness and C. Simpson, "On the Effects of Dimension in Discriminant Analysis", *Technometrics* 18 (1976), 21, 175-87.

the pooled estimate of the covariance matrix used by the Discriminant Analysis algorithm is dependent on both the sample size and the number of dimensions (variables) included in the Discriminant Function. As the latter number grows in relation to sample size, the sample covariance matrices move toward singularity. Consequently, the Discriminant Analysis algorithm tends to deteriorate as has been convincingly shown by Van Ness and Simpson.[14] To quote them, there are to date "very few guidelines as to how many dimensions one should use", and to quote another authority, "training sample size of, say, 10-40 are not unusual with a number of variables ranging from 10 to 200".[15]

Thus, though several "rules of thumb" have been proposed, the theoretical foundations for obtaining a proper sample size in the area of multivariate analysis are still poor and for most and widely used statistical methods no explicit way of determining sample size exist to date. A further complication is introduced by the fact that even determining the significance of results is very often based on statistics whose distribution, under the null hypothesis, is only asymptotically known (for example, the $\chi^2$-statistic employed in Discriminant Analysis). Thus, a minimal number of observations is needed to guarantee a good approximation of the actual significance of results. Yet, the functional dependence of the error of this approximation on the number of observations is unknown in most multivariate techniques.

We tried to overcome this obstacle in four ways.

Firstly, adopting a very conservative attitude we never rejected the null hypothesis of homogeneity unless the significance level achieved was very low. We thus took good care against committing an error of specifying results as significant lest this be caused by the use of statistics associated with distributions whose exact structure is unknown.

Secondly, by utilizing a wide array of techniques of univariate and multivariate analyses, several of which are statistically relatively independent, we made it our rule not to reject the null hypothesis of homogeneity unless some acceptable degree of agreement was reached between these techniques. Consequently, the actual overall type I error probability was considerably diminished. The consistency, which actually emerged in such varied techniques with regard to the research hypotheses, adds force to the conclusions detailed in Section 3.4.6.

Thirdly, with respect to Discriminant Analysis, which yields such a large portion of the evidence on which our conclusions rest, we took a most judicious stand concerning the number of variables allowed into the Discriminant Function. The authorities quoted above[16] have demonstrated

---

[14] See the proceding note.

[15] J. W. Van Ness, "On the Effects of Dimension in Discriminant Analysis for Unequal Covariance Populations", *Technometrics* 21 (1979), 1, 119-27.

[16] See the preceding note.

for their specific case that increasing the number of variables beyond five results in a sharp decrease of the average percentage of correct classifications both for linear and quadratic Discriminant Analyses. After taking much counsel we therefore decided not to allow more than five variables to be employed in the Stepwise Discriminant Analysis algorithm used. In view of the routine use of Discriminant Analysis as revealed in the second of the aforementioned quotations our policy may be seen as a sufficiently sound safeguard against the hazards referred to in the second paragraph of this Section.[17]

Finally, as one more cautionary device to compensate for the low number of samples ('observations') available, we embarked, after statistically evaluating the research hypotheses, upon an exploratory course. It was intended to raise a possible new set of hypotheses to follow from the natural grouping of samples as obtained through various descriptive measures or clustering techniques. What was exposed to view by them will be summarized in Section 3.4.4. This fourth precaution, while essentially not resulting in any new hypotheses, enhances the credibility of the findings flowing from statistical analyses of the research hypotheses.

Hoping to have refuted one serious objection which may be raised by statisticians and gained their approval, albeit *ex post factum,* of what we have done, we now wish to summarize this Part of the present volume for the benefit of Bible scholars. Unaccustomed to statistical procedures and confused — by ourselves, to be sure — by the wealth of material submitted to them, they, we are afraid, may be at pain to see the wood for the trees.

## 3.4.2. PRELIMINARY

Initially, we based our work on one putative claim: that our criteria set describes the language behavior of the Biblical text well enough to create 'families' of cognate text samples and to single out 'loners' from these 'families', in other words, borrowing a metaphor from the Jacob's Cycle, to separate the black lambs and spotted goats from the white flock. This claim was held up by the fact that our criteria were capable of drawing a sharp line between the words of the narrator ($N$) and those of the speakers, namely human ($H$) and Divine ($D$) direct speech, although this intensity of differentiation was not expected by us in the first place.

We approached the problem of the book's unity in two stages, Phases I and II. Phase I probed the book *ex hypothesi,* that is, specifically, following Wellhausen's *Quellenscheidung* in Genesis into three Documents, namely *J,* the Jahwist, *E,* the Elohist, and *P,* the Priestly Writer. In the course of Phase I, incidental, but ever growing attention had to be paid to the differences between

---

[17] J. D. F. Habbema and J. Hermans, "Selection of Variables in Discriminant Analysis by *F*-statistics and Error Rate", *Technometrics* 19 (1977), 3, 487-93.

the three Sorts-of-Discourse (*N, H, D*) and between the three Divisions, viz. *I* (chs. 2-11), *II* (chs. 12-36) and *III* (chs. 37-50). Our second approach, in Phase II, was inductive. We disregarded here such preconceived notions as those tested in Phase I, and aimed, in their stead, at detecting groups of samples which were akin to each other by virtue of their common linguistic properties. What we hoped for was that the results of both Phases would ultimately confirm each other, and it is with much content that we note that this hope was fulfilled.

### 3.4.3.  PHASE I

In Phase I, essentially two procedures were followed: Univariate Analysis of Variance (ANOVA) of the One-Way and the Two-Way kinds and Multivariate Analysis of Variance (MANOVA), including Factor and Discriminant Analyses. Each of these produced the same verdict: Genesis does indeed exhibit a diversified language behavior in all three respects, Documents, Sorts-of-Discourse and Divisions alike, in each, though, to a varying degree of intensity.

Since the main point at issue is the Documentary Hypothesis, let us begin with *J, E* and *P*. ANOVA found *J* and *E* indistinguishable from each other, but *P* strikingly unlike either, and, moreover, *NP* heterogeneous — most unlike its corresponding subcategories *NJ* and *NE*. MANOVA demonstrated the very same pattern of differences between Documents. More subtle insight was offered by Discriminant Analysis. It showed *P* to be relatively uniform across Sorts-of-Discourse — only quite a small number of variables set *NP* apart from *HP* and *DP*. It also emerged that *P* significantly differs in each of these from their parallel subcategories in *J* (*NJ, HJ, DJ*) and *E* (*NE, HE, DE*). So dissimilar was *P* to *J* and *E* that very rarely was a *J*-sample or an *E*-sample misclassified as *P*'s. At the same time, *J*- and *E*-samples were often confused with each other with regard to their hypothesized Documentary origin. Moreover, no one among 39 variables differentiated between *J* and *E* at the 0.01 level of significance. *P*, then, appeared to be an independent source while *J* and *E* bore so close a resemblance to each other that it would be thoroughly unfounded to distinguish between the two, were it not for one fact: a certain distinctness manifested itself between *NJ* and *NE*.

Ignoring this for a while, should then not Wellhausen's tripartition of Genesis into *J, E* and *P* be discarded in favor of a bipartition of the book into *P* and the rest? We do not think so and believe the latter to be unwarranted for reasons to be stated later.

But let us concern ourselves first with the just mentioned distinctness between *NJ* and *NE*. Too much weight need not be accorded to it. *NE* begins to play a substantial part no earlier than at the mid-point of Genesis and a predominant one from ch. 37 onward, that is, where the narrator starts to deal with Jacob's old age and then proceeds to tell the detailed life story of

Jacob's son, Joseph. In contrast, most of *NJ* stems from the early chapters, i.e., the tales of Paradise, the Flood, the Tower, Abraham and the young Jacob. Herein, Abraham is depicted (unlike Jacob, the Proto-Jew) in universal and almost monumental terms. Thus, *NE* takes over when *NJ* fades out and precisely where a break occurs in the treatment of the central figures. This interpretation receives support from the mild, yet still significant interaction effect between Divisions and Documents disclosed by Analysis of Variance (Table 3.8). Little wonder, then, that *NJ* is not uniform with *NE*, and there is no reason why the two should be ascribed to two different hands. To every intent, therefore, *J* and *E* seem to be one.

Carrying this reasoning further, one may add that it explains also the seemingly singular language behavior of *P*. This Document consists, in its greater part, of *N*-portions, and relates in the main genealogies where comparatively few words only are uttered. A glance at Table 1.3 is enough to confirm this assertion: *HP* is represented by no more than two samples (360 words), *DP* by three (611 words), but *NP* by twelve (2408 words). This last subcategory (*NP*) is supplied to a considerable extent by chs. 5, 10, 11, 35 and 36, all lists of rather obscure people, clans and foreign kings. If such is the state of affairs, then the unique character of *P* must be due to the lack of balance in subject matter between what Documentarians ascribe to the Priestly Writer and what they credit to the Jahwist or the Elohist. A comparison between texts makes sense only on the condition of *ceteris paribus* (see Section 1.1.6.1. end) which obviously is not the case here. In sum, thus far the Documentary Hypothesis is not borne out.

What of the Sort-of-Discourse hypothesis?

*N* was found lacking the slightest trace of similitude to *H* and *D* in whatever Document, with no misclassification at all of *N*-samples into the categories *H* and *D* nor *vice versa*, and with as many as 17 out of 39 variables presenting themselves as powerful discriminants (at the 0.01 level of significance!) between *N* and *H* + *D*. When *N* was broken down into subcategories per Documents, and when these were tested for inner homogeneity, *NJ* turned out highly homogeneous, *NE* moderately so, and *NP* highly non-homogeneous. In inter-subcategory comparisons between the three, *NP* came out totally different from either *NJ* or *NE* while these two proved to be of so great a mutual affinity that the program misclassified half the *NE*-samples into *NJ*. It is only in the first eleven chapters that *NJ* seems somewhat related to *NP* — and how could it be otherwise when there alone *P* is a storyteller proper (except for ch. 23)?

*H* and *D* were found indistinguishable by both ANOVA and MANOVA. In the breakdown of *H* into *HJ, HE* and *HP*, each emerged highly homogeneous within itself, with *HJ* and *HE* so greatly alike that two thirds of all *HJ*-samples were mistaken by the program for *HE*, but none of either subcategory for *HP*. This last phenomenon, however, must again not be interpreted as a sign of *P* being a source in itself, because what has been argued before about *P* in general applies here, too.

The main thrust of our study of the Sort-of-Discourse hypothesis is that the narrator behaves linguistically in a significantly different fashion from the speakers. This statement will sound like a truism to Discourse analysts. But the fact itself, it seems, has been given too little attention by Scriptural analysts, and that it must of necessity affect the final answer to the question of whether the Documentary Hypothesis is valid or not goes without question.

To what degree do the distinctive traits of the three Divisions *I, II* and *III* bear upon our judgment vis-à-vis the Documentary Hypothesis?

Let us first recall that splitting Genesis into three Divisions (see Section 1.4.1.) seemed justified, though not statistically tested, by Figure 3.1 which manifested two consecutive cycles of *E, J* and *P*. Upon closer examination, all samples of the first cycle are found to belong to, and to be about equally divided between, Divisions *II* and *III*. As regards the second cycle three quarters of its samples derive from Divisions *I* and *II*, again about equally divided between the two.

Coming now to statistical analysis proper, both ANOVA and MANOVA brought to light the fact that Division *I* comported itself linguistically unlike Divisions *II* and *III*, but MANOVA provided once again more detailed information: six among the 39 variables distinguished between *I* and *II + III* at the 0.01 and another ten at the 0.10 level of significance, whereas only two variables did so between *II* and *III* at the stricter, and nine more at the milder level of significance. Discriminant Analysis corroborated these results: it definitely set apart *I* from *II* and *III*, but failed to demarcate *II* from *III*. Not one sample of *I* was misclassified into *III* or *vice versa* and by far more misclassifications occurred between *II* and *III* than between *I* and *II*.

The implications of all this with regard to the Documentary Hypothesis are doubtless momentous. It assigns all of *I* to *J* or *P* and most of *III* to *E*. In *II*, the Elohist is said to make his first literary appearance as late as ch. 20 and from there on to have a roughly equal share in *II* with the Jahwist. Yet all this is hardly tenable now.

We have spoken of the distinctive traits of the three Divisions. What we referred to was that typology characterizes Division *I*, that there is a gradually increasing individuation in Division *II* and true life portraiture in Division *III*. Put differently, content and its presentation range from the quasi-mythical to the semi-heroic to the fully human. Now, these three literary techniques, slowly and almost unperceptively shading one into the other, cut across the Documents and greatly obliterate their alleged pecularities. That literary treatment varies from the beginning of Genesis to its end has of course been recognized by practically all Biblical scholars, but the preoccupation of many among them with the quest for marks of Documents must be the reason why they have overlooked or underrated the transition from one *genre* to another at least as an allied factor in the variation of what they prefer to call style. This oversight leads inevitably to identification of a certain "style" with a certain author or Document.


## 3.4.4.  PHASE II

In this Phase, we were not concerned with the Documentary or any other hypothesis, as already stated in Section 3.4.1.  Our aim was here to examine and process text samples in such a way as to let them arrange themselves in affinity groups as if of their own and as if neither champions nor challengers of Wellhausen had ever existed.  Yet for this very reason, the task of formulating concise and definite, let alone definitive, conclusions is so difficult.  In Phase I, the three investigated dimensions, i.e. (*J, E, P*), (*N, H, D*) and (*I, II, III*), serve as a sort of compass for reaching one crucial *locus* after the other.  In Phase II, not without reason titled "exploratory", we enter a jungle of some one hundred text samples and try to find our way through it.

Five analyses, each employing a number of modes, were administered: Analysis of Pattern Vector Distribution, Cluster Analysis, Smallest Space Analysis, Reliability Analysis and Factor Analysis.  Whichever was used, the results were unequivocal as attested to in the respective resumés.  They are briefly summed up at the end of Section 3.4.6 so that a treatment of each analysis seems superfluous here, although each may have added something new to the overall picture.  We shall therefore deal in this summary only with the first two of the above five analyses as they are the most easily comprehensible.

Analysis of Pattern Vector Distribution elicited which samples were so "mal-behaved" as to be labelled deviant in relation to the general language habits of Genesis. A full ten of the twelve *NP*-samples fell into this class. One exception was sample no. 5, most noteworthy as we shall see; the other was no. 8, of lesser interest since it is spread over eleven chapters and thus rather incoherent.  This deviant nature of *NP* has already been diagnosed and explained in Phase I.  A certain deviation also emerged in *NJ* of Division *I* — hardly a surprise because *NJ(I)* was previously found much like *NP*.

For non-statisticians, it is probably Cluster Analysis that is most revealing.  Its procedure is not difficult to follow and its computer output easy to survey at one single look and quite as easy to interpret.  Hence, we shall dwell upon it at some length.

Cluster Analysis resulted in the 96 samples forming — autonomously, so to say — three well-defined clusters in accordance with their affinity to each other in language behavior.

The first cluster comprised no more than the three *NP*-samples nos. 1, 2 and 4 — see Figure 3.12 — which have absolutely nothing in common with other *NP*-samples or with all the remaining ones.  This looks most intriguing until the three are located in the book.  Nos. 1 and 2 are supplied mainly by ch. 5, a list of names, ages and dates of birth of the "Ten Generations from Adam to Noah", and no. 4 is identical with ch. 11, another list of the same sort, this time of the "Ten Generations from Noah to Abraham" — surely two text blocks most unlike any other in Genesis. So far, so good, but, one may ask, why is it then that the program did not let no. 10(*NP*), i.e., ch. 36, join this cluster when this chapter, too, is a genealogy followed by a series of names of kings? Ch. 36, to venture a guess, is in reality not quite as similar to chs. 5 and 11 as all that, inasmuch as it lists names, but no ages or dates, possibly enough to effect a change in the realizations of several variables. Incidentally, no. 10 is in a sense also isolate: it is the very last to amalgamate with all other samples in Figure 3.11.

The singularity of the first cluster, i.e., samples nos. 1, 2 and 4, is therefore specious. But why is no. 3(*NP*) absent from this otherwise coherent cluster? Its provenance is the Flood Story, generally viewed as a mixture of *P*- and *J*-blocks, the latter providing sample no. 35(*NJ*). Hence, since plainly different in content from nos. 1, 2 and 4, no. 3 has no place in the first cluster. Tellingly, Figure 3.11 shows that the proximity between samples nos. 3(*NP*) and 35(*NJ*) is medium and of the same order of magnitude as that between nos. 39 and 41, two almost adjacent samples and, what is more, said to be the work of one and the same author, namely the Jahwist.

The second cluster encompasses most of the remaining *N*-samples outside *P*. What is remarkable from our point of view is that *NJ* and *NE* alternate in the sequence of their accession to the cluster as if they were written by the same hand; that here and there an *NJ*- and an *NE*-sample, drawn from the same text segment, follow each other consecutively in the cluster, yet another sign of how much the influence of Documentary origin is neutralized; and finally that, with one exception among 26 cases, the entire second cluster includes only samples from Divisions *II* and *III*, as if this twofold origin in the book's structure did not matter in the least. It follows that the surmised difference between a Jahwist and an Elohist does not govern the conglomeration of samples at all, but that differences between Sorts-of-Discourse and between Divisions, especially *I* vs. *II* + *III*, are decisive in the grouping process.

We turn now to the third cluster. It comprehends all *H*- and *D* samples, regardless of whether they come from *J* or *E*. The lonely two *HP*- and three *DP*-samples are interspersed among them. Why there are a few *N*-samples also scattered in Cluster 3 is too wide a subject to be discussed here, but, it is evident, sample clustering is once more dominated by Sorts-of-Discourse and Divisions and not by Documents. Figure 3.11 underscores this contention: the two samples to converge first, before all the other ninety-four do, in the amalgamation process of almost 100 steps are one of *HJ* and one of *HE*. This adds force — if it were still needed — to the impression that the Jahwist and the Elohist were each other's *alter ego*.

Finally, a few words about the remaining three analyses. The eight rather self-explanatory Figures 3.16-23 which demonstrate the results of Smallest Space Analysis uphold previous observations, time and time again: *N* is opposed to *H* + *D*, *NP* to *NJ* + *NE*, and *J* equals *E*. Reliability Analysis provides another check as does Factor Analysis, except that it also underlines the juxtaposition of Division *I* against Divisions *II* and *III*. This outcome matches that of MANOVA and Discriminant Analysis in Phase I. With respect to Factor Analysis, though, a clarification of the second factor of the *P*-analysis was promised in Section 3.3.7.2.2. There, *NP*-samples of Division *I* created one factor together with all *DP*-samples. Now, a look at Table 1.3 shows that the latter are predominantly derived from the same Division. Let us note, then, that it is the Divisions that are responsible for producing a factor.

### 3.4.5. SUGGESTIONS FOR FURTHER INVESTIGATION AND TWO EXAMPLES

All this does not exhaust by far what can possibly be inferred from the wealth of data of Phase II. They are a rich treasury, the threshold of which we have hardly reached when concentrating almost exclusively on their bearing upon the validity of the Documentary Hypothesis. Thus, many, if not all, samples deserve more intense scrutiny regarding their conformity to, or divergence from, their peers and pairs, and individual variables merit a survey of their realizations throughout Genesis, in sample groups or in samples posing exegetical problems. This task, however, lies beyond the scope of our undertaking and must be left to others. But two examples might be cited to illustrate this point.

For the first, and in order to show how much light is cast on troublesome issues by exploiting the data, let us for a moment gaze at one curious case in point as if through a microscope. There is one chapter in Genesis, ch. 14, which the Documentary School is at a loss to which of the three sources to attribute. Its allegedly heavy and ostentatiously learned style does not fit into *J*'s vivid nor into *E*'s emotional way of storytelling and would rather point into the direction of *P*, were it not that its subject matter is war. Depicting, as it does, Abraham as a warlike hero, it is unique in the book. By the same token, it is out of character with the peace-loving late Priestly Writer and can therefore not be attributed to him either. Most critics would concur with Speiser that it

> stands out alone among all accounts in the Pentateuch.... Its setting is international... and the narration notable for its unusual style and vocabulary ....
> [It] has to be ascribed to an isolate source.... A ranking documentary critic is inclined to dismiss the story as a late scholastic reconstruction.... For one thing, the account is admittedly not the work of *J* or *E*, let alone *P*.[18]

To Speiser, ch. 14 is the last addition to the mosaic of Genesis, affixed to it by a probably post-exilic editor, and its content is a spurious, fanciful glorification

---

[18] E. A. Speiser, *Genesis* (Garden City, New York: Anchor Bible 1, Doubleday, 1964), 105.

of Abraham's military exploits.   However, the recent discovery of the Ebla tablets appears to substantiate a diametrically opposed view and sharply to reduce this chapter's incompatibility with the rest of the Abraham Cycle. Freedman, for instance, conjectures that ch. 14, far from being an *addendum* dated in the Second Commonwealth, "should be understood in the setting of the third millenium".[19]   These vacillations, fascinating as they are, are not of our concern.   Let us trace, instead, which side of the controversy is supported by our analyses.

Ch. 14 provided sample no. 5.   Because its 311 words are, except for very few, the narrator's, it naturally fell into $N$.   We put it, for the sake of convenience and for lack of any better, into $P$ so that it was finally marked an $NP$-sample of Division $II$.   Now, as it may be recalled, no. 5 figured prominently again and again in our enquiry.   Found (a) alien by Reliability Analysis and (b) solitary by Cluster Analysis as the only sample not of $NJ$- or $NE$-origin in the otherwise extraordinarily compact second cluster (see Figure 3.12), it was (c) practically unique within $NP$, according to the Analysis of Pattern Vector Distribution, in view of its non-deviant nature.   What then is so odd about sample no. 5?   Strangely enough, and paradoxically as it sounds, the answer is that it is not odd at all, but fully harmonizes with $NJ = NE$ — see (b) above — and is out of tune with $P$ — see (c).   In short, ch. 14 is as "normal" within Division $II$ as any other ($NJ = NE$)-sample, and this can mean one thing only: it is, if we rely on statistical linguistics and neglect all other considerations, neither an archaic relic nor a late postscript, but part and parcel of Genesis.   It is hard to overstate the significance in Biblical criticism of this deceptively minor case.   That it leaves the historicity of the events described in ch. 14 and its "setting" in time indeterminate is understood.

The example shows how effective an instrument is available to us when we apply the data gathered to numerous other moot cases.   To do this, however, demands writing a comprehensive 'statistical-linguistic' commentary on Genesis, a task we do not feel equal to.

The second example is of a different sort: it does not concern one single sample, but all of them, and instead of supplying new information on a specific worrying detail all it does is clearing up the general make-up of the book. Consider once more Figure 3.11.   Arrived at in the explorative stage, it is superior to other charts in two respects: (a) it is based upon the original data, prior to any mathematical transformations and (b) includes every sample, offering thus an overall panorama of the sources of heterogeneity as found in Genesis.   The main feature it manifests is that the 96 samples fall into two classes.   One consists of samples sharing a common character which results in a large cluster encompassing almost half the number of all samples — see the amalgamation process starting from sample no. 5($NP$, $II$) on to sample

---

[19] D. N. Freedman, "The Real Story of the Ebla Tablets: Ebla and the Cities of the Plain", *Biblical Archeologist* 41 (1978), 143-64.

no. 59(*HE, II*).  The other class is composed of "loners" which have so little in common that they join the main cluster one at a time.  We have drawn attention to this phenomenon before throughout the explorative stage, but wish to repeat it here: it must be seen as the final verdict on, and the summarizing picture of, the source of lack of homogeneous language behavior in Genesis.  What the background of this bipartition of samples is must be left for further study.

## 3.4.6.  FINAL CONCLUSIONS

The following conclusions are, we believe, well founded and cogent:

(1)  The three Sorts-of-Discourse fall into two parts, $N$ and $H + D$. The two are more distinct from each other than $P$ is from $J$ and $E$.  This distinctness is of the greater specific weight as the classification into ($N, H, D$) is based on data given in the text and hence not debatable, whereas the classification into ($J, E, P$) is being surmised by scholars.

(2)  The Divisions, too, display not three, but two manners of writing: Division $I$ is more dissimilar to Division $II$ than Division $II$ is to Division $III$. Genesis is admittedly not explicitly divided into these three parts (albeit they are indicated by the traditional Jewish "weekly portions"), but it makes good sense to divide them so and most Biblical scholars endorse it.

(3)  There exists a considerable interaction effect between the Sorts-of-Discourse and the Divisions, and of each separately or both together upon the Documents.

(4)  As to the Documents ($J, E, P$), there are, at best, signs that one, namely $P$, is a source apart, yet even these signs are more easily explained by arguing *ex genere scriptorum* than by arguing *ex auctore*.

Since (4) touches upon the central issue of our enquiry, namely the Documentary Hypothesis proper, a scholarly theory held in high esteem for over a century and taught world wide, it is only to be expected that it meet with strong opposition, particularly if the above apodictic formulation alone is read.  A few qualifications must therefore be spelled out in so many words:

(a)  We have been dealing with Genesis and no more.  Whether the Documentary Hypothesis is validated in the other four parts of the Pentateuch, especially with regard to the hypothesized Document $D$, remains to be seen.

(b)  The equation $J = E$ is founded on quantitative and unassailably objective data.  The case of $P$ is different.  That it must not be viewed as a separate source is a matter of interpretation, founded on the rule that a comparison between two different literary types is meaningless in an authorship study, no matter whether it results in statistical significance or not.

(c)   That in several places in Genesis, *E* cannot be distinguished from *J* is no *novum*.   In fact, it has become customary in Biblical criticism to mark these portions by the siglum *JE,* which, though, still implies that these two main sources are indeed distinct in other places.   It is this latter notion that was revealed to stand on shaky ground.

(d)   When we spoke of the book's homogeneity, what we had in mind was its overall fabric.   Results obviously do not guarantee the authenticity of every single word or even a passage here and there.

(e)   Let us reiterate that the existence of problems, especially of repetitions and contradictions, is not denied in, nor explained by, our investigation.   The discipline of statistics has nothing to contribute to their solution: it must be found elsewhere, and we believe it can.[20]

(f)   Neither does the book's homogeneity prove Mosaic authorship. However, if it had emerged heterogeneous, Moses could definitely not have been the writer.

(g)   We should be mindful of the fact that statistical procedures provide probability values and do not result in fully confident yes-or-no answers.

All these reservations notwithstanding, and with all due respect to the illustrious Documentarians past and present, there is massive evidence that the pre-Biblical triplicity of Genesis, which their line of thought postulates to have been worked over by a late and gifted editor into a trinity, is actually a unity.

---

[20] Consult, for instance, Y. T. Radday, "Chiasmus in Hebrew Biblical Narrative" in *Chiasmus in Antiquity,* ed. J. W. Welch (Hildesheim: Gerstenberg, 1981), 50-117, esp. 96-110.

PART FOUR

# Vocabulary Richness and Concentration

Moshe A. Pollatschek and Yehuda T. Radday

## 4.1. The Lexical Angle

### 4.1.1. SEMANTIC DIFFERENTIATION

The statistical investigations into the Book of Genesis, the subjects of Parts Two and Three of this volume, operate, with varying stress, on the phonological, the morphological and the syntactical levels. They do not pay any attention to two other aspects of language behavior, namely, the semantic and the lexical. There are good reasons for omitting the former. What a word really means frequently depends on the reader's opinion, the more so when the text is about three millennia old and in state and need of constant interpretation. To adduce one example: critics claim the two Hebrew nouns for "concubine" (*'amah* and *pileges̆*) to be synonyms, each exclusively employed by only one of the authors of the three presumably original Documents. Consequently, the occurrence of either noun in a certain passage is taken by these critics to be author-specifying enough to attribute that passage to this or that Document. This view may well be correct, but an alternative explanation is also conceivable: either noun may denote a concubine or a "second-rate" wife, but the use of the one or the other depends on the context, on the author's attitude or even on that taken by the husband toward the woman in question at a certain point of the story. Such uncertainties — and they are far from rare in Genesis — seem to be treacherous ground for the purpose of source criticism. Fine semantic distinctions between words of cognate connotations must therefore not be taken into account in our research, which intends to be guided by uncompromising objectivity.

### 4.1.2. LEXICAL DIFFERENTIATION

The lexical side of a text is a different matter. Here, the statistician finds himself on *terra firma,* since lemmata can clearly be distinguished, accurately counted, and their frequencies calculated. How, though, to describe the frequency distribution of distinct words is more problematic, as will be seen.

The present enquiry aims at complementing the preceding approaches to the study of the unity of Genesis by concentrating on the lexical corpus of the book.

How much valuable information is lost if the frequencies of lexemes are neglected is illustrated by the following example. In Gen. 6:17, we encounter two adjacent words, *ruaḥ ḥayyim,* "a breath of life". Both are nouns, the lenghts of which are four and six phonemes, respectively. Another pair of words, this time in Gen. 21:20, is *roveh qaššat,* "an expert archer", again two nouns and of the same lengths as the first pair. For all purposes, in all analyses and in all ensuing calculations performed in other Parts of this volume, these two word pairs were treated as fully alike and analogous. Such they indeed are except for one minor difference: the first noun in the first pair is in the construct and the first in the second pair in the absolute state. Yet there is an enourmous difference between the two pairs which has intentionally been overlooked in the statistical analyses of formal criteria. Each of the two nouns in the first pair is rather frequent in Genesis, occurring 11 and 20 times, respectively, whereas the two in the second pair are not found elsewhere — neither in Genesis, nor in the entire Hebrew Bible! Plainly, the two pairs are highly dissimilar from the point of view of vocabulary.

## 4.2. The Type-Token Ratio

Word occurrence frequency [1] in a text of given length is commonly called the Type-Token ratio and has, in the last two decades, occupied the minds of many linguists to a considerable extent. It measures the relationship of the number of different words to the total number of words in the text, or in other words, the repetitiveness of vocabulary. When the data are tabulated, a frequency profile obtains, an example of which is shown in Table 4.1 for the vocabulary of *D,* i.e., Divine direct speech, in Genesis. Here, 234 words occur only once (*hapax legomena*), 79 occur twice (*dislegomena*) and so on. Let the number of words occurring a certain number of times be named frequency (col. 1) and the actual number of these times be named occurrence (col. 2). The text size of *D* is 1919 words and the number of distinct words 470 (bottom line) (See Table 4.1, p. 193).

## 4.3. Describing the Vocabulary

## 4.3.1. PREVIOUS METHODS

An author's behavior in his oeuvre in regard to the inventory of different words used by him has been the subject of many investigations in the past, and various ways of describing it have been suggested. Among them are

---

[1] The subject of word occurrence frequency merits an incomparably more thorough treatment. For reasons of space, and because this collection focuses on one specific problem in Biblical philology and is not a treatise in statistical linguistics, a cursory and necessarily superficial outline must suffice.

Table 4.1: Frequency Profile of *D*

| Frequency | Number of Words | Vocabulary Total | Text Size Total | Percentage of Vocabulary Total | Text Size Total |
|---|---|---|---|---|---|
| 1 | 234 | 234 | 234 | 49.79 | 12.19 |
| 2 | 79 | 313 | 392 | 66.60 | 20.43 |
| 3 | 30 | 343 | 482 | 72.98 | 25.12 |
| 4 | 22 | 365 | 570 | 77.66 | 29.70 |
| 5 | 22 | 387 | 680 | 82.34 | 35.43 |
| 6 | 16 | 403 | 776 | 85.74 | 40.44 |
| 7 | 4 | 407 | 804 | 86.60 | 41.90 |
| 8 | 10 | 417 | 884 | 88.72 | 46.06 |
| 9 | 7 | 424 | 947 | 90.21 | 49.35 |
| 10 | 10 | 434 | 1047 | 92.34 | 54.56 |
| 11 | 6 | 440 | 1113 | 93.62 | 58.00 |
| 12 | 7 | 447 | 1197 | 95.10 | 62.37 |
| 13 | 1 | 448 | 1210 | 95.32 | 63.05 |
| 14 | 2 | 450 | 1238 | 95.74 | 64.51 |
| 15 | 1 | 451 | 1253 | 95.96 | 65.29 |
| 17 | 1 | 452 | 1270 | 96.17 | 66.18 |
| 18 | 2 | 454 | 1306 | 96.59 | 68.06 |
| 19 | 1 | 455 | 1325 | 96.81 | 69.05 |
| 21 | 2 | 457 | 1367 | 97.23 | 71.23 |
| 27 | 2 | 459 | 1421 | 97.66 | 74.08 |
| 28 | 2 | 461 | 1477 | 98.09 | 76.97 |
| 32 | 1 | 462 | 1509 | 98.30 | 78.63 |
| 34 | 1 | 463 | 1543 | 98.51 | 80.41 |
| 36 | 1 | 464 | 1579 | 98.72 | 82.28 |
| 41 | 1 | 465 | 1620 | 98.93 | 84.42 |
| 44 | 1 | 466 | 1664 | 99.16 | 86.71 |
| 53 | 1 | 467 | 1717 | 99.36 | 89.47 |
| 60 | 1 | 468 | 1777 | 99.57 | 92.60 |
| 67 | 1 | 469 | 1844 | 99.79 | 96.09 |
| 75 | 1 | 470 | 1919 | 100.00 | 100.00 |

Table 4.2: *Hapax Legomena* and Personal Names in *J, E, P*

| Category | Total Number of *Hapax legomena* (1) | Personal Names Occurring Once (2) | Percentage of (2) in (1) (3) |
|---|---|---|---|
| *J* | 314 | 49 | 15.61 |
| *E* | 329 | 11 | 3.34 |
| *P* | 248 | 114 | 45.97 |

— the average number of occurrences
— the pertaining standard deviation
— the coefficient of skewness of observed occurrences [2]
— the coefficient of their kurtosis [3]
— the number of *hapax legomena* [4]
— the *hapax legomena/dislegomena* ratio [5]
— the percentage of *hapax legomena* within the total number of different words [6]
— the Type-Token ratio [7]
— Herdan's characteristic [8]
— Yule's characteristic [9].

For details, see Appendix 4.A.

Discussion of the advantages and disadvantages of these numerous approaches would lead too far afield. In general, it may be claimed that almost without exception results of the calculations enumerated remain dependent on the size of the text examined, a most serious deficiency which precludes comparison of texts of different size and, consequently, the use of vocabulary properties as discriminants in authorship studies. Moreover, the data obtained from the said methods hardly ever represents the entire profile: some concentrate on the rarest words while neglecting those of high occurrences, and others pay more attention to the latter to the exclusion of the former. Why, it may be asked, should only the top or the bottom lines of a frequency profile be considered when either, both or those in between, may disclose characteristic traits of a writer? Another weakness of the above proposals is that they operate solely with empirical data and fail to offer a theoretical model of word distribution. However, the principal question left open is, How many parameters are altogether necessary in order to fully describe a writer's vocabulary?

---

[2] M. R. Spiegel, *Theory and Problems of Statistics* (New York: Schaum Publ. Co., 1961).

[3] D. J. Veldman, *Fortran Programming for the Behavioural Sciences* (New York: Holt, Rinehart and Winston, 1967).

[4] P. Guiraud, *Problèmes et methodes de la statistique linguistique* (Dortrecht: Reidel Publ. Co., 1959). The same method of describing vocabulary is also used in fitting the Waring distribution to word frequency data by G. Herdan, *Quantitative Linguistics* (Washington: Butterworths, 1964), 89.

[5] Also employed by Guiraud, *op. cit.*

[6] This statistic, too, was developed by Guiraud, *op. cit.*, as one which would be relatively stable over sample sizes up to 10,000 words.

[7] This is one of the oldest and most widely used language statistics already noted by J. Estoup, *Gammes statistiques* [5] (Paris: 1917). See also J. W. Chotloss, "A Statistical and Comparative Analysis of Individual Written Language Samples", *Psychological Monographs* 56 (1944), 17-38, and G. Herdan, *Type-Token Mathematics* (The Hague: Mouton, 1962).

[8] Developed by him in his *Quantitative Linguistics* (see note 4), esp. p. 83.

[9] Calculated originally by him in his *The Statistical Study of Literary Vocabulary* (Cambridge: Cambridge University Press, 1944).

## 4.3.2.  ZIPF'S LAWS

Zipf was the first to reveal that a relationship exists between the number of word occurrences and their frequencies.[10]  His first law says that plotting the logarithms of word ranks against those of frequencies results in a straight line.  In accordance with his second law, an approximately straight line obtains when the logarithms of occurrences (1,2,... in Table 4.1) are plotted against the logarithms of frequencies (234,79,... in Table 4.1).  Following Zipf's second law, we arrived, for the vocabulary of $D$ in Genesis, at Figure 4.1 (p. 196).

Mandelbrot, continuing Zipf's line of reasoning, correctly derived the second from the first law.[11]  Both, however, were severely criticized — most notably by Herdan[12] — because the deviation from the straight line cannot be easily dismissed: too many occurrences are associated with one word only, i.e., the tail of the distribution, — see Figure 4.1.

## 4.3.3.  OTHER THEORETICAL DISTRIBUTIONS

Several other theoretical distributions have been put forward and used for giving a better fit to empirical data instead of simply stating that the log-log plot is linear.  Among them, those by Yule,[13]  Good,[14] and Simon[15] are the best known.  Yet not one appears to be wholly satisfactory.

Our immediate purpose, then, is to search for a theoretical distribution that is free of the imperfections pointed out above.

## 4.4.  The Sichel Distribution

## 4.4.1.  DESCRIPTION

A newcomer among the theoretical distributions is the one worked out by Sichel.[16]  We believe it to be the best suited to our purpose, and, should this

[10] G.K. Zipf, *Selected Studies of the Principle of Relative Frequency in Language* (Cambridge, NA: Harvard University Press, 1932).

[11] B. Mandelbrot, "On the Theory of Word Frequencies and on Related Markovian Models of Discourse" in R. Jakobsen (ed.), *Structure of Language and its Mathematical Properties* (Proceedings of Symposia in Applied Mathematics, vol. 12, American Mathematical Society, 1961).

[12] G. Herdan, *The Advanced Theory of Language as Choice and Chance* (Berlin-Heidelberg-New York: Springer-Verlag, 1966), 438-45, esp. 439.

[13] G.U. Yule, "Mathematical Theory of Evolution Based on the Conclusions of Dr. J.C. Willis FRS", *Philosophical Transactions of the Royal Society of London*, Sec. B, 213 (May 1924), 21-87.

[14] I.J. Good, "Statistics of Language", in *Encyclopaedia of Linguistics, Information and Control* (Oxford: Pergamon, 1969).

[15] H.A. Simon, "On Class of Skew Distribution Functions", *Biometrika* 42 (1955), no. 3-4, 425-40.

[16] H.S. Sichel, "On a Distribution Law of Word Frequencies", *Journal of the American Statistical Association* 70 (1975), 542-47.

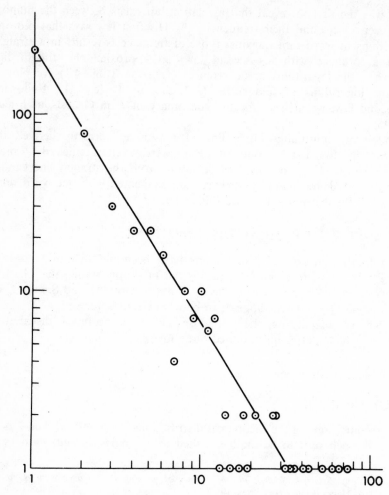

Figure 4.1: Demonstration of Zipf's Second Law for *D*

claim be substantiated, shall use it for studying the vocabulary of Genesis and that of the book's parts, in order to finally compare the vocabulary of one part with that of another.

The Sichel distribution involves two positive parameters, $\alpha$ and $\theta$, where $\alpha$ has no upper bound, while $\theta$ is always less than 1 (typically very close to 1). A third parameter, $\gamma$, may be either positive or negative, but when dealing with word occurrences, we may assume $\gamma$ always to be $-\frac{1}{2}$. This gives very good results. Thus, $\alpha$ and $\theta$ characterize the Sichel distribution. Their mathematics are given in Appendix 4.B. (Bible scholars should perhaps be explicitly reminded that the Greek letters used here do not stand for what they do stand for in their field.)

Sichel shows a superb fit of his distribution to numerous word occurrence data from different texts, but he does not interpret his parameters, nor does he explain how to compare texts with each other and what may be learned from such a comparison between two pairs of his parameters when each emerged from a different text. We believe that one may indeed interpret $\alpha$ and $\theta$ to the advantage of the linguist, the literary critic and, in the present case, the Bible scholar.

Figure 4.2 presents four theoretical distributions on log-log grid for four different sets of values of $\alpha$ and $\theta$. (See Figure 4.2, p. 198).

Note that the tail slope is defined by $\theta$ alone whereas the head slope by $\alpha$ alone. In addition, by an appropriate choice of the pair $(\alpha, \theta)$, any deviation from the straight line on log-log grid can be achieved.

It should be obvious that $\alpha$ is a measure of vocabulary richness by showing the slope for words of higher occurrences: the higher $\alpha$ is, the higher vocabulary richness, or, differently expressed, the more words occur with low frequencies. Conversely, the higher $\theta$ is, the higher vocabulary concentration or the higher the proportion of the most frequent words in the text. Thus, the superiority of the Sichel distribution is unmistakable since it allows any combination of richness and concentration.

From the excellent fit of this theoretical distribution to many empirical data follows that $\alpha$ and $\theta$ describe the frequency of occurrences in full and that the two together represent the total word count in contrast with what is accomplished by other methods.

## 4.4.2. ESTIMATION

Given an empirical word count as shown in Figure 4.1, two parameters, $\alpha$ and $\theta$, are sought so that the theoretical distribution may fit the empirical as well as possible. This procedure is called estimation.

Such estimation was until recently not a simple task since it involves modified Bessel functions of the second kind with non-integer orders (see Appendix 4.B). Nowadays, computer routines are fortunately available for this purpose. Exhibit 4.1 shows the output of a typical routine. Its input are the occurrence frequencies of Table 4.1 (Divine direct speech). (See Exhibit 4.1, p. 199).

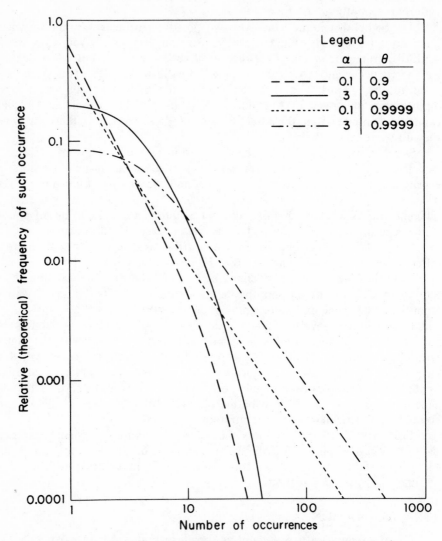

Figure 4.2: Four Examples of the Theoretical Occurrence Frequencies
of the Sichel Distribution

| | ABSOLUTE | INDIVIDUAL FREQUENCIES | RELATIVE | CUMULATIVE |
|---|---|---|---|---|
| | OBSERVED | EXPECTED | OBSERVED | EXPECTED |
| 1 | 234 | 234.00 | .4979 | .4979 |
| 2 | 79 | 77.74 | .6660 | .6633 |
| 3 | 30 | 39.05 | .7298 | .7464 |
| 4 | 22 | 23.95 | .7766 | .7973 |
| 5 | 22 | 16.37 | .8234 | .8321 |
| 6 | 16 | 11.97 | .8574 | .8576 |
| 7 | 4 | 9.16 | .8660 | .8771 |
| 8 | 10 | 7.25 | .8872 | .8925 |
| 9 | 7 | 5.88 | .9021 | .9051 |
| 10 | 10 | 4.87 | .9234 | .9154 |
| 11 | 6 | 4.09 | .9362 | .9241 |
| 12 | 7 | 3.48 | .9511 | .9315 |
| 13 | 1 | 3.00 | .9532 | .9379 |
| 14 | 2 | 2.61 | .9574 | .9434 |
| 15 | 1 | 2.28 | .9596 | .9483 |
| 16 | 0 | 2.01 | .9596 | .9526 |
| 17 | 1 | 1.79 | .9617 | .9564 |
| 18 | 2 | 1.59 | .9660 | .9598 |
| 19 | 1 | 1.43 | .9681 | .9628 |
| 20 | 0 | 1.28 | .9681 | .9655 |
| 21 | 2 | 1.16 | .9723 | .9680 |
| 22 | 0 | 1.05 | .9723 | .9702 |
| 23 | 0 | 0.96 | .9723 | .9723 |
| 24 | 0 | 0.87 | .9723 | .9741 |
| 25 | 0 | 0.80 | .9723 | .9758 |
| 26 | 0 | 0.73 | .9723 | .9774 |
| 27 | 2 | 0.67 | .9766 | .9788 |
| 28 | 2 | 0.62 | .9809 | .9801 |
| 29 | 0 | 0.57 | .9809 | .9814 |
| 30 | 0 | 0.53 | .9809 | .9825 |
| 31 | 0 | 0.49 | .9809 | .9835 |
| 32 | 1 | 0.45 | .9830 | .9845 |
| 33 | 0 | 0.42 | .9830 | .9854 |
| 34 | 1 | 0.39 | .9851 | .9862 |
| 35 | 0 | 0.36 | .9851 | .9870 |
| 36 | 1 | 0.34 | .9872 | .9877 |
| 37 | 0 | 0.32 | .9872 | .9884 |
| 38 | 0 | 0.30 | .9872 | .9890 |
| 39 | 0 | 0.28 | .9872 | .9896 |
| 40 | 0 | 0.26 | .9872 | .9902 |
| > 40 | 6 | 4.32 | 1.0000 | 0.9993 |

| | |
|---|---|
| NUMBER OF TYPES | 470 |
| NUMBER OF TOKENS | 1929 |
| SAMPLE MEAN | 4.104 |
| CHI SQUARE | 21.63 |
| DEGREE OF FREEDOM | 13 |
| GREATEST DIFFERENCE BETWEEN CUM. PROB. | 0.0207 |
| ALPHA | 0.365876 |
| THETA | 0.972884 |
| 10,000-EQUIVALENT ALPHA | 0.823878 |
| 10,000-EQUIVALENT THETA | 0.994652 |

Exhibit 4.1: Frequencies: Absolute, Individual, Relative, Cumulative

A few explanations are in order for a better understanding of this exhibit.

— "Observed" denotes the empirical data as it appears in Table 4.1.
— "Expected" refers to the theoretical frequency according to the Sichel distribution.
— "Absolute" means the frequency as defined before, and
— "Relative" the frequency as a proportion of the whole sample.
   Thus, of 470 different words, 234 appear only once which gives 234/470 = .4979, i.e., approximately 50% of the word total.
— "Cumulative" signifies that the frequencies are added up, e.g., 343 of all different words occur at the most three times.
— "40" is the number of all words occurring more than 40 times.
— "Types" are the number of different words.
— "Tokens" gives the sample size in terms of words.
— "Mean" indicates the average word occurrence.

All these details are included in the exhibit for general information.


The three following lines of the output assess the goodness of fit of the theoretical ("Expected") to the empirical ("Observed") word occurrence distribution.

Our main interest lies of course in $\alpha$ and $\theta$ which are .365876 and .972884, respectively, for the vocabulary of $D$ (Divine direct speech) in Genesis.

The last two lines contain even more important information, the nature of which demands some elaboration.


## 4.4.3.   THE SICHEL DISTRIBUTION AND TEXT SIZE

As has been noted before and as common sense confirms, sample size strongly influences the occurrence frequencies: the vocabulary at the disposal of a writer is perforce limited while the length of the text which he may compose is theoretically unlimited. It follows that the longer the text, the fewer words will occur that are new and hitherto not used. It is evident that, had the author of $D$ written, in the same fashion and on the same topics, a text of 10 000 instead of the actual 1919 words, the relative frequencies of word occurrences would be different from those in $D$ as in fact found in Genesis. In that case, $\alpha$ and $\theta$ would also differ and comparing these two values as obtained in $D$ with, say, those of $H$ (human direct speech) would not only be misleading, but completely senseless, since the $H$-text is not equal in size to $D$-text. For this reason, $\alpha$ and $\theta$ as calculated so far will not do in comparisons of texts of unequal lengths.

It is true that Sichel proves that the two quantities related to $\alpha$ and $\theta$ still remain constant for any text length, but, regrettably, they do not signify for him vocabulary richness and concentration.[17]  Nevertheless, it is feasible to derive from them what $\alpha$ and $\theta$ would be, if the length of the text were exactly 10 000 words.  These two new parameters — called the 10 000-equivalent $\alpha$ and $\theta$ — appear in the last two lines of Exhibit 4.1.  And these two new parameters and not the former, original $\alpha$ and $\theta$ must be used in comparisons of texts.  $\alpha$ and $\theta$ will henceforth have the meaning "10 000-equivalent".  Thus, the way is opened for performing such comparisons between texts regardless of their length.

## 4.4.4.  HOMOGENIZED SUBTEXTS

In spite of what has just been said, a few problems still remain to be solved.  To carry out a comparison between, say, $D$ and $H$, each should be divided into at least two subtexts, that is, into $D_1$, $D_2$, $H_1$ and $H_2$.  It is now convenient to plot each subtext on a graph where the horizontal axis refers to $\theta$ ( = concentration) and the vertical to $\alpha$ ( = richness).  According to the values of the pair ($\alpha$, $\theta$), each of the four subtexts is then represented by a point.

If the distances $D_1 - D_2$ and $H_1 - H_2$ are smaller than the distances across the two text categories, then $D$ and $H$ are suspect of being heterogeneous in relation to each other, i.e., of dealing with two different subject matters or of being written by two different people (or in two different manners of expression).  The smaller the intra-$D$ and the intra-$H$ distances in comparison to the inter-$D$-$H$ distance, the more our confidence grows that $D$ and $H$ differ from each other in one or more of the said respects.  In any case, mapping the texts or subtexts on the $\alpha$-$\theta$ grid offers an easily visualized, lucid and powerful way of representation and comparison.

The greater the sample size, the better the estimate.  Therefore, it is not advisable to subdivide the text into too many subtexts: two to four seem to give the best results.

But it is not only necessary to carefully weigh the number of subtexts: their composition, too, must be borne in mind.  Yule's 'spread sample' technique is probably the best.[18]  It proceeds as follow.  Assuming text $D$ to contain 10 000 words, we wish to divide it into two subtexts $D_1$ and $D_2$.  We first divide $D$ into 10 equal parts, $D_a$, $D_b$, ... $D_j$, where $D_a$ stands for the first 1000 words, $D_b$ for the second 1000 words, etc.  We then combine $D_a$, $D_c$, $D_e$, $D_g$, $D_i$ to form one subtext, $D_1$, and $D_b$, $D_d$, $D_f$, $D_h$, $D_j$ to form the other, $D_2$.  In this manner, the two subtexts are homogenized.

Several authors recommend taking into account only one single type of words for word occurrence analysis, for instance *mots forts,* to the exclusion of the rest, particularly proper names.  Whatever their reasons be for limiting

---

[17] A personal communication by Professor Sichel and hereby gratefully acknowledged.
[18] G. V. Yule, *The Statistical Study of Literary Vocabulary* (see note 9).

the analysis in this way, we believe that in Hebrew this restriction is not commendable and that all words should be included. Whether the case of English is different must be left to experimentation because in this language, some words, such as the definite and indefinite articles, are so predominant that their inclusion may cause an extremely long tailpiece and be thus bound to distort the estimate. It is probably impossible to advocate one and the same practice for all languages. Several alternatives should be examined and the one that gives the most easily explainable results be followed.

Satisfied that the Sichel distribution is indeed a useful tool for describing a writer's vocabulary behavior *in toto,* that is, for measuring both its richness and its concentration, there is hope that Sichel's two values, $\alpha$ and $\theta$, taken together, may serve as a discriminant between two writers and/or two literary types. Experiments to this effect were performed by us in several Biblical books. They are too few in number to provide an unqualified affirmative answer to the hope expressed, but their results are encouraging enough to continue the same experiment in Genesis.

## 4.5. The Vocabulary of Genesis

### 4.5.1. GENERAL

The vocabulary of the Book of Genesis was examined by us, by means of the Sichel distribution, in two dimensions: one, when the text was separated into the three categories of Discourse, namely, the words of the narrator ($N$), human direct speech ($H$) and Divine direct speech ($D$); the other, in pursuance of the primary objective of the enquiry, when the text was divided among the three Documents $J$, $E$ and $P$ in accordance with the Wellhausen hypothesis. Each of these six vocabulary inventories was then divided into two homogenized subtexts as delineated above so that two diagrams resulted, one for each of the two triads. Points in the diagrams represent the subtexts. Vocabularies of subcategories such as $NJ$, $NE$ etc. were not analyzed because approximately estimating the parameters of the Sichel distribution requires large samples.

### 4.5.2. THE VOCABULARY OF DISCOURSE

What emerged from applying the Sichel distribution to the word inventories of $N$, $H$ and $D$ is shown in Figure 4.3 (p. 203).

The first feature attracting notice in Figure 4.3 is that, in contrast with what perhaps could have been expected, vocabulary richness ($\alpha$) and vocabulary concentration ($\theta$) are not negatively correlated. In fact, any of the four possibilities may characterize a text, although three only are visible in Figure 4.3. There, we find low richness going with low concentration in $N$, low richness with high concentration in $H$, and high richness with high concentration

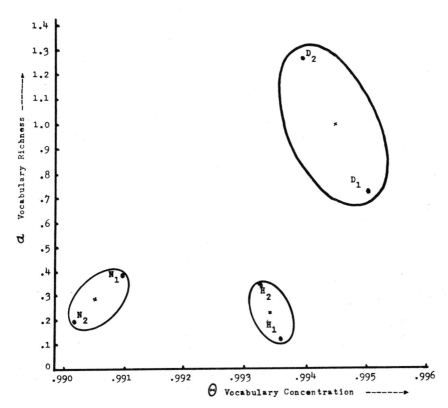

Figure 4.3: Vocabulary Richness and Vocabulary Concentration in *N, H, D*

in *D*. Upon further reflection, this need not surprise us. A writer may have to deal with a great variety of topics, but may describe them with ever recurring words (*N*), one speaker may talk only of what lies most close to his heart — matters of family and livelihood, for instance — and use the same words over and over again (*H*), and another, (*D*), aloof, more restrained and less "interested" in mundane and therefore diversified subjects, may prefer a sublime manner of speech — what Theophrastes called *megaloprepes* — and studiedly choose words that are *recherché* so as not to repeat himself too often. Recalling what *N, H* and *D* stand for, we cannot but conclude that each of the three combinations of richness and concentration as displayed in Figure 4.3 makes a good deal of sense, fitting, as it does, the respective source of the three word inventories.

More unforeseen is a second feature of Figure 4.3. The two points of *N*, on one hand, and of *H*, on the other, lie extraordinarily close to each other. The two points of *D*, it is true, are more distant. All the same, in all three cases, the Euclidean distance between the pair of points within each area is smaller than the one between the centroids of each pair. In short, the three areas not only nowhere overlap, but are unmistakably separated.

This observation — that is, that *N, H* and *D* exhibit three entirely different ways of behavior as to their vocabulary properties — deserves more attention than just stating the fact.

A story writer who intersperses his narrative with direct speech may well endeavour to let his personages speak in a different manner from the one he employs when speaking himself. He may do so for instance, by shortening their sentences, by letting then speak *staccato* or by putting into their mouths a special vocabulary such as slang, coarse terms, learned words and the like, none of which he himself would ever use in narration. Doing this demands of the writer a conscious effort which, given his skill, may not be beyond his capacity. Yet the measures of concentration and richness of vocabulary have nothing to do with the choice of a specific kind of words. Such choice is very much under the writer's control, but vocabulary richness and concentration are quantitative characteristics which he can hardly be aware of. What a writer is not aware of is by definition not provable. Studies of vocabulary to this effect are also so rare in professional literature that none can be adduced to evidence the claim of unawareness, although, we feel, common sense would confirm it. The more marvel, then, when a text excels to such a degree that we find in it, regarding vocabulary richness and concentration, not one, but two different ways of expression because it is virtually inconceivable that they are the result of manipulation by the author: if this were the case, he would merit very high marks indeed. In Genesis, however, we meet not two, but three manners of writing, each neatly distinguished from the other, each consistently emanating from a different Sort-of-Discourse and each most appurtenant to the Sort-of-Discourse from which it stems. This seems to us an outstanding and almost inexplicable literary feat, its uniqueness unfortunately can again not be proven since, as far as our knowledge goes, no other piece of literature has to date been subjected to an equally close scrutiny. But more on this point will follow.

The third, and not less startling, feature of Figure 4.3. is that it shows $N$, $H$ and $D$ to behave each so consistently throughout the book. If it is difficult to conceive that one writer could have achieved what has been discussed in the foregoing paragraph, how much more improbable is it that several writers — who, in the opinion of the Documentary school, allegedly have had a share in composing Genesis — have been favoured with such skill and, in addition, employed it in exactly the identical vein. This reflection together with the fact that the Sichel distribution was capable of so elegantly sorting out $H$ from $D$ and from $N$ naturally evokes our curiosity to find out what the same technique might produce when applied to the second dimension into which the book was divided.

## 4.5.3.  THE VOCABULARY OF THE DOCUMENTS

### 4.5.3.1.  **The Vocabulary of the Three Categories in General.**  When Sichel's technique was administered to the three corpuses $J$, $E$ and $P$, the result was Figure 4.4  (p. 205).

At first glance, Figure 4.4 appears to contradict what was argued in the preceding paragraphs. There, the consistency in vocabulary behavior, existing within $N$, $H$ and $D$, respectively, was emphasized, and doubts were raised whether this phenomenon — rare in literature — may not undermine, to some measure, the Documentary Hypothesis which, if valid, would credit as many as three different writers with the same competence. Now, Figure 4.4 manifestly settles these doubts: $J$, $E$ and $P$ occupy in this graph areas tidily separated from each other. A second glance will show that the matter is not so simple.

Regarding concentration, the range between the minimum and the maximum values (.9917 and .9942) is .0025, whereas the range between the corresponding values in Figure 4.3 (.9909 and .9951) is .0042, that is, almost twice as much. That all four values of $\theta$ are so close to each other is no reason for overlooking the difference between the two ranges, as it will be recalled (see Section 4.4.1.) that $\theta$ tends always to be very close to 1. As far as concentration is concerned, we learn from Figure 4.4 that $P$ conforms with $E$, with $J$ lying slightly apart in the direction of lower values.

### 4.5.3.2.  **The Vocabulary of $P$ in Particular.**  With regard to vocabulary richness, the configuration is the opposite: $J$ and $E$ behave in an almost identical way and $P$ exceeds both by far. That it is exactly $P$ of the three corpora that tops the other two in vocabulary richness is quite a surprise. The Documentary school — see Part One, Section 1.2. — has a rather low opinion of $P$'s literary skill, calling it repetitive and lacking imagination. If true, these

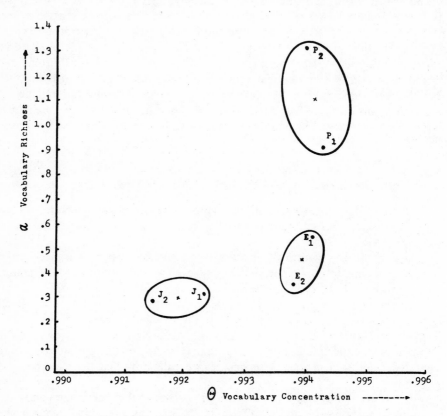

Figure 4.4: Vocabulary Richness and Vocabulary Concentration in *J, E, P*

traits may be expected to result in lower values of $\alpha$ than those found for $J$ and $E$ and not the opposite. Yet $P$'s high values of $\alpha$, far from contradicting the Documentarian view, are in fact its very result. Once all genealogies in Genesis, that is, all text blocks where dozens of personal names occur just once (or twice) without ever being mentioned again in the book are apportioned to $P$, it is only natural that, with each of these many names being reckoned as a new and distinct word, $P$'s rare words occupy a high proportion of his total vocabulary and, *ipso facto,* add to its richness. But before jumping to unwarranted conclusions, we counted the once-words as well as the personal names in $J$, $E$ and $P$ each and calculated the proportion of the latter in the former — see Table 4.2.

The number of personal names occurring only once in $P$ is three times higher than in $J$ and twelve times higher than in $E$, as foreseen. Vocabulary richness in $P$ is therefore due to the long name rosters and but ostensibly high. Consequently, its outlying values as shown in Figure 4.4 need not trouble us any longer. Incidentally, an outlier is, in statistical terminology, an observation suspiciously unlike the bulk of observations of which it is supposed to be a part.

At this point, it may be a good idea to devote also some attention to $P$'s vocabulary concentration. As has just been mentioned, it conforms to that of $E$, and thus does not seem to present any problem or contain valuable information. Further examination proves the opposite.

There is ample evidence in professional literature that the ten to twenty words ranking highest in a frequency list of a given language are dictated by its structure and must hence be the same in any literary work written in that language. These include mainly prepositions, pronouns, conjunctions, articles, etc., all depending on whether these word categories do in fact exist in it. Furthermore, it stands to reason that the percentage they take up in a written text necessarily remains constant. Now, the frequencies of these words of highest ranks determine, to a great extent, the values of vocabulary concentration. Because of these considerations, we arranged the twenty most frequent words in $J$, $E$ and $P$, and, for the sake of completeness, in $N$, $H$, and $D$, in descending order and thus obtained Table 4.3. The absolute frequencies are also given. (See Table 4.3, p. 208).

The cumulative relative frequencies of these most frequent words in the three Documentary categories are

$$J: 33.45\% \qquad E: 34.84\% \qquad P: 42.48\%$$

Not that Table 4.3 and the above three values resulting from it are of overwhelming importance in our enquiry, but they are quite informative and shed a certain light on the nature of the Document $P$.

With the corresponding values in $N$, $H$ and $D$ also fluctuating around 35%, we may claim that in a normal, random sample of a Biblical narrative text, roughly one third is covered by the twenty most frequent words. Not so,

Table 4.3: The Twenty Most Frequent Words in *J, E, P* and *N, H, D* and Their Absolute Frequencies

| Rank | J | | E | | P | | N | | H | | D | |
|------|------|-----|------|-----|------|-----|------|-----|------|-----|------|-----|
| 1 | את | 401 | את | 269 | את | 196 | את | 611 | לי | 219 | את | 75 |
| 2 | אמר | 332 | אמר | 221 | בן | 152 | אמר | 507 | את | 203 | כל | 73 |
| 3 | אל | 262 | אל | 207 | שנה | 103 | אל | 325 | אל | 162 | אשר | 60 |
| 4 | לי | 197 | לי | 163 | ארץ | 88 | בן | 261 | אשר | 150 | ארץ | 53 |
| 5 | אשר | 183 | אשר | 148 | כל | 84 | אשר | 205 | כי | 138 | כי | 44 |
| 6 | על | 163 | כי | 120 | היה | 82 | כל | 199 | לא | 120 | אל | 42 |
| 7 | כל | 149 | יוסף | 108 | אשר | 76 | היה | 190 | את | 90 | על | 41 |
| 8 | כי | 146 | על | 104 | אלהים | 69 | על | 189 | היה | 90 | היה | 36 |
| 9 | היה | 142 | כל | 102 | הויה | 59 | ארץ | 168 | ארץ | 89 | הנה | 36 |
| 10 | הויה | 140 | היה | 91 | לי | 59 | עם | 166 | אלהים | 89 | לא | 34 |
| 11 | ארץ | 138 | אלהים | 88 | אלה | 57 | לי | 163 | עם | 88 | על | 32 |
| 12 | בן | 137 | לא | 86 | אל | 50 | יעקב | 157 | כן | 87 | עשה | 28 |
| 13 | עם | 122 | את | 85 | עם | 49 | יוסף | 142 | על | 85 | ידי | 27 |
| 14 | אך | 109 | ידעי | 83 | בן | 47 | צבא | 133 | את | 82 | בין | 23 |
| 15 | לא | 108 | ארץ | 82 | חי | 47 | אלהים | 120 | הנה | 80 | עם | 21 |
| 16 | את | 91 | בן | 76 | משה | 46 | יהיה | 116 | עם | 78 | הברית | 21 |
| 17 | כן | 86 | אתו | 75 | אמר | 44 | אך | 108 | כן | 71 | כן | 19 |
| 18 | איש | 86 | את | 72 | אמר | 44 | יום | 108 | בן | 70 | בן | 18 |
| 19 | אמה | 80 | איש | 64 | כלוף | 43 | כי | 105 | כל | 70 | אתה | 18 |
| 20 | לפה | 75 | ותו | 62 | מאלהים | 40 | באלהים | 103 | אם | 68 | גוי | 17 |

though, in *P* where this sort of 'concentration' is 30% higher. The question must be asked why this is so. Let us postpone the answer for a while and look at the words themselves as they appear in the six columns of Table 4.3.

We immediately observe that in five columns, that is, except in column *P*, the same words are almost invariably listed in the first decade. Among these ten, seven are *mots de structure* which is only fit as no coherent text of sufficient lengtht can do without a high proportion of conjunctions, prepositions and similar particles. The remaining three are the Hebrew verbs *hayah* and *'amar* (the latter is absent in *H*, i.e., in direct speech, for obvious reasons) — which all makes good sense. Once again, however, *P* does not follow the routine. Of its ten most frequent words, six are *mots forts*, whereas the ubiquitous conjunction *ki*, the verb *'amar* and the prepositions *'el* and *'al*, all so necessary in Hebrew syntax in general and in narration in particular, are missing. True, *'el* ranks in the *P*-column only a little lower (no. 12) and *'amar* quite lower (no. 18), but *ki* is entirely absent from this part of the list. Such minor fluctuations, one might think are immaterial. They are not, particularly since these words not only occupy the highest, but almost the same ranks in all other columns (except *'amar* in column *D*, since it obviously must be rare in Divine direct speech). Whence, we feel prompted to ask again, stems this irregularity of *P*? How could the Priestly Writer have done without precisely those words that are the most indispensable in narration? To use a simile, how can one erect a proper building of nothing but unhewn rocks without using the necessary amount of cement? It is difficult, in these circumstances, to stifle the suspicion that an independent *P*-Document may never have existed. But let us leave this point to the discretion of those whose exclusive preserve is the study of Scripture.

Assuming, though, for the sake of the argument, that there was indeed such a Document comprising mostly dates, ages, clan and family lists to the exclusion of anything else, it is only natural that *mots de structure* were then of such low an incidence that they failed to climb up the frequency ladder to reach one of its uppermost rungs and that their places there were taken by *mots forts* such as *ben* (no. 2), *šanah* (no. 3) and *holid* (no. 11). By the same token, the so reconstructed *P*-Document deserves by all means to be called pedestrian, just as a telephone directory is. Yet, as the very same critics assert, *P* comprised also narrative matter: a great part of the Flood Story (chs. 6 and 9), the Covenant of Circumcision (ch. 17), written, as it is, in elaborate chiastic manner, the superb tale of the Sale of the Cave (ch. 23) with its subtle humorous touches, and the lofty hymnic "Account of Creation" (ch. 1, although omitted in this enquiry). All these attest to the Priesty Writer's gift as a storyteller, and poet to boot. If, therefore, *P* in its original form contained, exactly like *J* and *E*, variegated literary genres, it must or should also have contained the indispensable amount of *mots de structure*. If this is not the actual case, as shown in Table 4.3, it can only be due to the fact that the segments earmarked as *P*'s in Genesis (see Table 1.1) are a biased selection from the hypothesized original $P$-Document. The latter, as conceived of by the critics, can hardly stand on its own feet, so to speak, and owes its survival in fragments to the tendentious treatment of the text.

Arguments such as just made which are based on no more than what is absent in the list of the ten most frequent words in $P$ are not sufficiently substantiated to giving up the possibility that $P$ may have existed. But they find also some support in Figure 4.4 which astonished us by $P$'s rich vocabulary. If indeed two opposing language behaviors are present in $P$ because this source, by the Documentarians' own admission, comprises both tribal pedigrees and artistic narration, then the first may be responsible for $P$'s high concentration as well as for the high ranks occupied by words belonging to the semantic group "kinship" and the paucity of grammar words, and the other, together with the long lists, for $P$'s surprisingly high vocabulary richness.

These reflections go a long way to induce us to disclaim that $P$ is an independent source and rather to suggest that the $P$-segments should preferably be assigned, one way or the other, to $J$ and $E$. Since these segments seem to occupy a mediating position between $J$ and $E$, their assignation to them would cause the two encircled areas of $J$ and $E$ to move closer to each other. This experiment, though, is not feasible under the ground rules of this study, i.e., not to tamper with data to achieve convenient evidence.

4.5.3.3. **The Vocabularies of $J$, $E$, $P$ and $N$, $H$, $D$.** The preceding paragraphs dealt with the surprisingly deviant comportment of $P$'s vocabulary. It was argued, though, that it is only seemingly surprising and in fact the outcome, to be expected, of *a priori* assumption: when text blocks of a peculiar vocabulary are set apart, it is little wonder that a peculiar vocabulary will characterize these text blocks. This is but one of quite a few charmed circles in which some branches of Biblical scholarship have become entangled.

Yet there remains the undeniable fact that separate fields are occupied in Figure 4.4 by $J_1 + J_2$ and $E_1 + E_2$, which is plainly not consonant with the main thrust of Parts Two and Three of this volume, on the grounds of which one would have looked forward to $J$ and $E$ showing a more uniform tendency also in regard to vocabulary properties.

Let us begin with re-stating two observations. Concerning vocabulary richness there is no difference at all between $J_1$, $J_2$ and $E_2$, while it is slightly higher in $E_1$. What really makes for the disconnectedness between the two areas are their values of vocabulary concentration.

The problem boils down to the question whether or not we are entitled to call one distance slight and another disconnecting, or, statistically speaking, whether or not the differences, specifically between centroids, are significant. Unfortunately, the theory of statistical significance tests of the Sichel distribution used here has not yet been sufficiently developed in this direction.

We recall that the rather high degree of conformity which was elicited between $J$ and $E$ emphatically in other aspects of language behavior and the fact that $P$'s $\alpha$ is so much out of step with those of $J$ and $E$ did not ensue from

*P*'s different provenance, but from its content. Therefore, one would greatly wish to show that an explanation of the latter kind offered itself for *E*, too.

Let us frankly admit that we failed in this effort. Yet the experience gained in other and analogous vocabulary studies in the Hebrew Bible [19] did actually demonstrate that the same author's vocabulary behavior responds susceptibly to a wide range of factors which at times can be detected only by luck. A case in point is a test carried out by Michaelson and Morton. [20] When they investigated language consistency in Sir Walter Scott's writings they were struck by the narrow variation in his use of the collocation "*The* followed by an adjective". In one case, however, among many, this feature figured to an annoyingly higher incidence. They then discovered, almost by chance, that Scott never referred there to his two main personages by their proper names, but simply called them "The Old Man" and "The Old Woman". The embarrassing anomaly was due to such an apparently insignificant mannerism. It is not impossible that more discerning readers than the present writers may be able to define the locus of a similar anomaly in the text blocks which make up *E*, especially $E_1$.

Until then, a rough and ready "rule of thumb" is available for assessing whether or not the disjunct areas of *J* and *E* perforce typify two different authors: compare Figures 4.3 and 4.4. The former describes the vocabulary of *N, H, D,* the latter that of *J, E, P.* The fundamental difference between the two lies in that the former is based upon unquestionable data given in the very text of Genesis, the latter upon scholarly surmises concerning the book's author(s). Which of the two carries more weight? Surely the former! If this were not enough, comparison of the two diagrams shows that the Euclidean distances between points of each pair of homogenized samples are quite narrow in five among the six cases (except *D*). So there exists the same high measure of uniformity in each. But when the Euclidean distances are measured between centroids, we obtain that

$$J \longleftrightarrow E \text{ is by 30 p.c. narrower than } N \longleftrightarrow H,$$

$$J \longleftrightarrow P \text{ is by 17 p.c. narrower than } N \longleftrightarrow D,$$

$$E \longleftrightarrow P \text{ is by } 7 \text{ p.c. narrower than } H \longleftrightarrow D,$$

which amounts to underlining that the breaks between the three Sorts-of-Discourse are deeper than those between the three Documents.

---

[19] See for instance Y. T. Radday and M. A. Pollatschek, "Frequency Profiles and the Five Scrolls", *Revue de l'organisation internationale pour l'étude des langues anciennes par l'ordinateur* 2 (1978), 1-35; *id.,* "Vocabulary Richness in Judges", *Minḥat Kodesh,* ed. C. Rabin and B. Z. Fischler (Jerusalem: Council for the Diffusion of Hebrew, 1979) 108-12 (Hebrew); and *id.,* "Frequency Profiles a A Key to the Structure of Lamentations", *Balšanut Ḥofšit* 12 (1977), 24-35 (Hebrew).

[20] S. Michaelson, A. Q. Morton and N. Hamilton-Smith, *To Couple is the Custom* (Edinburgh: Dept. of Computer Science, University of Edinburgh, 1978).

In contrast to many Bible scholars who have never given much attention to what havoc the variance between $N$ and $H$ may play with their theories, professional linguists will not be surprised at all by the configuration shown in Figure 4.3, except, perhaps, by the remoteness of the $D$-area from the $H$-area, and rather hold that common sense necessitates it. But in Section 4.5.2. (end) this configuration was claimed to be unique.

To substantiate the claim that it indeed is, an extensive survey would be needed of those Biblical books that abound in direct speech, but this is not the place for embarking on it, and one example must suffice. Let us choose the Scroll of Esther.

In Esther, $N$ numbers 2255 and $H$ 770 words. We divide $H$ into two samples (350 and 420 words, respectively) and $N$ into six (five of 350 each and one of 505 words), all consecutive within the category, mutually exclusive and exhaustive. We calculate for each the 10 000-equivalents of $\alpha$ and $\theta$ (see Section 4.4.3.), comprehend the six $N$-samples into two groups of three and calculate the means of the 10 000-equivalents of $\alpha$ and $\theta$ for each group. Thus, points for $H_1$, $H_2$, $N_1$, $N_2$ and for the centroids of each pair obtain as shown in Figure 4.5. (p. 213).

Figure 4.5 gives occasion for a number of observations. Among these, the most obvious one, the inordinately high vocabulary richness value of $H_2$, is not of our present concern. More to the point is that the areas of $N$ and $H$ (there is no $D$ in Esther) are again discrete — note the great distance between their two centroids — but overlap a little. It follows that both claims made above are valid: the linguist's — namely that the two areas must be discrete in any case — and our own — namely that the configuration in Figure 4.3 is "unique", since in the case of Esther they do slightly encroach upon each other. The specific features apparent in Figure 4.5 of course merit a more detailed treatment.

What bearing has all this on our problem? The assumption, insufficiently substantiated by the single example of Esther, that $N$ and $H$ are separate by necessity, but may occasionally lie close to each other, leads us conclude that the configuration of the three fields as displayed for Genesis in Figure 4.3 is extraordinary. Yet, in following the Documentarians' viewpoint, we would be forced to conclude that this extraordinary skill must be considered not the achievement of one, but of three writers. This is so hard to conceive that our feeling grows that, despite the complexity of the issue, the three Sorts-of-Discourse play a by far greater role in the diversity of vocabulary behavior in Genesis than the three Documents supposedly underlying the book in its present form.

To sum up: from whatever angle we look at the issue — separateness of areas, distances between centroids, comparison between Figures 4.3 and 4.4 or comparison between Figures 4.3 and 4.5 — the final judgment is one: the difference between $N$ and $H$, and between both and $D$, is so incisive and decisive that these three Sorts-of-Discourse would have to be attributed each

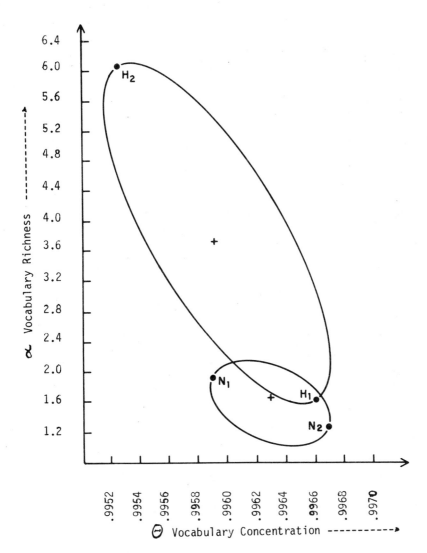

Figure 4.5: Vocabulary Richness and Concentration of *N* and *H* in Esther Exhibit 4.1

to a different author if this were only plausible which it is plainly not.  Hence, and *a fortiori*, it is even less arguable for *J, E* and *P,* the distances between which are throughout smaller.  In other words: if we have good reason to view the six points $N_1$, $N_2$, $H_1$, $H_2$, $D_1$ and $D_2$ in Figure 4.3 as representative of six samples drawn from the work of one and the same person (whose vocabulary behavior varies to a greater or lesser extent) despite the great distances between the centroids and despite the small ones between each pair ($N_1$, $N_2$ etc.), how much more so for $J_1$, $J_2$, $E_1$, $E_2$, $P_1$, and $P_2$ in Figure 4.4.

For the frequency lists themselves, see Appendix 4.C.


## 4.6.  Conclusion

The examination of vocabulary richness and vocabulary concentration in Genesis has shown that, as far as these two linguistic properties are concerned, assigning the words of the storyteller, the utterances of the story's personages and those of Deity each to a different writer is at least as justified as ascribing the text of the book to the three different sources *J, E* and *P,* postulated by the Documentary Hypothesis.  While solely on these grounds this hypothesis can not be rejected out of hand, such serious doubts regarding its validity have arisen that neither can it any longer be accepted as unreservedly as it has been hitherto.

PART FIVE

# An Interim Postscript

YEHUDA T. RADDAY and HAIM SHORE

Having reached the end of the statistical investigations, we may be allowed, also on behalf of the authors of Parts Two and Four, to abandon the dispassionate posture fit for researchers and to terminate on a somewhat personal note.

Trying to imagine the present state of mind of the reader who had no previous training in statistics we are more than a little apprehensive and feel rather apologetic. It is a fair guess that we have failed in the task we set ourselves right at the beginning, that is, to write readable prose, and that we have often confused the reader who must have found some of the material submitted to him esoteric.

We can only hope that now, at the end, he is less bewildered than he was when he had read halfway through this investigation. When section after section used the same raw data again and when the same terms recurred an endless number of times, he must have slowly become acquainted with statistical terminology, techniques and the statistician's way of thinking.

Nor ought statistics be esoteric. Its principal ideas are not too numerous and are, so we believe, within the range of comprehension of any intelligent person. Since the reader is not required to perform statistical analyses himself, it suffices, for following the argument, that he understands the meaning of a dozen basic concepts. That such understanding is a challenge to humanists and especially Bible scholars we are prepared to concede, expecting them, in exchange, to concede that a minimum of statistics is nowadays a *sine qua non* in most branches of knowledge.

The reader may, furthermore, find our discussion dry, if not tedious. Let the first charge be admitted: as procedure follows procedure, each reworking the same material in a different way, but presenting that way almost always in the same fashion — description first, results and summary afterwards — the final product must of necessity be dry. For its increased dryness we ourselves are to blame when, in the process of examining the validity of a widely accepted and dearly-held hypothesis in Biblical scholarship, we firmly resisted, almost to the very end, the strong temptation to raise Biblical hypotheses of our own in its stead. Much as such were permanently in our minds, we deemed them to be beyond our terms of reference and better be left to those whose primary concern is the study of Scripture.

Is computer-aided statistical linguistics tedious when it is trying to trace the fingerprints of authors? That we ourselves do not think so goes without saying. Quite to the contrary: we were fascinated, as we progressed, step by step, by observing how the various procedures began slowly to unravel the book's inner unity — or shall we still say, disunity? Suspense could have been enhanced, had we given our presentation a more polemical slant. Instead, we preferred writing technical reports *sine ira et studio* which may indeed make for some tedium.

But as one analysis was receiving reinforcement from the other, it must have become ever clearer to the reader that the prodigious amount of long lists, perplexing diagrams and tiny percentages is in reality anything but short of explosive substance.

To recognize this, the reader, faced by data exceeding tenfold the number of words in Genesis, is called upon, first of all, to separate the wheat from the chaff. Much of what is included particularly in Part Three, it is true, could have been eliminated or shortened, had we not decided to let it stand for the sake of completeness and for the benefit of colleagues. Who knows whether they, infected by our belief that, buried under the heap of digits, a hidden treasure lies of still untapped information, may not one day wish to base their research on our data and further exploit them.

The quintessence of our endeavours is that the Documentary Hypothesis, subscribed to if not by orthodox scholarship, then by scholarly orthodoxy, is not demolished, but severely weakened by the results of our computations. Performed in rigorous laboratory conditions — *in vitro,* so to say — they proclaim that Wellhausen's tripartition of Genesis into *J, E* and *P* is of high improbability. However, the same computations isolated facts which only added to the complexity of the issue. Language behavior in Genesis is indeed not at all uniform. There is a significant break between how the narrator tells his story and how the protagonists of the story speak. We have also witnessed that the book's so-called style changes abruptly with the appearance of Abraham on the scene (ch. 12) and for a second time, although less forcefully, with the beginning of the only short story in the Pentateuch, the Joseph Cycle (ch. 37). Whether one has reason to ascribe these variations to multiple authorship or whether they are necessitated in accordance with the theory of literature and discourse is not for us to determine. Personally, we feel like favoring the second alternative, against the first. We believe that ignoring the interplay between form and content, on the one hand, and between description and speech, on the other, reducing the lack of fixity in language usage encountered in any book to a plurality of sources, and resolving it by mechanistically assigning this or that part to various authors are hardly signs of a proper comprehension of what literature is and how a writer works. Such an approach, be it ever so ingenious, to a literary creation bespeaks no little naïveté in matters of art, a human dimension so sophisticated that it easily eludes the grasp of philologists and, for that matter, statisticians — with respect.

One thing is certain: the method is sound. After it established, operating with the very same criteria and much to the satisfaction of the critical school, that Judges, Isaiah and Zechariah are each not of one fabric,[1] its trustworthiness cannot be questioned when it overturns deeply entrenched concepts, much to that school's discomfort.

The cornerstone which these concepts rest upon in our case, is the duality of *E* vs. *J*, and this stone, as has been shown, is quite shaky. To demand of the community of Bible scholars to be moved, in the wake of this study, to abandon overnight the postulate that there existed an Elohist and a Jahwist would of course be unrealistic. On the contrary: the conclusion that the two — not cogently, though most probably — were one will predictably be repudiated. Such dysfunction is not unique in scholarship. Even scientists tend to shut their eyes to data liable to collide with an existing cherished theory. "After Sir William Herschel had discovered Uranus...it was found that the planet had been actually sighted twenty times before...but...its movement was simply suppressed as a fact".[2]

To be sure, there is no denying that what has been presented here does not deliver the *coup de grâce* to the Documentary Hypothesis. For this, the number of tantalizing puzzles in Genesis, all commending that hypothesis, is too great. They were not even touched upon, let alone solved, in our work, dealing, as it did, with the overall picture of language habits and no more. The dilemma boils down — be the slight distortion of their original meaning permitted — to which of the two of the "Hermeneutical Thirteen Rules" enumerated in the Baraita of Rabbi Ishmael in Sifra (introd. 5) to follow. The one infers particulars from a general proposition, the other *vice versa*. The general proposition in this argument is that Genesis appears to be more or less of one piece, the particulars are the said puzzling details. It cannot be gainsaid that these, by virtue of their sheer number, may outweigh the proposition. Detectives are often faced by the same predicament: are several clues enough to render a certain person suspect as the culprit, when committing that specific crime is entirely out of his or her character? By and large, the global make-up of the personality would mostly override minor discrepancies in the suspect's evidence, a weak alibi and similar indications. All these, the investigator would first try to account for by other means before arraigning in court someone who had previously undergone a gruelling cross-examination and been found intrinsically incapable of doing wrong.

So Genesis will continue to be a rich field for research, and all the four of us researchers can look forward to is to have supplied it with some new fertilizer.

---

[1] See Part One, note 30.

[2] E.E. Harris, *Hypothesis and Perception* (1970), 209, quoted by M. Tsevat, "Ishboshet and Congeners", *Hebrew Union College Annual* 46 (1975), 73.

# PART SIX

## Linguistic Aspects

### Chaim Rabin

A text is of course phrased in a language, more precisely in the form that language has at a certain time. However, the fact that statistical analysis can be applied to texts in order to establish their authorship shows that a language at any time is built in such a way that the same statement can be made in different ways. This may refer to the amount of details supplied, or to the order in which bits of information are arranged, but the differences which play a role in statistics are the choices of words, grammatical forms, syntactic structures, degrees of emphasis, and the like, i.e., purely linguistic features. This means that a language supplies alternative ways of saying the same thing, more means of expression than are necessitated by the need of describing the "world" in which the text functions. Of course there are not alternative expressions for every lexical item or for every grammatical or syntactical category, but only for a certain percentage of these. Moreover, the different ways of making the same statement, though they can be proved true or untrue by the same facts, may differ in connotation.

An author's personal style (in the sense in which it is investigated by literary statistics) is only one of the possibilities of choice that a language offers. The structured systems of choices, or language varieties, have been attracting much interest on the part of linguists and sociolinguists in recent years. They include local dialects (which have been investigated for a long time), the differences in the speech of social classes (sociolects), of people of different degrees of education, of different ages, of men and women, as well as differences connected with religion, with political outlook, etc. Another important class of varieties are connected with the purpose for which something is spoken or written and the social relations between the speaker or writer and the person or persons addressed. These are called registers, and a person is generally able to express him- or herself in different registers according to the social circumstances. The register differences — which may be considerable — are superimposed on the dialect, sociolect, etc., which are typical for the speaker or writer in the period during which the communication takes place. The linguistic realization of the register will thus vary according to who uses it. The concept of register is closely related to that of Form or

*Gattung* which was introduced into Bible research by Hermann Gunkel several decades before the concept of register was developed by linguists. The "Sitz im Leben" of the Biblical literary forms corresponds closely to the social circumstances of the theory of registers. In both cases the linguistic marking of the language is evidence that the purposes and circumstances of the act of communication were recognized by contemporary society as behavioral patterns clearly identifiable and requiring distinctive marking, which besides language also included clothing, movements, positions, or places, all according to the interaction, its purposes, and its importance in social life.

Literature is a special group of patterns of social interaction, and in all societies we know is marked by special language, differing according to the type of literature: prose and poetry, narrative, admonition, instruction, lyrical expression, etc. Like the set of registers, so the set of literary genres is different from culture to culture and from period to period. Also different is the degree to which certain verbal activities are considered literary, and the strictness of adherence to a certain linguistic pattern in each genre. On the whole, the more archaic the culture, the more the language of literary genres is regulated, the later the culture, the more freedom is allowed. In contrast to registers, literary genres are more independent of the spectrum of personal language varieties which characterize the speaker or writer. This is probably due to the more complicated and conscious processes by which the ability to handle literary language is acquired.

To the extent that literature represents life and social circumstances, there arises the problem of representing the registers in which the interactions described in a piece of literature are conducted. Just as the narrator and poet must represent actions in a way that their social meaning can be recognized, he also has to represent what the actants of his description say or write. The problem becomes even more involved where the author makes himself part of the action and his words become part of the linguistic happenings, and thus liable to be taken as expressing register. Literary register becomes stylized linguistic reality, transformed in accordance with the aesthetic needs of literature, over-characterized in order to be quickly identified in absence of the other markings or paraphernalia accompanying that register in reality, and partially adapted to the conventions of literary style. Again, the more archaic the literature, the more the depiction of registers in it will tend to be formalized, impersonal, representing a class rather than a personality. The foolish king, Ahasverus, still has to speak like a king, even if the content of his words betrays his foolishness; heroes, however simple their origin, have to speak like aristocrats, in rich language and in parallelisms.

But what of the speech of those who are not heard in real life, and therefore their register cannot be observed and subjected to literary stylization? Here the writer must invent registers, or at least adapt them from existing registers in a way that will give his listeners or readers an immediate identification by association. The serpent in the Garden of Eden speaks in what must have been recognizable as the language of the skilled negotiator, the she-ass of Bileam in the way a servant would speak to his master (while Bileam speaks in this verse like the master to his servant). Foreign kings speak in the same way as the kings of Judah and Israel, though in the Books of Kings they are occasionally characterized by not speaking fully acceptable Hebrew, for instance the Aramaic king of Damascus uses še-, a vulgarism in Hebrew, instead of the accepted 'ašer of the literary language (2 Kings 6:11), though this form did not serve in Aramaic.

The most important one of these registers is, however, that used for the speech of God. Since the present investigation of Genesis has shown that there are no really significant differences between texts attributed to the three major Sources in narration and in human speech, it is impossible to say whether the uniformity of the features investigated throughout Divine speech is due to the general uniformity of the features of like registers in Genesis, and whether, if the narrative had been different according to Sources, also Divine speech would have been different. To settle this question, it would be necessary to extend the statistical investigation to Divine speech in other early narrative books of the Bible. The important result of the present investigation is to have shown that Divine speech differs in the statistical features from human speech throughout the book. To recognize the significance of this, we have to show the reasons why speech has to differ statistically from narrative prose.

Narrative is in the third person (sg. and pl., masc. and fem.), while speech employs all persons of the verb and of the pronouns. This multiplicity of pronominal reference leads to a much higher percentage of independent and especially suffix pronouns in speech. Also demonstrative pronouns are rare in narrative, but frequent in speech, where they link the content of the sentence to the outside world and to what has been said.

The typical Biblical Hebrew alternation of finite verbal forms with w-(wa-yiqtol, we-qatal) at the beginning of a clause and forms without w-(qatal, yiqtol) in non-initial position works mainly in narrative, but is much rarer in speech, where the individual "turn" is usually too short to provide opportunity for the sequences which have given the w- forms in traditional Hebrew grammar the name "waw consecutive". Moreover, the imperfect tense, which expresses the future and the present, is for logical reasons infrequent in narrative, but frequent in speech, and the same applies to the employment of the ordinary or the "shortened" imperfect forms for expressing modus. In narrative the yiqtol form occurs mainly to express protracted or repeated action (durative aspect), which in itself is not too frequent.

The brevity of most of the turns in human speech causes sentences to be short, with few subordinate clauses, and therefore also comparatively few conjunctions. The rhythm of human speech is staccato, while that of Biblical narrative is flowing.

These features are not part of a description of a register, but partly derive from the nature of conversation as such, and partly from the dramatic style of the conversations in Genesis, which are repartee rather than conversation. Even the speech of God is generally in short units in Genesis, quite different from the speech of God in the Latter Prophets, with long units stating a case, and often what might be called narrative speech, of which in Genesis we have only one real example in human speech, Gen. 24:34-49, which in its statistical features seems to be much more like narrative prose.

Register enters the description of speech in the form of the distinction between human and Divine speech which the statistical analysis shows. We may speculate whether Divine speech, in the form in which we have it in Genesis, was not developed by those who spoke for Him, namely the priests, and that what we have before us is not simply priestly rhetoric as used in teaching the people. It would then be a real register in origin (and not literary stylization of a register) adopted for this special purpose.

The speech of God differs statistically from the speech of men already through the greater average length of the individual pronouncements. In almost all cases, God is the initiator of the conversation where there is a dialogue, and there are many "monologues" among the instances of Divine speech in Genesis, while there are hardly any attributed to human beings. It is customary nowadays to evaluate samples of speech on the basis of "rules of conversation", which relate to turn-taking and to the way each speaker relates to what has been said previously by the other speaker. It would be difficult to imagine that the ancient Israelite author subjected Divine speech to rules applying in his society to mortals, and this may be one of the reasons why even in dialogues the Almighty speaks at greater length, and the phrasing is less dependent on what was said by the human partner. Divine speech employs much more widely the future tense and the imperative, never requests, and therefore lacks the standardized phrases often appearing when a request is made. But Divine speech frequently explains the reasons for God's decisions and thus more sentences are inserted for the purpose of logical structure. This greater explicitness expresses itself at times in involved sentences, such as Gen. 3:11.

Another register feature of Divine speech in Genesis is that it often has rhythm, and at times parallelism. It was customary until recently to see every use of parallelism as a sign that the passage in question was poetic. This also forced Biblical scholars to discuss the question why the Israelite prophets delivered their speeches in poetry. Recent studies have questioned this,[1] and it now seems that parallelism was a feature of rhetoric rather than of any particular literary genre. In contrast to poetry, which is a textual property,

---

[1] James L. Kugel, *The Idea of Biblical Poetry: Parallelism and its History* (New Haven: Yale Univ. Press, 1981). Cf. also C. Rabin, "Discourse Analysis and the Dating of Deuteronomy", in J.A. Emerton and S.C. Reif, ed., *Interpreting the Hebrew Bible,* essays in honour of E.I.J. Rosenthal (Cambridge: C.U.P., 1982), 175.

and which we therefore expect to apply to a complete text or to well-defined structural portions within it (e.g., verse summaries at the end of a text), rhetoric can be applied at will, serving to foreground a section of a statement. This is the way it appears in Divine speech in Genesis, as can be seen by considering the parts of Divine pronouncements set as poetry in the text of the third edition of the Biblia Hebraica. On the other hand in Genesis the use of such rhetorical devices in human speech is very rare (e.g., 2:23).

Rhetoric in itself is conducive to the stabilization of sentence forms and phraseology. A striking instance of this is the high rate of repetition of parallel word-pairs in the Hebrew Bible, combined with the fact that many of these pairs are found also in other Semitic literatures which have parallelism. Since borrowing is unlikely in this case, it may be surmised that these word-pairs were inherited from an older stage of Semitic poetical activity, along with a fair number of lexical items not found in Biblical Hebrew outside parallelism. This is the phenomenon which has been treated in biblical research and in the history of literatures as "formulaic language". This conservativism does of course contribute to the statistical uniformity of Divine speech in Genesis and its statistical difference from human speech.

If Divine speech exhibits features of being a register, this is not true of the samples of human speech in Genesis. These are diversified within the general pattern of conversation, according to the personalities involved and their relations to each other, according to the characterization of the speaker intended by the narrator, and according to the social purposes the conversation serves in each case. Only the last factor involves registers, but as stated above, registers stylized for literary purposes. In principle it is possible to study the linguistic and textological features of each corpus of statements by one person, or of the register of each conversation, as well as the features exhibited by the persons of lower status speaking to persons of higher status, or vice versa. Because of the small size of the corpuses involved, this would probably have to be done descriptively rather than quantitatively. Even word frequency would have limited significance in such small totals of words. For our present subject of linguistic evaluation of the study of the Sources of Genesis, this would contribute little, because all the above features occur across the delimitations of the Sources.

A feature of greater significance is the general way in which conversation is represented by a writer. Modern studies in Conversation Analysis have shown that spontaneous talk is so full of ellipses, repetitions, uncompleted sentences, and implications that when written down literally from recordings, it is largely incomprehensible to the untrained reader. All talk in written narratives, even the most "realistic" one, is revised in the direction of standard written style. To do so without destroying the illusion that this is spontaneous talk, each language and each period has conventions marking the stretch of written text as spoken language, except in periods of literature when the convention was that all dialogue was in the same formal language as the rest of the narrative, or that dialogue was put into the form of indirect speech, which naturally was in formal language. The conventions suggesting spontaneous speech consisted of syntactic and grammatical concessions to the irregularities of natural speech, and were in themselves just as highly regulated as the formal language employed in the narrative, a kind of secondary normative system marked "conversation".

Our intuitive impression, reinforced now by the results of the statistical analysis, shows that Genesis belonged to the literatures which had such a secondary system. This does not necessarily apply to Biblical literature as a whole: the Book of Ruth, for instance, does not seem to have such a system of differences between narrative and dialogue. We can therefore see the relative uniformity of human speech throughout the three supposed Source corpuses as a possible proof that those three corpuses, if not from the same hand, were at least written in the same period (not necessarily a short one). Had the material attributed to the Priestly Source been written, as is widely thought, in the post-exilic period, we might expect it to be at the formal level of the conversation of the Book of Ruth, rather than at the relatively informal one of the conversation in *J* and *E*. It is true that one might reply to this that the Priestly Source could have been unique among the known writings from the later periods in trying to have more naturalism in the dialogue. One might even point to the early Midrashim, written somewhat later in Mishnaic Hebrew, with their even more "natural" dialogue — but then Mishnaic Hebrew was in the Tannaitic period still fairly close to the contemporary spoken Hebrew of Judaea, and what applied to a text written in it is unlikely to have applied to a text written in a Hebrew which, if we place the Priestly Source in the post-exilic period, would have been a highly archaic language as measured against the contemporary colloquial.

We may accept, on the other hand, the thesis of A. Hurvitz,[2] who on linguistic grounds dates the Priestly Source in the pre-exilic period. This would remove the difficulty created by its having the same attitude to spoken dialogue as *J* and *E*, as also Samuel and Kings have the same attitude of a secondary normative system, and the similarity of statistical features would not prove common authorship with *J* and *E*. It is doubtful whether a parallel statistical investigation of the dialogue in Samuel and Kings would help us to decide the problem of common or separate authorship. If the statistical results for the latter were to turn out markedly different from *J*, *E*, and *P*, this would perhaps make it slightly more probable that the three Sources of Genesis come from one hand, but would not prove it conclusively, as there may be other explanations. Great similarity between human speech in Sam.-K. and in *J-E-P* would make the similarity between human speech in *J-E* and *P* devoid of significance. The most spectacular result could be that

---

[2] *A Linguistic Study of the Relationship between the Priestly Code and the Book of Ezekiel* (Paris: Gabalda, 1982 [Cahiers de la Revue Biblique, 20]).

*P* lies somewhere between the set of features for *J-E* and those for Sam.-K., as this would increase substantially the probability that *P* is separate from the two other Source of Genesis.

Narrative is the most difficult of the three corpuses to evaluate linguistically. On the one hand there is no doubt that narrative is, especially in ancient texts, of the nature of register. It is, however, a register with particularly wide possibilities of variation, as its linguistic features are influenced by the subject matter and locale, which involve both terminology and standard phrases, as well as by the speed of action, quantity of detail, level of tension, and other features of story-telling. All these may influence statistical data. Anyone who compares the narrative styles of Genesis and Kings will be struck by their difference, but closer inspection will show that this derives to no small extent from the subject matter: here history of a patriarchal family in a pastoral economy and with a slow pace of life, varied mainly by contacts with exotic royalty; there administration, wars, diplomacy and court intrigue, and therefore a much faster pace.

It seems that an analysis of narrative unaffected by content can be achieved by the techniques of Discourse Analysis (DA). These techniques have only just begun to be applied to Biblical texts. There is however another problem which affects the use of DA in connection with statistical analysis: it has not, to the best of my knowledge, been investigated whether the features investigated by DA affect in any way the statistical facts used by the present research. DA itself is amenable to statistical treatment, and it seems to me that only an experiment subjecting the same text to both types of statistics can show whether results point in the same direction.

PART SEVEN

# A Bible Scholar's Evaluation

SHEMARYAHU TALMON

## 7.1. Concerning the Documentary Hypothesis in General

Modern techniques of the computer-age have caught up with humanistic studies, notwithstanding the humanist's aversion toward the subjection of matters with which he is concerned to the impersonal approach and scrutiny of statisticians and computer technicians. It must be conceded that the invasion of the time-honoured fields of scholarly endeavour, especially of literary criticism, by these novel methods, has indeed produced useful gains. Suffice it to mention the comparative ease of computer-aided production of tools and aids for textual studies, such as concordances and dictionaries, in an incomparable shorter time-span and at sharply reduced cost. Scholars got used to availing themselves of these welcome services of contemporary science in a wide range of divisions of the humanities. However, one yet seems to maintain a standoffish stance when the living matter of breathing literature itself, which one is accustomed to approach with great reverence for its contents and artistic beauty, is being submitted, as it were, to "vivisection", or worse to "autopsy", so as to lay bare its linguistic intricacies.

An important branch of the new science — statistical linguistics — has been applied with significant results to the field of ancient and modern literatures for the purpose of verifying conjectures about the multiple authorship of discrete units of writing. Saying this, the possibly paramount importance of statistical linguistics for the study of Biblical literature springs to the eye. Since the inception of critical Old Testament research some three centuries ago, much, maybe too much, scholarly energy has been invested in exactly defining the contours of "sources", "strands" or "*Überlieferungen*" which are taken to constitute the literary weave of the Biblical books in their present form, as handed down by tradition over the ages. It may be said that no other literary creation ever was submitted to as intensive a search toward the unravelling of the individual threads which make up its warp and woof as have been the books of the Old Testament, foremost of the Pentateuch. Hence, it stands to reason that Biblical literature should be considered a most attractive and promising object for investigation by statistical linguistics.

It should be stressed from the outset that the grid of linguistic criteria which the statistical linguist uses in the analysis of a given text, in no way can be considered to be of an altogether revolutionary nature. After all, like him, Biblical scholars have been intensely occupied with gaging differences in vocabulary, morphology, sentence structure etc. as indicators of an assumed diachronous or synchronous diversity of authorship between diverse Books of the Old Testament and, what is more important in the present context, between components of one and the same book. It would seem, however, that their interest centered predominantly on in part consciously achieved idiosyncrasies of that or the other author, and on diachronic linguistic developments of a general nature. In contradistinction, the science of statistical linguistics is concerned solely with "involuntary" speech habits. By thus nullifying or at least significantly reducing the influence an author's mannerism may have exerted on the text under review, a measure of "objectivity" is achieved which cannot be attained by an analysis which is based on the criteria employed by established Old Testament scholarship.

To this must be added the fact that a computer-aided linguistic study can encompass a much greater variety of linguistic data than an analysis carried out by traditional means, since it dispenses with much of the otherwise required immense investment of time and manpower. Therefore, statistical linguistics can give an altogether new dimension to the literary inquiry into the Biblical writings.

When applied to modern writings, the statistical-linguistic analysis in some cases achieved results which buttressed a supposition, grounded on historical, stylistic, ideonic or other criteria, that a given literary work which had been suspected not to be of one cloth, indeed betrayed signs of multiple authorship.[1] It is in the nature of things that in reference to ancient and mediaeval literary works, similar conclusions, arising from whatever method of investigation is used, cannot be corroborated by any tangible means. The presumed author or authors of a work of antiquity cannot be brought into the witness box. Thus, there is no way of eliciting from him or them or any other reliable witness, evidence which could prove or disprove claims based on whatever technique of scholarly analysis. Hence, all inferences which emanate from the prevailing methods, all of which belong in the realm of the non-exact humanities, by necessity, are hypothetical.

In distinction, the proponents of statistical linguistics maintain that their procedures deserve to be classified with those of the exact sciences, since their validity can be checked under laboratory conditions. It is on record that investigators using statistical linguistics were able to determine the multiple authorship of a given piece of writing which for the purpose of the experiment had been penned *ad hoc* by different writers. The Old Testament scholar who lives with and almost loves the doubts and the unavoidable divisions of

---

[1] For pertinent literature, see: Y. T. Radday's book on Isaiah, supra, Part I, n. 30, and D. Wickmann, supra, Part I, n. 29 and 49.

opinions which the historical-literary inquiry into any part of the Bible is bound to arouse, cannot but cock his ears and marvel at the brazen statement, that when examined by statistical linguistics "habits of speech and writing become as recognizable as fingerprints".[2] It would be most reassuring if the student of the Bible could accept at face-value the linguistic statistician's self-assurance and professed certainty respective to the reliability of results attained by the method he employs. With such an investigative instrument at hand, the settling of yet unsolved problems respective to the composition of Biblical books to the satisfaction of all savants in the field, would be just a matter of time.

However, can one really acquiesce in the above, almost preposterous claim, as it stands? Or should one ask for further checks and tests by which to prove the efficacy of that technique? The hesitancy to which these questions give expression, arises not alone from the uneasiness of the scholar who spent a lifetime working with other methods in his study of the Old Testament, when he suddenly encounters an altogether novel, perplexing and at the same time awe-inspiring investigative technique. A call for caution is justified when one is confronted with disparate, discordant even contradictory results which emanate from the application of several such modern — not necessarily identical — modes of analysis to the selfsame material. In the present context, it suffices to set against one another the conclusions arrived at, on the one hand by François Chenique, and on the other by the collaborators in the present "Genesis-Project": the first submits that an analysis carried out with a *calculateur électronique* underpins the Documentary Hypothesis respective to Genesis ch. 1-11;[3] the latter claim to have seriously undermined or actually disproved the reliability of that hypothesis by putting its conclusions with regard to the Book of Genesis to the teststone of statistical linguistics. The non-exact humanistic scholar contentedly smiles at finding the exact scientists at loggerheads, a situation which he knows too well from his own bailiwick.

Notwithstanding such diverging views, the Old Testament scholar is well advised to heed the exhortation of H. de Wouters and H. Cazelles voiced in a review of F. Chenique's book: "Notre discipline doit être ouverte à toutes nouvelles techniques".[4] The advisability of keeping an eye open for the potentialities of statistical linguistics in the domain of Biblical research is underscored by the conclusions reached in the examination of other Biblical books which contributors to the present volume carried out prior to the analysis of Genesis. In some significant instances concerning "classical"

---

[2] M. Copeland, *Beyond Cloak and Dagger: Inside the CIA* (New York: 1975), 59-60, apud: Y.T. Radday - G. Leb - D. Wickmann - S. Talmon, "The Book of Judges Examined by Statistical Linguistics," *Biblica* 58 (1977), 469, n. 1.

[3] F. Chenique, *Principes et methodes de l'étude de la bible massorétique sur les calculateurs électroniques* (Diss. Strasbourg: 1967).

[4] *Vetus Testamentum* 18 (1968), 562-564.

cases of conjectured multiple authorship — e.g., the Books of Judges,[5] Isaiah[6] and Zechariah[7] — the outcome of an analysis by statistical linguistics dovetailed with suppositions previously established by means of a literary-critical investigation, and thus confirmed them. The corroboration of their theses provided by objective science certainly will be greeted with satisfaction or at least be tacitly recognized by proponents of Old Testament scholarship, a branch of the non-exact or subjective humanities. However, by the same token, the professional Bible scholar must take notice of queries raised by the statistical-linguistic tests, and of conclusions which put in question axioms considered to have been proven by techniques of investigation that are customary in his own field of learning.

To return to the issue under review. Gaging the unity or diversity of Old Testament Books like Isaiah, Judges and Zechariah is of secondary importance compared with the submittance of a Book of the Pentateuch to a statistical-linguistic probe, since in that latter instance, the investigator actually puts the entire Documentary Hypothesis to the acid test. Moreover, this latter endeavour is infinitely more complicated than dealing with Isaiah, Judges and Zechariah. In those cases, the inquiry pertains to substantial consecutive blocks of text, sufficiently large for sustaining statistical measurements, and similar in their literary constitution to non-Biblical works of literature which had been submitted to the same investigative procedures. Thus, in the Book of Isaiah, chs. 1-33 (or 35) could be compared with the undoubtedly different part starting with ch. 40; in Zechariah chs. 1-8 could be pitted against the equally distinct chs. 9-14; the "Saviour-traditions" set up vis-à-vis "the appendixes" of the Book of Judges (chs. 17-21).

When it comes to the Books of the Pentateuch, the situation changes completely. The Documentary Hypothesis draws demarcation lines not only between appreciably comprehensive blocks of text, ascribed to different authors (or schools), which a redactor ($R$) had culled from historical accounts ($J, E, P, D$) that at one time presumably had existed as separate entities and were yet available to him. It also separates smaller units and even parts of verses which hail from one source and found their way into text segments identified as belonging to a different source. As a result, the Books of the Pentateuch achieved their present form in a conjectured long process of intersplicing of those narrative strands. In the final mosaic or patchwork, few sufficiently extensive units of text can be identified which conform to the customary minimum requirements for analysis by the method of statistical linguistics.

---

[5] *Biblica* 58 (1977), 469-499 (supra n. 3).

[6] Y. T. Radday, *The Unity of Isaiah in the Light of Statistical Linguistics* (Hildesheim: Gerstenberg, 1973).

[7] Y. T. Radday - D. Wickmann, "The Unity of Zechariah in the Light of Statistical Linguistics", *Zeitschrift für die alttestamentliche Wissenschaft* 87 (1975), 30-55.

For this reason, it was considered improbable even only a few years ago, that the assumed diversity of authorship of a Pentateuchal book ever could be tested by statistical linguistics.[8] It is to the credit of the collaborators in the "Genesis-Project" that they succeeded in devising a type of analysis and a battery of criteria with the help of which the language behavior that characterizes Genesis could be adequately charted. Respective to comprehensiveness and finesse, this battery goes far beyond the range of criteria which had been employed in the earlier studies mentioned above. The infinite care taken by the investigators in checking and rechecking their findings, analyzing text-units or "cells" which were defined and redefined by the application of various division-standards — amongst them those of the Sources theory — leaves no doubt that every precaution was taken to refrain from making insufficiently documented assumptions. The basic agreement between the results achieved by taking these diverse approaches, enhances the reliability of the final conclusions.

## 7.2.  Concerning the Documentary Hypothesis in Genesis

It is eminently logical to make the Book of Genesis the yardstick for an assessment of the validity of the Documentary Hypothesis. The central position accorded to this book in the history of modern critical Biblical studies, shows already in the pioneering works of Spinoza[9] and Hobbes[10] in the late seventeenth century. In his *Commentary on the Pentateuch,* written in the early eighteenth century, H. B. Witter demonstrated the existence of two parallel Creation Accounts, derived from two separate *Quellen* which can be identified by the employment of different Divine appellations. This commentary never got beyond the end of Gen. ch. 17.[11] It thus was left to Jean Astruc to lay the foundations of the Documentary Hypothesis in his *Conjectures sur les mémoires dont il paroit que Moyse s'est servi pour composer le livre de la Genèse,*[12] again by identifying in the First Book of Moses two major sources which he designated *A* and *B,* later to be termed the *E*(lohist) and the *J*(ahwist). While there is no need to highlight here any further the pivotal role of the Book of Genesis in critical Old Testament research, mention should be made of B. W. Bacon's *The Genesis of Genesis,*[13] followed by O. Eissfeldt's

---

[8]  Y. T. Radday, *Biblica* 58 (1977), 471.

[9]  B. Spinoza, *Tractatus Theologico-Politicus* (Amsterdam-Hamburgi: *apud* H. Kunraht, 1670).

[10]  Th. Hobbes, *Leviathan* (London: Crooke, 1651).

[11]  H. B. Witter, *Juro israelitarum in Palaestinam* (1711).

[12]  (Bruxelles: Fricx, 1753).

[13]  (London, 1892).

study which carries an identical German title — *Die Genesis der Genesis*,[14] since these publications underscore the importance accorded to the analysis of this book in the evolution of the Documentary Hypothesis.

In view of these facts, it can cause no wonder that the criticism levelled in diverse quarters against this hypothesis, to a significant degree derived its ammunition from a probe into the Book of Genesis. The counter arguments adduced by D. Hoffmann at the beginning of the twentieth century,[15] by M. H. Segal[16] and others[17] several decades later, found their most poignant expression in U. Cassuto's *La questione della Genesi*,[18] B. Jacob's *Das erste Buch der Tora*[19] and Cassuto's partial commentary on Genesis (chs. 1-12),[20] to mention only a few. Since those authors were suspect of being motivated by apologetic tendencies — which to a large extent indeed was the case — their protest fell on deaf ears. They propagated the unity of the Pentateuch and its Mosaic authorship, and hence were so much out of tune with the reigning theory that the scholarly guild did not consider theirs and similar studies as "ernsthafte Beiträge zur Lösung des Pentateuchproblems".[21]

Not much better fared students who were well within the fold of Old Testament scholarship, but posed irksome questions concerning the Documentary Hypothesis *in toto* or some of its aspects. The present context does not call for a survey of that trend. But one work should be cited which appears to have a special bearing on the research-project under review here: P. Volz and W. Rudolph, *Der Elohist als Erzähler — ein Irrweg der Pentateuchkritik? An der Genesis erläutert.*[22] In the title of this work is encapsuled a second, possibly even weightier reason for making the Book of Genesis the launching-pad of an inquiry like the one carried out in the present research project. This statement requires some further explication. No other Biblical book besides those contained in the Pentateuch can be made the primary teststone for validating or invalidating the Documentary Hypothesis, since in the other Biblical writings a widely varying measure of literary variation is

---

[14] (Tübingen: J.C.B. Mohr, 1961).

[15] *Die wichtigsten Instanzen gegen die Graf-Wellhausensche Hypothese*, Berlin. Rabbiner Seminar. Jahresbericht pro 5673,5674-5 (Berlin: Itzkowski, vol. I, 1903; vol. II, 1914).

[16] *The Pentateuch, its Composition and Authorship and other Studies* (Jerusalem: Magnes Press, 1967).

[17] *e.g.*, J. Goldmann, *In the Beginning* (Philadelphia: Jewish Publication Society, 1949).

[18] (Firenze: F. de Monnier, 1934); *id., The Documentary Hypothesis*, tr. by I. Abrahams (Jerusalem: Magnes Press, 1961).

[19] *Das erste Buch der Tora — Genesis* (Berlin: Schocken, 1934), esp. the Anhang: "Quellenscheidung," pp. 949-1049.

[20] *A Commentary on Genesis*, tr. by I. Abrahams. Part 1: *From Adam to Noah*; Part 2: *From Noah to Abraham* (Jerusalem: Magnes Press, 1961-1964).

[21] O. Eissfeldt, *Einleitung in das Alte Testament*[3] (Tübingen: J.C.B. Mohr, 1964), 220.

[22] *Beihefte zur Zeitschrift für die alttestamentliche Wissenschaft* 63 (Berlin: Töpelmann, 1933).

found, but not the Documents themselves. Therefore the debate about that theory, in the last count and by right revolves on the Five Books of Moses. Among those five, Genesis stands out as being almost in its entirety a work of prose narration, laced occasionally with longer or shorter insets of a poetic nature, such as Gen. ch. 49; 4: 23-24 (cp. further, e.g., 4:3-5; 9; 6:25-27), of the (civil or cultic) legal genre (e.g., 9:3-6; 17:9-14) and genealogical lists which are considered a hallmark of *P*. These latter are to be found mostly in the first part of the Book (chs. 1-11) whose language behavior anyhow was shown to be significantly distinct from that of the remaining chapters. Because of this characteristic, the Book of Genesis is a most suitable object for a statistical-linguistic investigation in which the Narrator (*N*) and his speech habits are at the very center of the undertaking.

## 7.3.  Sources, Divisions and Discourse

The results of the present inquiry prompt the question of how they could effect Biblical studies as such, and especially whether in their wake the Documentary Hypothesis should be subjected to incisive scrutiny with respect to the reliability of the linguistic-stylistic-theological criteria on which it is founded.

In view of the fact that no tangible difference in language behaviour between the discourse of the *N*(arrator) and the recorded speeches originating with the *D*(ivinity) or a *H*(uman) *dramatis persona* could be established by submitting passage conventionally ascribed to *E, J* and *P* respectively to a linguistic-statistical analysis, it would indeed seem that the very fundaments of the Documentary Hypothesis have been called in question. One must bear in mind that while at the inception of this theory, the discernment of two different Divine appellations — *E*(lohim) and *J*(hwh), or their combination in one dual name — triggered the search for comprehensive diverse *Quellen* which constitute the weave of the Book of Genesis (and for that matter, of the entire Pentateuch) in its present form, in the ensuing stages of the *Quellenscheidung,* the emphasis to an increasing measure was shifted to the identification of conceptual and linguistic characteristics to *E* which differed from those exhibited by *J* and/or *P*. Now, if the statistical linguistic investigation does not verify or even disproves the presence in Genesis of tangible idiosyncratic language behaviors by which one presumed *Source* can be told from another, the entire theory of the one-time existence of yet separable full-dress historical accounts ascribed to different authors (or schools) loses credibility.

However, an invalidation of the Documentary Hypothesis, if indeed this should be considered the upshot of the statistical linguistic investigation, does not yet prove the original unity of the Book of Genesis, nor does it have any bearing on the traditionally accepted Mosaic authorship of the Pentateuch.

Any such claim based on this investigation would be a *non sequitur*. The present research, in fact has buttressed the generally posited linguistic-literary diversity of the Book of Genesis by highlighting the telling disparity of the *N*arrator's language behaviour vis-à-vis the one which characterizes *D*ivine and *H*uman speeches recorded by him. The consistency of divergence in these speech patterns requires an explanation. While the statistical linguist can consider this problem as being beyond his call of duty, it must exercise the mind of the Bible scholar. It would be premature to attempt putting forward any detailed proposals for solving the question before the new evidence has been fully digested. But it may be in order to point out an approach to the issue which might be further investigated to some advantage. To this end, attention should be directed to one other well recognized way of subdividing the Book of Genesis which was indeed followed in the present study and which arises quite logically from its content, viz. the three-part division into an "Account of Creation and Pre-history" (Gen. chs. 1-11), the "Patriarchal History" (chs. 12-36) and the "Joseph Cycle" (chs. 37-50). Since, in the main, the Book of Genesis consists of narration, it cannot cause any surprise that in all three parts *N* predominates, accounting for 53% of text in Division *III*, 56% in Division *II*, 74% in Division *I* and totalling 61% in the Book as a whole. What strikes the eye is the marked difference in the amounts of text in the three Divisions which can be identified as *H* and *D* material. An increase of *H* matter from 5% in Division *I* to 34% in Division *II* and 47% in Division *III*, runs parallel to a decrease in the amounts of text ascribed to *D*: from 21% in unit *I* to 10% in *II* and its complete absence from *III*.

The internal consistency in language behaviour of *H* and *D* respectively and their both being different from the Narrator's language, provokes the conclusion that *N* made use of pre-existing materials which he incorporated into his account, by practically quoting from them *D*(ivine) and *H*(uman) speeches or utterances. This leads to the supposition that the imbalance in the presence of *H* and *D* matter in Divisions *I* and *III* inhered already in the *Vorlagen* to which *N* had recourse in the process of composing his tale. This supposition can be underpinned by the following considerations which mutually strengthen each other:

1. It is indisputable that Divisions *I* and *III*, i.e., chs. 1-11 and 37-50 respectively, show more pronounced affinities with extra-Israelite ancient near-eastern literary traditions than does Division *II* (chs. 12-36) which centers altogether on Israelite affairs proper, viz. the history of the Patriarchs.

2. The question of whether or not the Creation tradition, the Flood story and other segments of the "pre-history account" (Division *I* — chs. 1-11) are indeed surviving remnants of an Israelite (national) epic does not need to concern us here.[23] But it is *communis opinio* that this part of the

---

[23] For my views on this matter, see: "Did There Exist a Biblical National Epic?", *Studies in the Bible and the Ancient Near East* (Jerusalem: Magnes Press, 1981), 41-61.

Book of Genesis reflects, or at least shows an acquaintance with, mythopoeic traditions known from Mesopotamian and Cananite literatures. In those cosmogonies, the "gods" acted not unlike and interacted with humans on diverse and multifaceted levels. Therefore it stands to reason that in drawing on such *Vorlagen* in composing his own account, the Biblical Narrator would necessarily chance upon a good deal of "Divine oratory" which he assimilated in part into his presentation. This would go a long way in explaining the comparatively high 21% of *D*-material in Division *I*.

3. Von Rad's suggestion that the "Joseph cycle" exhibits traits which characterize Egyptian and Biblical *Weisheitsliteratur*[24] could provide the explanation for the fact that almost half of Division *III* (47%) consists of *H*-speeches, whereas *D*-material is conspicuous by its total absence. The anthropocentric nature of Biblical and extra-Biblical ancient Near Eastern wisdom literature does not need to be stressed here. It is as evident as is the pronounced toning down of man's dependence on the Divine and God's deciding on the fate of man.[25] The probability that *N* leaned heavily on wisdom(-type) literature may have brought about the quite different linguistic-literary constitution of the "Joseph Cycle" relative to the *Urgeschichte* and also the "Patriarchal History".

4. Notwithstanding the percentagewise discrepancies between *N, H* and *D* in Division *II* (chs. 12-36), that part of Genesis presents the most balanced picture of the three. This linguistic-literary peculiarity vis-à-vis Divisions *I* and *III* dovetails with the exclusively Israelite orientation in content to make the "Patriarchal History" the best and possibly the sole representative of genuine Israelite story-telling in the Book of Genesis. It could be considered a prime example of narrative prose which Biblical authors fostered especially over and against the ancient Near Eastern epic style with its mythopoeic overtones.[26]

## 7.4.  A New Insight

This brings us to the assessment of what in this writer's opinion constitutes the major contribution of the Genesis-Project to Biblical studies — directly with respect to the literary structure of Genesis, and indirectly to any other Biblical, or for that matter extra-Biblical, book in which narration predominates. The marking of every single word in Genesis with one of the sigla *N, H, D,* thus to

---

[24] G. von Rad, "Josephsgeschichte und ältere Chokma," *Supplements to Vetus Testamentum* 1 (1953), 120-27.

[25] See also: S. Talmon, "Wisdom in the Book of Esther," *Vetus Testamentum* 13 (1963), 419-55.

[26] See Talmon, "Epic" (above n. 23), 57ff.

identify it as a component of the Narrator's, Human or Divine speech — a strategy which the investigators present as having resulted from an "afterthought"[27] — in fact should be deemed the most salient achievement of the study. While these criteria initially were conceived in the orbit of language, they quite obviously (also) pertain to literature pure and proper. By introducing these analytical touchstones into the discussion, the linguists did what Old Testament scholars should have done before them: they provided some congenial tools for investigating and appreciating Biblical narrative literature *qua* literature. Their linguistic enquiry blends remarkably well with literary regards. Consequently, the present study bears on a legitimate concern of Old Testament research which for far too long has been overshadowed by the overriding preoccupation with *literarhistorische Probleme*. It thus links up with the "corrective" process which was set on foot by H. Gunkel and his followers,[28] but actually can be traced back to the seminal work of E. König.[29]

Since those days, our discipline has come a long way. More and more contemporaneous investigative efforts are being channelled into the assessment of the truly literary-structural characteristics of the Biblical writings. Triggered by developments in the wider discipline of literary criticism generally, diverse schools in present day Biblical studies evince the burgeoning interest in researching the Old Testament books as literature: what with *Werkinterpretation*,[30] rhetorical criticism,[31] structuralism,[32] holistic interpretation and others.

---

[27] See supra, 1.4.1.

[28] *inter alia*: "Die Grundprobleme der israelitischen Literaturgeschichte," *Reden und Aufsätze* (Göttingen: Vandenhoeck & Ruprecht, 1913), 29-38; *Die Psalmen*[4], *Göttinger Handkommentar zum Alten Testament* II, Bd. 2 (Göttingen: Vandenhoeck & Ruprecht, 1929); *Die israelitische Literatur* (Stuttgart: Teubner, 1925).

[29] *Stilistik, Rhetorik, Poetik in Bezug auf die biblische Litteratur komparativistisch dargestellt* (Leipzig: Weicker 1900).

[30] e.g. M. Weiss, *Hammiqrā' kidmūtō* (Jerusalem: Bialik, 1962); Y. Zakovitch, *The Life of Samson* (Jerusalem: Magnes Press, 1982 [Hebrew]).

[31] The founder of this school of interpretation which developed especially in the U.S.A. is J. Muilenburg. A concise presentation of his method may be found in his essay "A Study in Hebrew Rhetoric," *Supplements to Vetus Testamentum* 1 (Leiden: Brill, 1954), 97-111. See further: B.W. Anderson & W. Harrelson, eds., *Israel's Prophetic Heritage — Essays in Honor of J. Muilenburg* (New York: Harper & Brothers, 1962); J.J. Jackson & M. Kessler, eds., *Rhetorical Criticism — Essays in Honor of J. Muilenburg, Pittsburgh Theological Monograph Series*, Number 1 (Pittsburgh: Pickwick Press, 1974).

[32] See *inter alia*: J.P. Fokkelmann, *Narrative Art in Genesis — Specimens of Stylistic and Structural Analysis* (Assen-Amsterdam: van Gorcum, 1975); *id., Narrative Art and Poetry in the Books of Samuel*, vol. 1 — *King David* (Assen: van Gorcum, 1981); R. Alter, *The Art of Biblical Narrative* (London-Sydney: Allen & Unwin, 1981); J. Calloud, *Structural Analysis of Narrative*, tr. D. Patte (Philadelphia: Fortress, 1976); R.C. Culley, *Studies in the Structure of Biblical Narrative* (Philadelphia: Fortress, 1976), where a representative listing of pertinent literature may be found.

Intertwined with this pursuit is the orientation towards interpreting and evaluating — "wie sie sind" — comprehensive units of writing as they present themselves to the viewer in the books of the Bible. Indeed, one does not lose sight of "kleinere" and even "kleinste Einheiten" [33] which have been incorporated into the larger frames. However, the pursuance of matters which relate to a book as a book, its structure and inner cohesion, appears to gain steadily in impetus. A high-mark of this renewed interest in an interpretation which relates to larger literary units in their entirety, may be perceived in Brevard Childs' recent call for "canonical criticism". [34]

The "afterthought" which produced the explanation of linguistic (and stylistic, even conceptual) differences in the Book of Genesis as arising out of a Narrator's recording Divine and Human speech without neutralizing their respective pecularities, makes the linguistic-statistical inquiry presented here an important stepping stone in contemporary Biblical research.

---

[33] See: O. Eissfeldt, "Die kleinste literarische Einheit in den Erzählungsbüchern des Alten Testaments," *Theologische Blätter* 6 (1927), Sp. 333-337 = *Kleine Schriften* 1 (Tübingen: Mohr, 1962), 143-149.

[34] *Introduction to the Old Testament as Scripture* (Philadelphia: Fortress, 1979), esp. 46ff.

# The Raw Data of Realizations in 96 Samples of 54 Variables
## (in Percentage - see Section 1.5.2.)

Sample nos. are marked by squares. Read percentages in each sample from left

| 12 | 13 | 14 | 15 | 16 | 17 |

# APPENDIX 1.A

| 18 | 19 | 20 | 21 | 22 | 23 |

24  25  26  27  28  29

APPENDIX 1.A

| 30 | 31 | 32 | 33 | 34 | 35 |

36 | 37 | 38 | 39 | 40 | 41

42    43    44    45    46    47

# APPENDIX 1.A

54

55

56

57

58

59

60 61 62 63 64 65

66   67   68   69   70   71

72  73  74  75  76  77

| 78 | 79 | 80 | 81 | 82 | 83 |

# Symbols Used in the Summary Output of the Discriminant Analysis (Section 3.2.3.2.2.)

*Eigenvalue*: a statistical measure computed in the process of deriving a Discriminant Function which represents the amount of total variance accounted for by that Function.

*Canonical Correlation:* a measure of association between the single Discriminant Function and the set of $(g - 1)$ dummy variables which define the $g$ groups participating in the Discriminant Analysis. It indicates the Function's ability to discriminate between groups.

*Percentage of Trace:* the relative contribution in percents of the Discriminant Function to the total discriminant variance, traced by all Discriminant Functions. The percentage of trace of the $i$-th Function equals

$$\lambda_i / \sum_{j=1}^{n} \lambda_j$$

where $n$ Functions were derived and where $\lambda_i$ is the root (*eigenvalue*) of the $i$-th Function. In our analyses $n$ equals 2.

*Wilks's Lambda:* an inverse statistic which measures the amount of residual discriminating power still retained in the data after discriminating variance, accounted for by earlier Discriminant Functions, has been removed. The smaller this statistic, the higher the residual discriminating power of the variables.

*Chi-square:* a statistic based of Wilks's Lambda and calculated to assess the significance of the latter. Found non-significant in the $i$-th step, it indicates that only the first $(i-1)$ derived Discriminant Functions are significant.

*Significance:* the probability of obtaining such a value of Wilks's Lambda or a smaller one under the null hypothesis that no further discriminating information may be accounted for in the population by an additional Discriminant Function.

*Discriminant Score:* the scores of the observation calculated from the first Discriminant Function (the horizontal axis) and from the second (the vertical axis).

$P(x/G)$: given that the observation originated in the population (group) to which it has been actually classified, this value yields the probability of obtaining the discriminant score (or the distance from the centroid) which the observation actually has.

$P(G/x)$: given the discriminant scores of the observation, this value yields the probability that the observation originated in the population (group) to which it has actually been classified.

*Centroid:* the average of the group samples in the feature space, i.e. in the reduced space, the axes of which are the two Discriminant Functions.

## Location of Points in the Reduced Space Diagram and Allied Statistics (Section 3.3.5.2)

### Fig.3.16

| Sample no. | Sub-cat. | Point | Distance from C | Dimension 1 | Dimension 2 |
|---|---|---|---|---|---|
| 1 | NP | 1 | 34. | 41.22 | 76.17 |
| 4 | | 2 | 35. | 53.84 | 76.59 |
| 8 | | 3 | 54. | 86.88 | 78.56 |
| 12 | | 4 | 58. | 53.15 | 100.00 |
| 16 | N E | 5 | 48. | 72.35 | 1.15 |
| 17 | | 6 | 51. | 96.98 | 32.21 |
| 21 | | 7 | 48. | 88.05 | 16.74 |
| 25 | | 8 | 45. | 89.11 | 26.84 |
| 29 | NJ | 9 | 45. | 66.16 | 83.33 |
| 33 | | 10 | 43 | 54.18 | 85.03 |
| 37 | | 11 | 53. | 99.87 | 45.68 |
| 41 | | 12 | 48. | 95.34 | 46.43 |
| 44 | | 13 | 45. | 97.92 | 21.83 |
| 48 | | 14 | 25. | 69.57 | 54.43 |
| 52 | | 15 | 55. | 88.76 | 6.12 |
| 55 | | 16 | 52. | 96.28 | 24.34 |
| 56 | HP | 17 | 45. | 17.66 | 8.51 |
| 60 | H E | 18 | 45. | 6.11 | 23.27 |
| 64 | | 19 | 35. | 23.40 | 68.46 |
| 68 | | 20 | 49. | 0 | 30.11 |
| 71 | | 21 | 41. | 9.05 | 57.45 |
| 72 | | 22 | 43. | 4.74 | 45.48 |
| 76 | HJ | 23 | 41. | 7.73 | 33.05 |
| 80 | | 24 | 50. | 14.16 | 5.00 |
| 84 | | 25 | 45. | 5.21 | 27.66 |
| 85 | | 26 | 50. | 5.20 | 15.84 |
| 87 | | 27 | 44. | 37.59 | 0 |
| 88 | DP | 28 | 44. | 25.78 | 81.06 |
| 89 | | 29 | 39. | 31.49 | 78.17 |
| 93 | DJ | 30 | 31. | 21.08 | 58.25 |
| 94 | | 31 | 34. | 13.51 | 42.39 |
| 96 | | 32 | 31. | 39.68 | 12.81 |
| Centroid | | | | 47.25 | 42.57 |

Normalized $\varphi$ = .04493 for 6 iterations
Coefficient of alienation = .296364E+00

### Fig.3.18

| Sample no. | Sub-cat. | Point | Distance from C | Dimension 1 | Dimension 2 |
|---|---|---|---|---|---|
| 56 | HP | 1 | 32. | 66.61 | 0 |
| 59 | H E | 2 | 3. | 56.06 | 32.54 |
| 60 | | 3 | 7. | 62.05 | 35.45 |
| 62 | | 4 | 30. | 37.23 | 7.46 |
| 65 | | 5 | 58. | 0 | 26.27 |
| 68 | | 6 | 20. | 40.07 | 40.15 |
| 71 | | 7 | 39. | 29.54 | 56.88 |
| 74 | HJ | 8 | 24. | 57.46 | 6.00 |
| 76 | | 9 | 20. | 56.73 | 49.72 |
| 77 | | 10 | 32. | 68.95 | 59.85 |
| 79 | | 11 | 29. | 78.96 | 49.82 |
| 83 | | 12 | 17. | 73.52 | 36.39 |
| 84 | | 13 | 31. | 28.04 | 21.20 |
| 85 | | 14 | 39. | 91.47 | 11.96 |
| 86 | | 15 | 23. | 72.63 | 13.29 |
| 87 | | 16 | 43. | 100.00 | 36.13 |
| Centroid | | | | 57.46 | 30.19 |

Normalized $\varphi$ = .02335 for 23 iterations
Coefficient of alienation = .214825E+00

### Fig.3.19

| Sample no. | Sub-cat. | Point | Distance from C | Dimension 1 | Dimension 2 |
|---|---|---|---|---|---|
| 88 | DP | 1 | 36. | 74.88 | 70.34 |
| 89 | | 2 | 43. | 56.51 | 84.70 |
| 90 | | 3 | 48. | 100.00 | 46.68 |
| 91 | DE | 4 | 31. | 42.11 | 12.41 |
| 92 | DJ | 5 | 39. | 21.69 | 66.23 |
| 93 | | 6 | 7. | 47.60 | 46.88 |
| 94 | | 7 | 52. | 0. | 42.22 |
| 95 | | 8 | 44. | 96.58 | 10.16 |
| Centroid | | | | 52.14 | 42.18 |

Normalized $\varphi$ = .01010 for 9 iterations
Coefficient of alienation = .141787E+00

### Fig.3.17

| Sample no. | Sub-cat. | Point | Distance from C | Dimension 1 | Dimension 2 |
|---|---|---|---|---|---|
| 1 | P | 1 | 53. | 62.40 | 83.79 |
| 2 | | 2 | 53. | 61.43 | 84.37 |
| 3 | | 3 | 37. | 78.85 | 43.54 |
| 4 | | 4 | 49. | 65.45 | 78.23 |
| 5 | | 5 | 31. | 27.41 | 8.56 |
| 6 | | 6 | 35. | 74.12 | 20.55 |
| 7 | | 7 | 45. | 81.17 | 12.06 |
| 8 | | 8 | 38. | 75.32 | 16.26 |
| 9 | | 9 | 49. | 83.90 | 9.18 |
| 10 | | 10 | 55. | 92.96 | 12.81 |
| 11 | | 11 | 39. | 68.66 | 6.07 |
| 12 | | 12 | 51. | 89.23 | 15.73 |
| 14 | E | 13 | 33. | 10.57 | 45.36 |
| 15 | | 14 | 39. | 25.95 | 70.34 |
| 16 | | 15 | 34. | 26.05 | 64.91 |
| 17 | | 16 | 19. | 24.53 | 43.07 |
| 18 | | 17 | 30. | 14.05 | 25.47 |
| 24 | | 18 | 44. | 10.06 | 4.95 |
| 25 | | 19 | 39. | 3.47 | 33.33 |
| 26 | | 20 | 39. | 6.70 | 52.11 |
| 27 | | 21 | 41. | 21.75 | 0 |
| 28 | | 22 | 9. | 34.18 | 31.64 |
| 30 | | 23 | 45. | 3.21 | 57.75 |
| 31 | | 24 | 34. | 46.86 | 1.95 |
| 32 | | 25 | 58. | 100.00 | 40.96 |
| 33 | | 26 | 47. | 81.83 | 60.27 |
| 34 | | 27 | 37. | 60.00 | 67.30 |
| 40 | | 28 | 20. | 26.62 | 47.75 |
| 41 | J | 29 | 27. | 22.31 | 53.03 |
| 42 | | 30 | 20. | 22.95 | 30.71 |
| 43 | | 31 | 34. | 9.42 | 26.00 |
| 44 | | 32 | 36. | 30.43 | .93 |
| 51 | | 33 | 33. | 9.19 | 35.81 |
| 52 | | 34 | 36. | 7.84 | 44.79 |
| 53 | | 35 | 47. | 0 | 14.06 |
| 54 | | 36 | 33. | 68.19 | 56.16 |
| 55 | | 37 | 32. | 38.23 | 3.50 |
| Centroid | | | | 42.31 | 35.22 |

Normalized $\varphi$ = .03799 for 6 iterations
Coefficient of alienation = .273009E+00

### Fig.3.22

| Sample no. | Sub-cat. | Point | Distance from C | Dimension 1 | Dimension 2 |
|---|---|---|---|---|---|
| 11 | NP | 1 | 52. | 36.62 | 95.13 |
| 12 | | 2 | 55. | 58.60 | 99.59 |
| 21 | N E | 3 | 46. | 5.13 | 45.83 |
| 22 | | 4 | 37. | 16.09 | 57.22 |
| 23 | | 5 | 42. | 19.23 | 73.64 |
| 24 | | 6 | 20. | 32.18 | 51.58 |
| 25 | | 7 | 42. | 9.90 | 37.72 |
| 26 | | 8 | 35. | 25.63 | 21.26 |
| 27 | | 9 | 22. | 32.12 | 57.40 |
| 28 | | 10 | 48. | 5.28 | 61.13 |
| 51 | NJ | 11 | 36. | 19.10 | 27.82 |
| 52 | | 12 | 50. | 13.85 | 12.15 |
| 53 | | 13 | 46. | 16.47 | 15.66 |
| 54 | | 14 | 34. | 57.41 | 79.34 |
| 55 | | 15 | 51. | 0 | 47.71 |
| 64 | H E | 16 | 24. | 74.19 | 52.18 |
| 65 | | 17 | 18. | 49.05 | 63.25 |
| 66 | | 18 | 55. | 98.69 | 73.11 |
| 67 | | 19 | 51. | 84.43 | 7.00 |
| 68 | | 20 | 33. | 81.36 | 32.34 |
| 69 | | 21 | 21. | 47.80 | 24.57 |
| 70 | | 22 | 35. | 84.86 | 38.18 |
| 71 | | 23 | 33. | 83.98 | 44.05 |
| 72 | | 24 | 36. | 73.97 | 72.65 |
| 73 | | 25 | 53. | 100.00 | 25.84 |
| 85 | HJ | 26 | 46. | 70.74 | 4.16 |
| 86 | | 27 | 47. | 98.19 | 43.65 |
| 87 | | 28 | 46. | 51.84 | 0 |
| 90 | DP | 29 | 50. | 94.12 | 71.67 |
| 96 | DJ | 30 | 40. | 88.14 | 30.37 |
| Centroid | | | | 50.97 | 45.55 |

Normalized $\varphi$ = .04181 for 6 iterations
Coefficient of alienation = .286126E+00

## Fig.3.20

| Sample no. | Sub-cat. | Point | Distance from C | Dimension 1 | Dimension 2 |
|---|---|---|---|---|---|
| 1 | NP | 1 | 51. | 79.74 | 84.60 |
| 2 | | 2 | 44. | 83.32 | 73.71 |
| 3 | | 3 | 34. | 84.80 | 47.67 |
| 4 | | 4 | 50. | 95.48 | 65.84 |
| 29 | NJ | 5 | 37. | 14.19 | 45.43 |
| 30 | | 6 | 56. | 13.41 | 1.69 |
| 31 | | 7 | 65. | 100.00 | 0 |
| 32 | | 8 | 28. | 41.93 | 16.17 |
| 33 | | 9 | 8. | 44.38 | 38.19 |
| 34 | | 10 | 16. | 38.20 | 52.20 |
| 35 | | 11 | 40. | 87.75 | 26.83 |
| 36 | | 12 | 48. | 74.92 | .57 |
| 74 | HJ | 13 | 58. | 0 | 16.33 |
| 88 | DP | 14 | 28. | 42.20 | 69.01 |
| 92 | DJ | 15 | 58. | 4.69 | 77.60 |
| 93 | | 16 | 41. | 17.88 | 67.09 |

Centroid 51.43 42.68
Normalized $\varphi$ = .02626 for 11 iterations
Coefficient of alienation = .2276438+00

## Fig.3.21

| Sample no. | Sub-cat. | Point | Distance from C | Dimension 1 | Dimension 2 |
|---|---|---|---|---|---|
| 5 | NP | 1 | 21. | 68.53 | 50.81 |
| 6 | | 2 | 50. | 79.64 | 82.90 |
| 7 | | 3 | 49. | 69.73 | 87.68 |
| 8 | | 4 | 48. | 77.08 | 82.31 |
| 9 | | 5 | 53. | 65.78 | 94.07 |
| 10 | | 6 | 55. | 52.08 | 98.66 |
| 13 | NE | 7 | 40. | 88.60 | 37.13 |
| 14 | | 8 | 42. | 86.67 | 25.51 |
| 15 | | 9 | 43. | 61.09 | 1.53 |
| 16 | | 10 | 38. | 70.26 | 11.26 |
| 17 | | 11 | 47. | 95.21 | 36.12 |
| 18 | | 12 | 36. | 67.28 | 12.24 |
| 19 | | 13 | 40. | 87.59 | 32.40 |
| 20 | | 14 | 22. | 54.92 | 64.29 |
| 37 | NJ | 15 | 36. | 84.97 | 49.83 |
| 38 | | 16 | 41. | 89.99 | 47.69 |
| 39 | | 17 | 42. | 89.45 | 31.15 |
| 40 | | 18 | 41. | 83.95 | 21.74 |
| 41 | | 19 | 46. | 90.96 | 23.33 |
| 42 | | 20 | 48. | 97.46 | 44.78 |
| 43 | | 21 | 42. | 89.62 | 33.34 |
| 44 | | 22 | 37. | 83.76 | 57.33 |
| 45 | | 23 | 33. | 81.95 | 37.49 |
| 46 | | 24 | 33. | 77.36 | 26.06 |
| 47 | | 25 | 37. | 82.14 | 25.71 |
| 48 | | 26 | 43. | 46.15 | 0 |
| 49 | | 27 | 37. | 85.18 | 35.89 |
| 50 | | 28 | 57. | 45.24 | 100.00 |
| 56 | HP | 29 | 28. | 21.59 | 37.86 |
| 58 | HE | 30 | 44. | 7.21 | 30.37 |
| 59 | | 31 | 50. | 0 | 35.25 |
| 60 | | 32 | 46. | 3.80 | 33.91 |
| 61 | | 33 | 46. | 7.43 | 23.14 |
| 62 | | 34 | 49. | 3.94 | 63.07 |
| 63 | | 35 | 49. | 6.64 | 18.85 |
| 75 | HJ | 36 | 45. | 4.04 | 48.24 |
| 76 | | 37 | 46. | 3.25 | 41.08 |
| 77 | | 38 | 40. | 11.69 | 58.53 |
| 78 | | 39 | 42. | 7.06 | 48.61 |
| 79 | | 40 | 40. | 13.19 | 25.80 |
| 80 | | 41 | 32. | 20.33 | 30.51 |
| 81 | | 42 | 15. | 39.22 | 54.71 |
| 82 | | 43 | 47. | 2.83 | 32.85 |
| 83 | | 44 | 39. | 14.08 | 25.38 |
| 84 | | 45 | 43. | 6.06 | 44.26 |
| 89 | DP | 46 | 51. | 14.35 | 80.14 |
| 94 | DJ | 47 | 41. | 13.47 | 64.44 |
| 95 | | 48 | 45. | 5.73 | 30.99 |

Centroid 49.14 43.32
Normalized $\varphi$ = .02917 for 6 iterations
Coefficient of alienation = .239754E+00

## Fig.3.23

| Sample no. | Sub-cat. | Point | Distance from C | Dimension 1 | Dimension 2 |
|---|---|---|---|---|---|
| 13 | NE | 1 | 23. | 76.23 | 40.89 |
| 14 | | 2 | 17. | 71.26 | 37.32 |
| 15 | | 3 | 31. | 47.59 | 62.90 |
| 16 | | 4 | 30. | 72.76 | 56.12 |
| 17 | | 5 | 6. | 60.70 | 33.01 |
| 18 | | 6 | 24. | 58.12 | 55.88 |
| 19 | | 7 | 19. | 73.85 | 33.36 |
| 20 | | 8 | 47. | 100.00 | 45.34 |
| 21 | | 9 | 31. | 47.53 | 1.99 |
| 22 | | 10 | 18. | 37.94 | 25.94 |
| 23 | | 11 | 28. | 27.22 | 28.77 |
| 24 | | 12 | 26. | 57.22 | 58.48 |
| 25 | | 13 | 6. | 53.23 | 38.40 |
| 26 | | 14 | 22. | 72.18 | 45.58 |
| 27 | | 15 | 32. | 60.65 | 63.53 |
| 28 | | 16 | 16. | 69.18 | 24.38 |
| 29 | NJ | 17 | 43. | 12.27 | 36.13 |
| 30 | | 18 | 25. | 39.71 | 52.18 |
| 31 | | 19 | 30. | 59.59 | 2.30 |
| 32 | | 20 | 56. | 0 | 41.93 |
| 33 | | 21 | 48. | 12.20 | 48.07 |
| 34 | | 22 | 38. | 17.25 | 36.53 |
| 35 | | 23 | 38. | 25.25 | 8.56 |
| 36 | | 24 | 35. | 29.30 | 8.02 |
| 37 | | 25 | 21. | 57.62 | 11.66 |
| 38 | | 26 | 12. | 62.65 | 22.83 |
| 39 | | 27 | 14. | 68.25 | 26.58 |
| 40 | | 28 | 10. | 58.06 | 23.22 |
| 41 | | 29 | 15. | 67.97 | 40.48 |
| 42 | | 30 | 17. | 61.67 | 17.20 |
| 43 | | 31 | 22. | 77.02 | 30.38 |
| 44 | | 32 | 12. | 53.08 | 20.09 |
| 45 | | 33 | 30. | 83.53 | 23.50 |
| 46 | | 34 | 36. | 79.04 | 21.13 |
| 47 | | 35 | 22. | 76.81 | 31.41 |
| 48 | | 36 | 37. | 30.05 | 59.32 |
| 49 | | 37 | 27. | 81.87 | 29.25 |
| 50 | | 38 | 52. | 14.70 | 0 |
| 51 | | 39 | 11. | 60.52 | 41.89 |
| 52 | | 40 | 27. | 82.06 | 32.29 |
| 53 | | 41 | 34. | 86.11 | 19.25 |
| 54 | | 42 | 36. | 22.13 | 47.14 |
| 55 | | 43 | 26. | 62.96 | 7.29 |

Centroid 55.06 32.34
Normalized $\varphi$ = .04850 for 6 iterations
Coefficient of alienation = .307658E+00

# Formulas for Type-Token Relations

Denote by f(r) the observed frequency of r occurrences, $r = 1,2,...,R$, where R is the most frequent word in the text. The number of types, i.e. of distinct words, is n and given by

$$n = \sum_{r=1}^{R} f(r),$$

while the number of tokens, i.e. the text length, is N and given by

$$N = \sum_{r=1}^{R} r \cdot f(r),$$

The number of *hapax legomena* is f(1), that of *dislegomena* is f(2) etc. The average number of occurrences is r and given by

$$\bar{r} = N/n$$

The variance $s^2$ is

$$s^2 = \frac{1}{n} \cdot \sum_{r=1}^{R} (r - \bar{r})^2 \cdot f(r)$$

and the standard deviation s is

$$s = \sqrt{s^2}.$$

The coefficient of skewness is calculated as

$$\frac{1}{n} \cdot \sum_{r=1}^{R} (r - \bar{r})^3 \cdot f(r)/s^3$$

and that of kurtosis as

$$\frac{1}{n} \cdot \sum_{r=1}^{R} (r - \bar{r})^4 \cdot f(r)/s^4 - 3.$$

Herdan's characteristic is

$$\frac{s}{r\sqrt{n}}$$

and Yule's,

$$10^4 \frac{\sum_{r=1}^{R} r^2 \cdot f(r)}{N^2 - \frac{1}{N}}.$$

## The Mathematics of the Sichel Distribution

The probability function of Sichel distribution in the general case is given by

$$\varphi(r) = [((1-\theta)^{\frac{1}{2}})^{-\gamma} \, K_\gamma \, (\alpha(1-\theta)^{\frac{1}{2}}) - K_\gamma \, (\alpha)]^{-1} \, \frac{(\alpha\theta/2)^r}{r!} \, K_{r+\gamma} \, (\alpha) \qquad (1)$$

$$r = 1, 2, 3, \ldots$$

where $\alpha > 0, 0 < \theta < 1$ and $K_\nu \, (x)$ is the modified Bessel function of the second kind of order $\nu$. The order is not integer in our case.

The modified Bessel function of the second kind is defined as

$$K_\nu \, (x) = \tfrac{1}{2} \, \Pi \, (\sin \nu \, \Pi)^{-1} \, [I_{-\nu} \, (x) - I_\nu \, (x)],$$

where $I_{-\nu} \, (x)$ and $I\nu \, (x)$ are the two independent solutions of the modified Bessel's differential equation:

$$x^2 \cdot \frac{d^2y}{dx^2} + x \cdot - \frac{dy}{dx} \, (x^2 + \nu^2) \, y = 0.$$

From (1), when $\gamma < 0$:

$$\lim_{r \to 100} \frac{\varphi \, (r+1)}{\varphi \, (r)} = \theta$$

and when $\theta \to 1$ and $\gamma = -\frac{1}{2}$

$$\frac{\varphi \, (2)}{\varphi \, (1)} = (1 + \alpha)/4.$$

Actually, (1) is obtained when the following is evaluated and 0-truncated:

$$\varphi\ (r) = \int_0^\infty \frac{e^{-\pi}\ \pi^r}{r!}\ f(\Pi)\ d\Pi \tag{2}$$

where

$$f(\Pi) = \frac{[2(\sqrt{1-\theta})/\alpha\Theta]^\gamma}{2K_\gamma\ (\alpha\sqrt{1-\theta})}\Pi^{\gamma-1} \cdot e^{\displaystyle -(\frac{1}{\Theta}-1)\ \Pi\ -\ \frac{\alpha^2\Theta}{4\Pi}} \tag{3}$$

It is possible to take account of the text length N. Then, instead of (2), we take:

$$\varphi\ (r) = \int_0^\infty \frac{e^{-N\Pi}\ (N\Pi)^r}{r!}\ f\ (\Pi)\ d\Pi. \tag{4}$$

When (4) is evaluated we obtain:

$$f(r) = \left[\frac{1-\Theta}{1+(N-1)\ \Theta}\right]^{\gamma/2} \cdot \frac{1}{K_\gamma(\alpha\sqrt{1-\Theta})} \cdot \left[\frac{\dfrac{N\alpha\Theta/2}{\sqrt{1+(N-1)\Theta}}}{r!}\right]^r \cdot K_{r+\gamma}\left[\alpha\sqrt{1+(N+1)\ \Theta}\right] \tag{5}$$

$$r = 0, 1, 2, ...$$

0-truncation results in

$$\varphi\,(r) = \psi\,(r)/\psi\,(0),\ r = 1, 2, ...$$

Comparison of (1) and (5) shows that the following quantities are independent of N:

$$\alpha\sqrt{1-\theta}\ \text{and}\ \theta/[1-\theta)\ N].$$

# The Frequency Lists

The vocabulary of Genesis is described and compared per Documents and Sorts-of-Discourse in Part IV, but the word frequency lists themselves cannot be rendered in full because they would occupy dozens of pages. The following Tables are designated to make up at least partially for this omission. They refer to the first 10, 50 or 100 most frequent words and are displayed here without comment. Inspecting them will confirm that (a) J and E are akin; (b) P's difference from J and E may well be caused by its special content; and (c) the variety of vocabulary between the three Sorts-of-Discourse being greater than that between the three Documents demonstrates itself already at the heads of the lists. Divine names, proper names and toponyms are excluded.

### (1)

### The 10 Most Frequent Words

| | | Documents | | | | Sorts-of-Discourse | | | | Overall |
|---|---|---|---|---|---|---|---|---|---|---|
| | | *J* | *E* | *P* | Total | *N* | *H* | *D* | Total | Total |
| 1 | אֵת | + | + | + | 3 | + | + | + | 3 | 6 |
| 2 | לוֹ | + | + | + | 3 | + | + | + | 3 | 6 |
| 3 | אֲשֶׁר | + | + | + | 3 | + | + | + | 3 | 6 |
| 4 | הָיָה | + | + | + | 3 | + | + | + | 3 | 6 |
| 5 | כָּל | + | + | + | 3 | + | — | + | 2 | 5 |
| 6 | אֶל | + | + | — | 2 | + | + | + | 3 | 5 |
| 7 | אֶרֶץ | + | — | + | 2 | + | + | + | 3 | 5 |
| 8 | כִּי | + | + | — | 2 | — | + | + | 2 | 4 |
| 9 | עַל | + | + | — | 2 | + | — | + | 2 | 4 |
| 10 | לֹא | — | + | — | 1 | — | + | + | 2 | 3 |
| 11 | אָמַר | + | + | — | 2 | + | — | — | 1 | 3 |
| 12 | בֵּן | — | — | + | 1 | + | + | — | 2 | 3 |
| 13 | אָב | — | — | — | 0 | — | + | — | 1 | 1 |
| 14 | אֵלֶּה | — | — | + | 1 | — | — | — | 0 | 1 |
| 15 | שָׁנָה | — | — | + | 1 | — | — | — | 0 | 1 |
| 16 | הוֹלִיד | — | — | + | 1 | — | — | — | 0 | 1 |
| Total | | 10 | 10 | 10 | | 10 | 10 | 10 | | |

## (2)

### The Frequency of Verbs

|  |  | J | E | P | N | H | D |
|---|---|---|---|---|---|---|---|
| Number of different verbs in the | first 50 words | 12 | 10 | 14 | 14 | 10 | 6 |
|  | second 50 words | 14 | 10 | 11 | 15 | 17 | 21 |
| Percentage of all verbal forms in the | first 50 words | 23.0 | 20.8 | 18.7 | 26.7 | 17.0 | 11.8 |
|  | second 50 words | 29.0 | 28.0 | 22.6 | 28.6 | 36.4 | 44.1 |
| Difference between percentages in p.c. |  | +17 | +35 | +21 | +7 | +114 | +75 |

## (3)

### Cumulative Frequencies of the First 50 Words

| Documents | Sorts-of-Discourse |
|---|---|
| J : 49.26% | N : 52.70% |
| E : 51.42% | H : 50.05% |
| P : 59.91% | D : 53.71% |

## (4)

### Communality between the 50 Most Frequent Words of Any Two Lists

| | | Of the 50 Most Frequent Words in | | | | | |
|---|---|---|---|---|---|---|---|
| | | J | E | P | N | H | D |
| also occur | J | — | 35 | 29 | | | |
| among the | E | 38 | — | 28 | | | |
| 50 most | P | 30 | 35 | — | | | |
| frequent | N | | | | — | 34 | 26 |
| words | H | | | | 11 | — | 29 |
| of: | D | | | | 23 | 37 | — |
| Average | | | (35) | | | (27) | |

(5)

## Rank Correlation between the 50 Most Frequent Words

| Documents | Sorts-of-Discourse |
|---|---|
| $J$ and $E$ : $+.398$ | $N$ and $H$ : $+.019$ |
| $J$ and $P$ : $-.380$ | $N$ and $D$ : $-.334$ |
| $E$ and $P$ : $-.270$ | $H$ and $D$ : $-.174$ |